My wife, Eleanor, and I
leadership and teaching at Trinity Streetsville since 1992; this man is so articulate and thoughtful in making God's written word both practical and applicable. Harold and I have been in a men's group together for over twenty years, and he has profoundly impacted my life in understanding leadership. If this book enables a new generation of Christian leaders to benefit from Harold's experience, it will be a great gift to the future of the church.

Paul Henderson
Canadian Hockey Legend

The ministry of Harold Percy has had an indelible impact on my own ministry. Harold brought the ministry of evangelism out of the "red light district" of the Canadian church, and for that we owe him deep gratitude. I distinctly remember walking through downtown Toronto one winter night nearly twenty-five years ago, when I was a student at Wycliffe College. I had been in Harold's class on evangelism, and he awoke in me such a hunger for the ministry of evangelism that, as I walked, I prayed to God that I could serve him in some small way in leading others to new life in Christ. Thank you, Harold. I commend this diverse volume to all readers as we seek to build on Harold's legacy.

Jenny Andison
Suffragan Bishop of the Diocese of Toronto

Another strong book on the mission of the church in the Canadian context! Even better, a book dedicated to Harold Percy, who personifies the effective leadership that is so crucial in the church of the twenty-first century. A must-read for anyone thinking of addressing the church's missional initiative in Canada and what it takes to bridge the gap between church and culture. The fact that all the contributors are Canadian writers and practitioners makes it all the more valuable a resource.

Gary Nelson
President, Tyndale University College and Seminary

The gospel as presented by Harold seemed so real, it was easy to accept it as a way of life. He transformed the way we worshipped at Trinity from the traditional to a more meaningful and contemporary worship service, and he did it with concern for the members.

Hazel McCallion
Former Mayor of Mississauga,
Chancellor of Sheridan College

Legacies are gifts, built up through hard work in the past, that enable and enrich present and future generations. Harold Percy is still very much contributing to the life of the church today, yet these essays honour and extend exactly what he has spent decades of ministry teaching us to pay attention to if the good news is to be effectively lived and proclaimed: leadership, discipleship, spirituality, congregational ministry, and reaching out. He models it himself and, thank God, not in the past tense.

Colin R. Johnson
Anglican Archbishop of Toronto

I have known Harold Percy for many years as friend, mentor, leader, and fellow worker in the vineyard. His irrepressible humour, and his depth of love for Jesus and Jesus' people, knows no bounds. As I read *Good News Church*, I was reminded once again of all the leadership Harold has offered to so many of us in a variety of ways throughout the years. Whether it be preaching, evangelism, prayer, or leading a faith community, Harold has shown the way—often to the chagrin of the institutional church. I commend *Good News Church* to all of us called to serve a changing church in this post-Christendom era.

Barry Parker
Rector, St. Paul's Bloor Street &
St. George the Martyr, Toronto

As a young Canadian church planter, I have enjoyed the privilege of being one of the later miners to break through the great underground shaft of reformation led by Harold Percy and his many fellow collaborators, represented in this book. I believe the perspectives in this unique volume are both a foretaste and a guide to the kind of kingdom theology we are seeing unfold today. God is on the move!

Graham Singh
Executive Director of Church Planting Canada &
Rector of St. Jax Montreal

GENERAL EDITORS
**JOHN BOWEN
& MICHAEL KNOWLES**

GOOD NEWS CHURCH:
CELEBRATING THE LEGACY OF HAROLD PERCY

Good News Church: Celebrating the Legacy of Harold Percy
Copyright ©2018 John P. Bowen and Michael P. Knowles

All rights reserved
Printed in Canada
ISBN 978-1-988928-00-5 Soft Cover
ISBN 978-1-988928-02-9 E-book

Published by: Castle Quay Books
Burlington, Ontario
Tel: (416) 573-3249
E-mail: info@castlequaybooks.com | www.castlequaybooks.com

Edited by Marina Hofman Willard and Lori Mackay
Cover design and book interior by Burst Impressions
Printed at Essence Publishing, Belleville, Ontario

All rights reserved. This book or parts thereof may not be reproduced in any form without prior written permission of the publishers.

Unless otherwise marked Scripture quotations are from the New Revised Standard Version of the Bible, copyright 1989, by the Division of Christian Education of the National Council of the Churches of Christ in the United States of America, and are used by permission. All rights reserved. • Scripture quotations marked MSG are taken from The Message. Copyright © 1993, 1994, 1995, 1996, 2000, 2001, 2002. Used by permission of NavPress Publishing Group. • Scripture quotations marked NTE are taken from The New Testament for Everyone. Copyright © Nicholas Thomas Wright 2011. • Scripture quotations marked NIV are taken from the HOLY BIBLE, NEW INTERNATIONAL VERSION ®. Copyright © 1973, 1978, 1984 by International Bible Society. Used by permission of Zondervan Publishing House. • Scripture quotations marked NLT are taken from the Holy Bible, New Living Translation, copyright © 1996, 2004, 2015 by Tyndale House Foundation. Used by permission of Tyndale House Publishers Inc., Carol Stream, Illinois 60188. All rights reserved. • Scripture quotations marked KJV are from The Holy Bible, King James Version. Copyright © 1977, 1984, Thomas Nelson Inc., Publishers. All rights reserved.

Library and Archives Canada Cataloguing in Publication

Good news church : celebrating the legacy of Harold Percy / general editors,
John Bowen & Michael Knowles.

ISBN 978-1-988928-00-5 (softcover)

    1. Christian leadership. 2. Church work. 3. Christian life. 4. Spiritual life.
5. Percy, Harold--Influence. I. Bowen, John P., 1946-, editor II. Knowles, Michael, 1956-, editor

BV652.1.G66 2018   C2018-900586-6

For Kathy

INTRODUCTION: HAROLD PERCY'S LEGACY   **19**
CARMEN AND PETER MASON

SECTION A: LEADERSHIP

LEADING CHANGE IN THE CHURCH   25
JOEL PERCY

THE GIFT OF LEADERSHIP   37
JAMIE HOLTOM

BEING INTENTIONAL IN LEADERSHIP   49
JUDY PAULSEN

THE PASTOR AS CONDUCTOR   63
DAVE TOYCEN

GIVING IT ALL AWAY: EMPOWERING OTHERS FOR MINISTRY   73
WALLY VOGEL

NEW WINE IN NEW WINESKINS:
DENOMINATIONAL LEADERSHIP AND NEW FORMS OF MINISTRY   87
LINDA C. NICHOLLS

SECTION B: DISCIPLESHIP AND SPIRITUALITY

MAKING DISCIPLES: AN URGENT NECESSITY   103
TIM DOBBIN

THE BUSINESS WE'RE IN:
PRAYER AND THE SPIRITUAL LIFE OF THE PASTOR   117
KELLY BAETZ

FIVE KINDS OF MENTORS: THE FIVE PEOPLE PRINCIPLE   131
BILL FIETJE

GROWING THE GIFT OF GENEROSITY: HAROLD PERCY AND MONEY   143
PETER PATTERSON

SECTION C: CONGREGATIONAL MINISTRY

WELCOMING AND INTEGRATING NEWCOMERS 155
DIANE TOYCEN

WORSHIP THAT MAKES DISCIPLES 165
JUDITH M. MACDONALD

BECOMING AN EFFECTIVE COMMUNICATOR OF THE GOSPEL 177
LANCE B. DIXON

GRACIOUS FORMS OF YES:
INVITATIONAL DOORS IN PREACHING AND WORSHIP 193
JOHN H. MCNALLY

SECTION D: REACHING OUT

THE EXIGENCIES OF OUR TIME: REFLECTIONS ON THE TWENTIETH 213
ANNIVERSARY OF *GOOD NEWS PEOPLE*
ANDREW STIRLING

HOW EVANGELISM CHANGES WITH CULTURE 227
JOHN P. BOWEN

ENGAGING OUR COMMUNITIES IN THE POWER OF GOD'S SPIRIT 245
DEBBIE JOHNSON

ALL DOORS OPEN: GOD'S CHILDREN, PEOPLE, AND REIGN—
A VIEW FROM A PROGRESSIVE URBAN PARISH 257
PETER G. ELLIOTT

THE REVEREND HAROLD J. PERCY, BA, MREL, STD

HAROLD PERCY IS PERHAPS BEST KNOWN FOR HIS PASTORAL MINISTRY AT TRINITY ANGLICAN Church in Streetsville, Ontario, between 1987 and 2010. He came to national prominence in 1991 as founding director of the Wycliffe College Institute of Evangelism. In that role, he led workshops and conferences across the country, as well as publishing numerous articles and books on the topics of congregational renewal, evangelism, and discipleship. He retired from the institute in 1998 in order to devote more time and attention to parish ministry.

Harold's educational background includes a BA from York University (1969) and an MRel from Wycliffe College (1975). For three years, he pursued doctoral studies in the New Testament with C. K. Barrett at the University of Durham, England, before deciding that his true calling in ministry was to parish leadership.

Following ordination in the Anglican Diocese of Toronto in 1975, Harold served as assistant curate at St. Bride's, Clarkson (1975 to 1977), as associate priest at Little Trinity in downtown Toronto (1980 to 1983), then as rector of St. James, Humber Bay, in Etobicoke (1983 to 1987), before being appointed as rector of Trinity Streetsville.

He is the author of *Following Jesus: First Steps on the Way* (1993), *Good News People: An Introduction to Evangelism for Tongue-Tied Christians* (1996), *Your Church Can Thrive: Making the Connections That Build Healthy Congregations* (2003), and (with John Bowen) *Just the Basics: Teaching the Faith to Beginners* (2004).

Harold and his first wife, Kathy, had four children: Joel, Ben, Rachel, and Rob. Kathy (to whom this volume is dedicated) was tragically killed in a traffic accident in 2004. Harold is now married to Heather Smith and is the proud grandfather of five grandsons and one granddaughter.

In retirement, Harold continues in various ministry roles, which include preaching, leading worship, and mentoring younger leaders. Since 2011, he has served as spiritual adviser to the senior leadership team of World Vision Canada.

Harold says of his own work, "My great joy in ministry is to lead God's people in worship, helping them to become intentional followers of Jesus and grow towards maturity in their faith." In 2000, Wycliffe College awarded him an honorary doctor of sacred theology degree, in recognition of his pioneering contributions to evangelism and congregational renewal.

(This bare list of names, dates, and titles is important, but, as always with such lists, it fails dismally to convey the substance of the person honoured. To learn more of "the real Harold Percy," read on!)

John Bowen
Michael Knowles
Pentecost 2018

CONTRIBUTORS

KELLY BAETZ IS THE PASTOR OF ST. THOMAS' ANGLICAN CHURCH, BRACEBRIDGE. SHE RECEIVED her MDiv (Hons) from Wycliffe College, Toronto, in 2006 and more recently completed courses for a certificate in missional leadership and formation. For three years, she was part of a small group that received formal mentoring from Harold Percy, and she has kept in regular touch with him since. Kelly's particular passions in ministry include preaching and providing opportunities for unchurched families to find a home among God's people. She lives in Muskoka with her children, Gregory and Claire.

JOHN P. BOWEN IS EMERITUS PROFESSOR OF EVANGELISM AT WYCLIFFE COLLEGE. HE IS THE author of three books, including *Evangelism for Normal People* (Augsburg Fortress, 2002), and editor of two more, most recently *Green Shoots out of Dry Ground* (Wipf and Stock, 2011). He worked with Harold for two years in the Institute of Evangelism at Wycliffe College and then took over as director in 1999. John's daughter is married to one of Harold's sons, so his relationship with Harold is now one for which there is no English word but Swahili calls a *mkwe*. Harold and John share two wonderful grandchildren, Owen and Moira.

LANCE B. DIXON IS CURRENTLY CONSULTANT OF RELIGIOUS EDUCATION FOR THE CALGARY Catholic School District in Calgary, Alberta. As an ordained Anglican priest, he served four parishes in the Diocese of Toronto, including five years (2003 to 2008) as associate pastor and director of Christian education at Trinity Streetsville with Harold. Prior to moving to Alberta, Lance initiated the Jeremiah Project, an urban missional community in downtown west Toronto. Lance lived for a year in South Africa as guest lecturer in mission studies at Transfiguration College. He holds an MDiv (Wycliffe College, 1996), an MRE (St. Michael's University College, Toronto, 1998), and a DMin (Gordon-Conwell Theological Seminary, Boston, 2011).

TIM DOBBIN IS CURRENTLY RECTOR OF ST. MARK'S ANGLICAN CHURCH IN BRANTFORD IN THE Diocese of Huron. Ordained in the Diocese of Canberra and Goulburn in Australia in 1997, he completed a DMin in pastoral counselling in 2004 at Waterloo Lutheran Seminary. He has been part of a mentoring group hosted by Harold Percy and John Bowen, which has played an instrumental role in focusing his parish ministry. He is married to Lynn; they are both kept on their toes by their young children, Sophie and Felicity.

PETER G. ELLIOTT HAS SERVED AS DEAN OF VANCOUVER'S CHRIST CHURCH CATHEDRAL since 1994. He worked with Harold on the formation of the LOGOS Institute, the Diocese of Toronto lay school (1986 to 1990). Later, when serving as director of ministries in church and society for the Anglican Church of Canada, Peter collaborated with Harold on the Canadian Anglican response to the "Decade of Evangelism" through the Primate's Commission on Evangelism and the Primate's Evangelism Network (1990 to 2000). Active in governance of the Anglican Church in his diocese, Peter served as prolocutor of General Synod and the priest member of the Anglican Consultative Council.

BILL FIETJE BECAME PRESIDENT OF THE ASSOCIATED GOSPEL CHURCHES IN JULY 2008. PRIOR to this role, Bill served for five years as the Canada East AGC superintendent. Before joining the AGC team, he was the national director of Overseas Missionary Fellowship (OMF) International—Canada for eleven years. He and his wife, Lois, also served for two terms with OMF in Thailand as church planters and developers. In 1999, Bill earned his DMin degree at Gordon-Conwell Theological Seminary. Bill and Lois attended Trinity Streetsville for five years under the pastoral care and teaching of Harold Percy. The Fietjes reside in Ancaster, Ontario, and have four adult children and eleven grandchildren.

JAMIE HOLTOM IS LEAD MINISTER AT NORTH BRAMALEA UNITED CHURCH AND CHAPLAIN TO the Brampton Fire Department. He is the author of two books, including one co-written with fellow minister Debbie Johnson, *Bullseye: Aiming to Follow Jesus: Six Markers of the Christian Life* (United Church of Canada, 2015). He and his wife, Katrina, have four children—Lucas, Leah, Cameron, and Caleb. Jamie considers Harold to be a great mentor who has not only talked leadership but exemplified what it means to lead in a faithful and impactful way. Jamie believes that Harold was talking about leadership in the church at a time when no one even used the word.

DEBBIE JOHNSON IS AN ORDAINED MINISTER IN THE UNITED CHURCH OF CANADA, SERVING at North Bramalea United Church. Harold has been one of her influential teachers and mentors, particularly in the areas of leadership development and congregational ministry. Debbie admires Harold's down-to-earth practicality and active faithfulness as a follower of Jesus. Debbie is co-author with Jamie Holtom of *Bullseye: Aiming to Follow Jesus: Six Markers of the Christian Life* (United Church of Canada, 2015).

MICHAEL P. KNOWLES CURRENTLY HOLDS THE GEORGE FRANKLIN HURLBURT CHAIR OF preaching at McMaster Divinity College in Hamilton, Ontario. Ordained within the Anglican Church of Canada, he completed an MDiv (1982) and a ThD in New Testament Studies (1991) at Wycliffe College. Between 1991 and 1997, he served with Harold Percy as assistant director of the Wycliffe College Institute of Evangelism. Michael's teaching and publications (including study guides for two of Harold's books) focus on homiletics, worship, and biblical interpretation, with particular attention to the theological foundations of the church's mission and ministry. He lives in Ancaster, Ontario.

JUDITH M. MACDONALD WAS DIRECTOR OF DRAMA AT TRINITY STREETSVILLE FROM 1991 TO 2000. She holds a four-year diploma in acting from Ryerson Polytechnical Institute (1979) and an MRel (1999) from Wycliffe College. As well as performing in theatre and opera, her experience includes writing drama for worship, including comedy sketches, dramatizations of Scripture, choral readings of Scripture, plays, and pageants. She has also taught drama for worship in college courses and workshops. She is now retired and lives in St. Louis, Missouri, with her husband, John, two cats, and a dog.

CARMEN AND PETER MASON GREW UP ON FARMS IN RURAL QUEBEC. THEY MET IN MONTREAL, where Carmen trained to become a nurse and Peter studied for the Anglican ministry. They served in the Diocese of Montreal, produced three children, and eventually moved to Halifax, where Peter became rector of St. Paul's Church and Carmen worked in medical research at Dalhousie University. In 1985, Peter was appointed as principal of Wycliffe College. In addition to her ministry to faculty, students, and college friends, Carmen found time to be secretary to two downtown parishes. In 1992, they moved to Kingston, where Peter served as bishop of the Diocese of Ontario for ten years. Ever the medical guru, Carmen worked for those ten years as office manager in a dental office. In retirement, they support local churches, sing in community choirs in Prince Edward County, and enjoy their three kids, four grandsons, and a celebrity sheltie dog named Charlotte.

JOHN H. MCNALLY IS ASSISTANT PROFESSOR OF PRACTICAL THEOLOGY AND DIRECTOR OF THE Mentored Ministry Program at Acadia Divinity College in Wolfville. He studied at Queen's University in Kingston (BA [Hons], 1990, and MPA, 1991), Wycliffe College (MDiv, 1994), and Acadia Divinity College (DMin, 2011). John was encouraged and challenged through Harold's evangelism classes, books, and articles. After twenty years of pastoral ministry in Canadian Baptist churches in Toronto and Nova Scotia, John is now focusing on equipping and accompanying Acadia students in deep spirituality and vitality in ministry for God's kingdom.

LINDA C. NICHOLLS IS THE BISHOP OF THE DIOCESE OF HURON, ONTARIO. HER BACKGROUND includes degrees in music and education as well as an MDiv and a DMin (Wycliffe). Linda served in parish ministry in the Diocese of Toronto for nearly twenty years, during which time she knew Harold as a colleague and assisted in visioning for the Institute of Evangelism. Prior to her translation to Huron, she served as suffragan bishop for the area of Trent-Durham, Diocese of Toronto, where she particularly enjoyed walking alongside Ryan Sim in the adventure of evangelism in new ways.

PETER PATTERSON QUALIFIED AS AN ACTUARY IN THE MID-1970S AND ENJOYED A SUCCESSFUL career in the insurance/reinsurance industry, including having global business responsibilities. Over the past two decades, Peter has served as chairman of World Vision Canada, volunteers as business director for Wycliffe College, and is a board member for Stonegate Ministry. Peter, Barbara, and their sons, Andrew and Paul, were inspired by Harold during his time at St. James, Humber Bay, and have been privileged to share ministry with Harold in their various roles at Wycliffe College, World Vision Canada, and several parish contexts.

JUDY PAULSEN IS PROFESSOR OF EVANGELISM AT WYCLIFFE COLLEGE AND DIRECTOR OF THE Institute of Evangelism, which exists to help churches share their faith more effectively through missional structures, community connections, personal evangelism, and effective communications. Judy holds a DMin in missional leadership from Fuller Theological Seminary and recently co-authored *Christian Foundations: A Grounding for a Life of Faith*, a small-group resource that teaches the story of the Bible, the creeds, church history, and Christian disciplines and discernment. An ordained Anglican priest, Judy served for two years with Harold Percy on the ministry team of Trinity Streetsville.

JOEL PERCY IS HAROLD'S ELDEST SON. HE CURRENTLY LIVES IN MACHA, ZAMBIA, WHERE he and his wife, Julianne, provide leadership for Macha International Christian School. They have three sons: Caleb, Micah, and Nathaniel. Joel has previously worked in corporate marketing roles with Loblaw Companies, Ltd., and Purolator Courier. He was also as a pastor at The Meeting House (Brethren in Christ) Church in Oakville.

ANDREW STIRLING IS THE SENIOR MINISTER OF TIMOTHY EATON MEMORIAL CHURCH IN Toronto and is ordained by the United Church of Canada. He is a lifetime fellow of Acadia Divinity College where he teaches the preaching master class. In 2008, he received an honorary DDiv from Wycliffe College. He has written over sixty academic and devotional articles and has authored three books. His areas of theological interest are homiletics, missions, ecclesiology, and the Trinity. Andrew has known Harold for twenty years, and his ministry has been enriched by Harold's wise counsel and inspired by his faithful publications.

DAVE TOYCEN RETIRED AFTER SERVING FORTY-THREE YEARS WITH WORLD VISION IN THE US, Australia, and Canada, where he was president and CEO for nineteen years. He completed a BA in philosophy at Lawrence University in Wisconsin and an MDiv from Fuller Theological Seminary in Pasadena. He has served in lay leadership positions in Pasadena and Melbourne and at Trinity Streetsville. He is married to Diane, and they have two children and four grandchildren. They have lived in Canada since 1988 and are proud Canadians. He is the author of *The Power of Generosity: How to Transform Yourself and Your World* (Harper, 2005).

DIANE TOYCEN IS RETIRED FROM SERVING WITH HAROLD PERCY FOR TWENTY-FOUR YEARS as director of programming and parish life at Trinity Streetsville. She graduated from Pepperdine University in Malibu, and, after teaching first grade for five years, worked as director of children's ministry in two churches: an Episcopal church in Pasadena, for ten years, and then as a volunteer at an Anglican church in Melbourne, for six years. She moved to Mississauga in 1988 and started attending Trinity Streetsville. She is married to Dave Toycen and lives in Mississauga. They have two children and four grandchildren.

WALLY VOGEL HAS BEEN AN ACTIVE MEMBER OF TRINITY STREETSVILLE FOR OVER TWENTY-FIVE years and was blessed to grow in faith under Harold's gifted leadership. Wally has been the founder and CEO of two software companies, Creditron and Sparcblock, but he devotes much of his time to lay leadership in the church, currently acting as rector's warden. He also volunteers his time as a founding board member of Kidney Cancer Canada, in addition to the Kidney Cancer Research Network of Canada and the Alumni Council of Conestoga College. Wally and his wife, Jane, have two daughters, who were baptized and raised in the Trinity family.

INTRODUCTION: HAROLD PERCY'S LEGACY
CARMEN AND PETER MASON

IN 1988, THE LAMBETH CONFERENCE—A WORLD-WIDE GATHERING OF ANGLICAN BISHOPS— called for the 1990s to be a decade of evangelism. This challenge prompted a variety of global responses: in some instances, monies were raised, leadership positions were created, slogans emerged, and rallies took place. Years later, it is easy to dismiss these well-intentioned efforts as naive attempts to reverse noticeable declines in church membership and Christian presence; skeptics are not lacking who take perverse delight in crying, "I told you so."

However, the decade of evangelism gave rise to at least two significant developments among Canadian Anglicans. First, Archbishop Michael Peers, then leader of the Anglican Church of Canada, established the Primate's Commission on Evangelism. He hosted several conferences across the country, bringing together a wide range of clergy and lay leaders to pray, study, worship, and brainstorm around creative possibilities for evangelism within our church. Among those conference leaders were Harold Percy and others who have contributed to this book.

Second, inspired by the decade of evangelism, Wycliffe College in Toronto established an Institute of Evangelism. Its mission was to teach evangelism to students preparing for leadership ministry, to offer courses and conferences for clergy and lay leaders, and to develop and promote an imaginative range of resources for the wider church. Thanks to the support of a generous Christian benefactor, Harold Percy, rector of Trinity

Streetsville, became the first director of the institute, on a part-time basis, ably assisted by Michael Knowles. Now, a quarter century later, and led by its third director, the institute represents a lasting legacy of the decade of evangelism and of the pioneering role of its founding director.

Down the ages and across the church, the very notion of "evangelism" has conjured up an entire gamut of reactions. Some wholeheartedly embrace the work of evangelism, traditionally understood as preaching the good news of salvation through Jesus Christ, testifying to his truth and power, persuading individuals to repent and turn to the Lord. Others, including many Anglicans, deplore traditional evangelistic methods as being overly focused upon an individual's response, detached from the life of the church. They rightly suspect the cult of personality that sometimes grows up around certain celebrity evangelists. And they detect manipulative, insensitive attempts to pressure potential converts into snap decisions.

One of Carmen's childhood memories illustrates a distortion of evangelistic fervour that persists to this day in some circles:

> My first experience of evangelism occurred when I was a child growing up in a multi-generational family. We regularly made visitors welcome and often invited guests to join the family in Bible reading and prayers before beginning the day's activities. One day, we had a lunchtime visit from a well-known Bible scholar and evangelist who was passing through our community with his entourage. After lunch, our guest was invited to read Scripture and pray for those gathered around the table. We were impressed with his verbatim recitation of a chapter from Romans and his fervent prayer. At the close of the prayer, he fixed his attention on my grandfather, who was sitting at the head of the table, and asked him point blank, "Brother, are you saved?"
>
> My grandfather, a dedicated church elder who read his own Bible every day, may have been suffering some justifiable resentment at this blunt question. He replied by quoting from Paul's second letter to Timothy: "I know whom I have believed, and am persuaded that he is able to keep that which I have committed unto him against that day" (2 Tim 1:12, KJV). The

silence was deafening, and the discomfort was palpable even for a young child. I have always wondered whether our guest wished he had phrased his question in a more tactful way.

That caricature of evangelism from a bygone age scarcely mirrors the ministry of Harold Percy. For one thing, Harold invariably located the ministry of evangelism within the life of the church. Early on, the Institute of Evangelism challenged the church to understand itself as an evangelizing community: personal witness, individual faith sharing, gospel living, preaching, and testimony all find their place within the fellowship of congregations, parishes, and wider expressions of the church.

At the same time, Harold did not hesitate to call out those situations where the church had become overly preoccupied with itself and had strayed from its mission of glorifying and following Jesus Christ as its indisputable Lord. He was an enthusiastic motivator and cast a compelling vision but had little patience for the minutiae of institutionalism, which too often consumes the time and energy of other clergy and lay people.

It is here that we perceive a tension: by definition, the gospel is about change—change of heart, change of practice, and change of direction and purpose in both personal and corporate life. To turn to Christ is to repent of past failures, mistakes, and priorities. Yet it is often difficult for a community such as a church to set out on that radical journey from a place of relative comfort to an uncertain waypoint where the Holy Spirit may be undertaking a new creation. Several of the following chapters illustrate from Harold's own experience how that journey can be taken, as long as every stepping stone—worship, preaching, education, leadership development, stewardship, pastoral care, and missional outreach—is shaped and fitted together by Christ.

The friends and peers who contributed to this book capture many of Harold's beliefs, ideas, methods, and priorities. There is, however, a deeper level to his ministry that many of them also reveal: Harold is a joyous, winsome personality, possessing an infectious laugh and an endless capacity for seeing the funny side of life. He is a man without pomp himself, but he spots it quickly in others. The sorrows in his own life have nurtured compassion for others; as a mentor to younger leaders, he speaks encouragement into some of their most difficult situations.

We have been richly blessed by our long friendship with Harold Percy and, more recently, with his wife, Heather. Whether sharing in ministry, travelling in Europe, or simply enjoying a meal together, we have been enormously enriched by this extraordinary pastor, who has helped so many others take first steps in following Jesus.

SECTION A
LEADERSHIP

LEADING CHANGE IN THE CHURCH
JOEL PERCY

MY FATHER WOULD LATER SAY THAT IT WAS HARD TO KNOW WHICH OF THE PROBLEMS TO address first. He was standing on the steps of Trinity Streetsville, in his early months there as rector, greeting people as they arrived for Sunday service. She was a long-time parishioner, unafraid to express herself to this upstart who was messing with her church. And while my father was certainly open to feedback, her choice of words was unfortunate: "If Jesus knew what you were doing to his prayer book, he would roll over in his grave."

One could, of course, point out that the prayer book had followed Jesus by a good sixteen hundred years and was therefore not exactly *his*. Or that, generally speaking, Christians would agree that he *does* know what is being done, so there was no need to speak in the hypothetical. But perhaps the error in the sentence that towered above the others was that the woman had decided to locate Jesus in the grave. Even if she imagined him as animated enough to do a little rolling around now and then, this might have been something worth covering in an upcoming sermon.

It was not the first time my father had come up against resistance to the changes he was making at Trinity. Certainly, it would not be the last. Those were the early days. The battles were small ones. Or rather, they were about small things. Could we change from the red to the green prayer book? Could we sprinkle in a song here and there that had been written in the present century? Would it be all right if he came down from the pulpit during the sermon, so we could stand on the same level and he could look us in the eye?

When my father arrived at Trinity in the late 1980s, it was a fairly typical Anglican church, a small congregation filled with long-time members. The previous rector was a faithful man who had served there for many years. It was a good and decent place to attend church. But if from time to time there were newcomers to welcome, it was most likely because a new Anglican family had moved to town. "Change" was not a big part of their vocabulary.

By the time my father retired from Trinity over two decades later, it was not the same church. Numerous ministries were active in reaching out to the community. The demographics had shifted—the core of aging retirees had been joined by a host of young families. Sunday attendance was pushing up towards a thousand people. The energy in the place was palpable.

This transformation, of course, was not brought about by switching the prayer book. That was one of innumerable small decisions, none particularly important on its own. But taken together, they had amounted to a significant culture shift at Trinity.

It would be easy to list the changes that happened at Trinity. I have mentioned the change from the red to the green prayer book.[1] The music changed, too. Not just a shift from hymns to contemporary choruses, though that did happen, but the creation of a music group that put on some real toe-tapping performances on Sunday mornings. A drama group was assembled and tasked with coming up with creative ways to supplement the sermons. Dress became more casual: priestly robes were set aside in favour of a suit and tie. Flyers inviting people to church were distributed in the surrounding neighbourhoods.

Many more could be added to the list. But in truth this list is not only incomplete but also misleading. It can be tempting to take any successful turnaround and make it a step-by-step formula for church renewal. But what happened at Trinity was more than this set of outward changes. It was the result of a new ethos that transcended any particular change. It amounted to a shift that, while it had numerous outward markers large

---

[1] That is, from *The Book of Common Prayer* (Toronto: Anglican Book Centre, 1962) to *The Book of Alternative Services of the Anglican Church of Canada* (Toronto: Anglican Book Centre, 1985).

and small, had at its core something more intangible. It was the idea that church could matter to people who had long ago given up on it. It expressed a belief that there could be a community that people would join not out of duty but because they actually wanted to, together with the conviction that a Sunday service could be exciting, surprising, funny, relevant, and even (gasp!) enjoyable.

There is a long-standing debate in the church about just how far we should go in adapting to the culture in proclaiming the gospel. Some will stop at nothing in the pursuit of cultural relevance, while others simply say that truth is truth and anything with even a whiff of contemporary culture about it puts us in danger of watering down the pure wine of the gospel.

Both these views are overly simplistic, and both ignore the myriad ways that *any* expressions of the gospel, including those that emerged from the mouth of Jesus himself on Galilean hillsides, are inextricably bound up with the cultures in which they are proclaimed. (After all, not even the most diehard purists today would limit themselves to speaking Aramaic when sharing the good news.)

Christians are no less steeped in contemporary culture than our neighbours. But sometimes it seems we have cast ourselves as omniscient guardians of timeless truth, then agreed that we should convene a symposium every few years to repackage such truth for a pesky culture that cannot seem to make up its mind about who or what it wants to be.

Much of what happened during the transformation at Trinity was certainly designed to make things more accessible to those who might be coming to church for the first time—or at least for the first time in a long while. But I would not describe the changes as watering anything down or as a strained overreaching for relevance. If anything, they represented not a bending to culture but a stripping away of culture. Practices that had developed over decades or even centuries of church tradition still made sense to those in the know, but they were baffling to the uninitiated. Removing or updating these was not a capitulation: it was simply an acknowledgement that in the time since these practices had first been introduced, the culture had moved on.

In some ways, I had a front row seat to the changes that happened at Trinity over the years. This was sometimes the view from beside the altar, where I sat as a server, looking out into the faces of a congregation that was by turns astonished or delighted or annoyed (but rarely bored) by the changes taking place in front of them. It was also the view from my seat at our kitchen table, where I listened intently as my father relayed to my mother the highs and lows of a church leader's life.

But it is also true that much of what took place in those early years at Trinity was closed to me. I was ten years old when we moved to Streetsville. I was not part of any meetings; nor was I consulted on any decisions. Besides, in those days I had more interest in collecting baseball cards or throwing a tennis ball at the strike zone I had chalked on the back wall of our house than I did in the vagaries of church leadership.

What I know of the transformation at Trinity comes not from any careful observation or study but simply from being one of the many people who were caught up in the life of the community during those days. I did not have much interest in the principles of leading change. But I was around enough—at Sunday services and youth group meetings and church picnics and holiday celebrations—to know that something special was going on.

In what follows, I do not offer a play-by-play history of the transformation at Trinity. Nor do I seek to extract from the process a set of timeless principles that leaders can take and apply in their own contexts. I offer, instead, a portrait of the man who led this transformation and highlight some of the qualities that made it possible for him to do so.

This is not meant as a blueprint but rather as a simple set of observations. No doubt there are as many ways to bring about transformation in a community as there are leaders. But this was my father's way. And it worked.

VISION

The first thing the leader needs before implementing change is vision. By this I do not mean that they need a well-crafted vision statement, hammered out on a leadership retreat or hanging on a plaque on the wall. This is fine, if you want to do it. But it is not what I am talking about. I am talking about vision in the most basic sense of "seeing." The leader must know what he or she wants the future to look like. It is often more a feeling than a sentence. A picture, not a statement. But it is, at least in the leader's mind, clear and compelling.

One immediate consequence of having this kind of picture of the future is that it shines a bright light on the current reality. The ability to see a new future creates an ability to see the present. A plain, clear-eyed view of the current situation is an almost inevitable consequence of having a clear view of the future. Things that have been taken for granted—that have always been just "the way we do things"—suddenly feel wrong and have to go. Other things that have been missing but not missed are suddenly felt as gaping holes. This clear-eyed *seeing* of the present gives the leader all the material he or she needs to get going on making changes.

In the case of Trinity, one of the things that was obviously missing was new people. The congregation was well established, and most of the people in the pews on Sunday morning were long-time members. Sure, from time to time a committed Anglican might move into the area and show up. But that was rare. I don't imagine that most parishioners walked into the sanctuary each Sunday and asked, "Where are all the new families?" But to my father, who had in mind a vibrant, healthy congregation that was there not just for itself but for the community around it, this was a glaring omission. It was time to get down to the business of inviting people to church.

This imperative brought with it another kind of seeing. Because once you know that you are going to start inviting people, it is only natural to sit in church on Sunday morning and see the service through their eyes. The experience is like suddenly realizing how messy our house is when we know company is coming over or discovering that a previously innocuous movie is wildly inappropriate once we sit down to watch it with our parents.

Every element of the service at Trinity was examined in this new light. Yes, *we* all know what it means. But what is it going to look like to the family who walks through those doors next week, having never been to church before? Is it going to appear relevant and compelling to them? Will they even know what we are talking about?

From the music and the prayers to the bulletin and the signage, everything had to be re-examined. Every little change was run through this filter.

INSTINCTS

Once a leader has adopted this new way of seeing, a second problem emerges. Rarely is it the case that everything is humming along magnificently and one or two tweaks will do the trick. Much more likely is it that the leader sees dozens or even hundreds of things that need to be changed. And some of those changes are likely to be whoppers.

This is where the second quality of the transformative leader comes in. The leader needs good instincts. Which changes should be made at once, and which battles are better left unfought? Is it better to start with a few small, incremental changes or to make a bold move that will send a message? How much is too much for people to handle at one time?

Naturally, some practical guidance can be helpful here. Many good leadership books will offer useful insight. Connect the changes to a larger purpose. Start with changes that key leaders support in order to create some quick wins and needed momentum. Choose areas where it is possible to start small—by running a test or pilot project that can easily be abandoned or reversed if it does not work out.

But at the end of all this, the leader will still need to make some decisions. While all of us would love to have the playbook that confirms we are on the right path, no such thing exists. One day he or she will have the luxury of hindsight by which to evaluate them, but in the moment, it will be decidedly unclear whether or not this or that move is the right one. Making good decisions is, at the end of the day, more art than science.

My father had very good instincts. Some things he did right away, like changing elements of the service to include language that would be more accessible to the non-churchgoer. But it was several years, as I recall, before the priestly robes were abandoned in favour of a suit and tie. Creative illustrations and demonstrations in the sermons were there from the beginning—he could not help himself. But it would be a while before a drama team was created and given free rein to unleash their creativity. A troupe of actors prancing through the aisles in giant apple, banana, and grape costumes, talking about the fruits of the Spirit, during his first weeks at Trinity would have been too much, too soon.

My father's instincts showed up in other areas, too. Years later, when the church suffered a massive fire right in the middle of a full-scale construction project, the fire was discovered to have been an act of vandalism by a local teenager. When the young man was tried in juvenile court, my father suggested that part of his sentence should be to help set up chairs each week in the school gym that would be the church's temporary home while the damage from the fire was repaired and construction completed. Embraced by the congregation and especially the volunteer team he worked with, this young man got to see firsthand the community he had affected. And the congregation received a visible reminder of what it meant to be a community of grace and forgiveness.

AUDACITY

Some people feel most comfortable preserving the status quo. Such people often like to remain in the background, to make sure everyone is happy, to avoid rocking the boat.

My father is not one of those people. For as long as I can remember—and if the stories are anything to go on, for much longer than that—he has been someone who likes to stir the pot. He asks the question that no one else will ask, says out loud the thing that is awkward to say.

This is not, I believe, an approach to life and leadership that he has intentionally fostered over the years. He did not read an article about the value of audacity in leadership and establish a program of developing it in himself. It is simply who he is.

He recalls sitting in a college lecture hall as a young man while an elderly professor admonished the students about the dangers of going to the movies. To hear him tell it, he heard a voice call out, "You should try the movies now, sir. They talk." As he looked down the row of desks to find the source of this witticism, he realized that the voice that had called out was his own. These things just come out of him. He cannot help himself.

My father has an audacity that allows him to jump in and get things going without worrying too much about what might go wrong. He is not careless or foolish. But neither is he afraid of tackling something big without seeing clearly beforehand how it is going to end. I fondly remember family vacations when I was a child that consisted of packing up the camping gear and hitting the open road, "just to see where we end up." There was no map, no itinerary, no plan. But with my father at the wheel, we all knew there were grand adventures ahead. For him, the uncertainty was part of the fun. To have the entire route mapped out ahead of time would have felt to him deathly boring, and it would not have been long before he grew restless and we were tearing up the plans and taking a detour somewhere.

I am not suggesting that planning is unimportant or that everyone needs to adopt my father's carefree approach or occasional lack of filter. This was him, and others will be different. But I do believe that without these elements of his personality, Trinity would not have developed the way it did or had the impact it has had. And I do believe that, whatever their personal style might be, an underlying audacity is required of leaders who would lead people successfully through significant change.

Early on in our family's time at Trinity, I remember being enlisted by my father to hand out flyers in the neighbourhoods around the church. A team of volunteers had been gathered, and we spread out to try to cover as many houses as possible. My father was right in there with the troops, with his kids at his side.

The flyers he had chosen were, for their time, downright edgy. A picture of Santa beside an image of Jesus, with the caption "Whose birthday is it, anyway?" A picture of the empty tomb beside some pastel-coloured jelly beans, asking, "Does Easter mean beans to your kids?" Or my personal favourite: a photo of six pallbearers carrying a casket, with the headline "Will it take six strong men to bring you back to church?"

These flyers were certainly polarizing. For some in the congregation, they were a breath of fresh air and a signal of exciting things ahead. But for others, they went too far and crossed the line of respectability. I imagine that my father wondered more than once whether he was making a mistake in using them.

But looking back, these flyers represented a defining moment. For one thing, they certainly conveyed to the people who found them at their front doors that they were not being invited to the same old, traditional church. More importantly, I think, they sent a message to those who were already in the church. The flyers said that the people out there in our neighbourhoods mattered to us, and we as a congregation would go to great lengths to gain their attention.

If everyone is on your side, if everyone is encouraging you, if everyone is telling you that you are on exactly the right path, then it is safe to say you are not leading anyone through any major changes. Because that is not what it feels like. There can be allies, of course. But there will also be opposition. There will be fear. There will be uncertainty about whether this thing you are undertaking is even going to work.

In those moments, there is no way around it. The leader needs to jump and to invite others to jump with him.

GRIT

If my father was bold in beginning, he was also determined in finishing. This quality goes by many names: persistence, stick-to-it-iveness, stubbornness, grit. Whatever you call it, my father had it to spare.

Among the highlights of my childhood were the times my father took me to watch the Blue Jays play at Exhibition Stadium in Toronto. We used to sit in the right field bleachers, which afforded a perfect view of my childhood hero, Jesse Barfield, and his famous cannon of an arm.

While all of these trips were wonderful, one stands out above the rest. On this particular afternoon, we found ourselves sitting a few rows behind an empty section of bleachers that had been roped off. Since he was with two small boys—my brother and me—who could not easily see over the people in front of us, sometime around the third inning Dad decided it would be easier for the three of us to move down to this empty section.

It was not long before an employee of the stadium came by to inform us that we were not allowed to sit there and ask us to return to our seats. The section had been reserved for workers of the Toronto Transit Commission, he explained, and was off limits to us. My father pointed out politely that it was already the third inning, and since the section (which probably seated five hundred people) currently contained exactly zero transit workers, it seemed unlikely that the reserved seats were going to fill up. "Now if you'll excuse me," he said, "I am going to watch the game with my boys."

What followed over the next hour or so was a procession of people of increasing importance. First another employee of the stadium, then his supervisor, and eventually a police officer were sent to reason with my dad. Each of them explained that we could not sit there. And each one listened to him explain that it was ridiculous not to give two small boys a spot where they could see the game when an entire section was sitting empty. They tried everything they could think of, short of physically removing him, but my father was unshakable. By this point, he was all in, and I think he just might have preferred being physically removed from the stadium in handcuffs to returning to his original seat.

As a boy of eight years old, I was fascinated by the whole thing. It also turned out that the crowd seated behind us was enjoying the show, and occasionally someone would chime in with their support for our cause. Eventually—and I still have no idea how this happened—the police officer decided that we could, in fact, stay where we were. I looked up admiringly at my dad. The section behind us erupted in cheers.

This was before my father took over as the rector at Trinity. But he brought this dogged determination with him when he came. I have no doubt that it played a big part in helping him shape the church the way he did. It was not that he was unwilling to listen to the opinions of others or that he liked a good fight for its own sake. But he steadfastly refused to give in on things that simply didn't make sense. And I am sure that more than once he had to stand his ground—sometimes for a very long time—on a decision that some in the congregation were not ready to accept.

This last quality is perhaps the most important of all in effecting real and lasting change. A leader like my father can see more clearly than those around him. He can have sharp instincts that allow him to make the right move at the right time. He can have the audacity to zig when others want him to zag. But if a leader cannot stick with it for the long haul and do the hard work of grinding it out, day after day, all may come to nothing in the end.

This determination is, of course, closely tied to the vision we discussed at the outset. For if a leader does not have a clear and compelling picture of the future that he or she is striving for, it is hard to find the motivation to stand firm against the opposition. Vision provides fuel for the grit.

My father has now been retired for many years. But if you visit Trinity Streetsville today, you will still find a thriving church. It is a church where Sunday morning services are still crafted with the newcomer in mind. It is a church where involvement in the community—whether through classes in English as a second language, practical help on getting out of debt, care and counselling for the grieving, or dozens of other ministries—is the norm. Most important, you will find a group of people who simply take it as a given that the church is there for others. These are people who know that they are living God's vision to the fullest when they are working for the benefit of someone who has yet to walk through the doors of their church. And they would be surprised if you told them that things had ever been any other way.

THE GIFT OF LEADERSHIP
JAMIE HOLTOM

WHEN I WAS AT SEMINARY, THE FIRST TIME I EVEN NOTICED THE WORD "LEADERSHIP" WAS in a course offered by Harold Percy and John Bowen. I was at Emmanuel College, the theological school for the United Church of Canada, and for some reason when I was choosing courses one term, this course really jumped out at me. I can't say that I knew much about leadership at the time, and certainly not the significance of leadership, but there was something about this course that seemed both practical and concrete.

That course on congregational leadership ended up being one of the best and most influential of the courses I took during my seminary days. I can't honestly say that I remember the actual content of the course. But what I do remember is being around a natural leader like Harold. There was something about the way he carried himself. He had a vision for the church that inspired me. He had a clarity of conviction, a focus on Christ and his mission, and a confidence to communicate these things. It all started to draw me in. As we moved through the course, I started to get hooked on the importance of leadership and the desire to grow in my own understanding and practice of leadership skills. God began to raise in me the conviction that the effectiveness of my ministry would depend on the principles that I was learning. Taking full responsibility to grow as a leader was no longer something I could avoid.

Over the years, I have been blessed to know Harold both as a mentor and as a friend. Every single conversation I am blessed to have had with him has led to new learning and continued growth. As I share some of these lessons, I hope that you also will be blessed.

THE IMPORTANCE OF LEADERSHIP

Many leadership gurus say that everything rises and falls on leadership. In my experience, that is absolutely true. It doesn't mean that other roles are not important. It doesn't mean that the leader carries out the vision alone. It doesn't mean that surrounding circumstances are not significant. However, as I look around, it is absolutely true that—whether in the church or in any other organization—everything seems to rise and fall on leadership.

In our own church, you could look behind or beneath any of our successful ministries, and can you guess what you would find? A leader! Behind every successful ministry, you will find a capable and gifted leader through whom God has done amazing things.

Let me offer some examples. (I suspect that there are similar examples in every church; perhaps developing a list like this would help all pastors increase their awareness of the importance of leadership within their own churches.)

- We have a baptism course for young parents, created by two leaders named Judy Reid and Joan Grandy, who made it their mission to help families grow in Christ through the baptismal process. They began this course more than ten years ago, as a result of which hundreds of parents and families have been blessed by God—all because these two leaders followed through with a great idea.
- A few times a year, we organize a clothing exchange that blesses the community around us. Each time, hundreds of people who could not otherwise afford new clothing show up to receive free clothes. Each time, a beautiful team of volunteers has a blast making it all happen. This ministry began and continues because a young leader named Alison McCulloch had a vision from God and acted on it.
- We have a music program that enables people to worship God, includes a range of ages in leadership, and blesses people Sunday

after Sunday, all because of faithful, passionate, and gifted leaders such as Bonnie Greene, Jose Shapero, and Steve Allin.
- As the financial situation of our growing church has become more and more complex, a dedicated team has emerged to manage this area of ministry. Today there are systems in place to help us track, manage, and grow God's resources, all because George Watson rolled up his sleeves and offered some fantastic leadership.

I could go on and on with real results from real leaders who have stepped forward to offer their ideas, skills, time, and energy.

As I look at congregations across our country, I see signs of hope and growth in various communities. Of course, I also see many challenges, and I see churches that are on a path toward closing down. In each case, however, the difference is neither location nor resources nor outside factors in general. The difference is always leadership, because everything really does rise or fall on leadership.

GOOD NEWS

The good news is that leadership can be taught and grown and shared. In fact, the good news is that good, strong, faithful leadership is God's idea. That is why, whenever God has something that needs to be done on planet earth, a leader gets tapped on the shoulder and raised up.

- Need to build an ark as part of saving the world? How about Noah? He is a good man who can do the job.
- Need to take the people from Egypt to the Promised Land? There's a fellow named Moses who might be up for the task. He may not think so, but let's tap him on the shoulder anyway.
- It's time for a message of challenge and hope because my people have wandered away from me (again!). Let me see . . . How about Jeremiah? Or Ezekiel? Or even Jonah? Done.
- Now for one of God's most creative projects ever: it's time for God to come to earth, and someone will need to make the delivery. How about Mary? She seems like a good choice!

Because leadership is God's idea, we are never alone in what God has called us to do: God calls us, invites us, challenges us, encourages us, *and* empowers us.

A LEADER'S GREATEST ASSET

After almost twenty years of Christian leadership, I have come to a conclusion that in my mind makes sense—in fact, so much sense that this next section is the most important in the chapter. In the context of church leadership (or anywhere else, to be honest), our greatest asset is without question relying on the power of God as the source of our wisdom, direction, confidence, energy, and life itself. So, the most important thing a Christian leader can do is to spend time with God in prayer, allowing Jesus to draw us near and the Holy Spirit to empower us for ministry.

In Acts 1, Jesus promises that he will give his disciples his Spirit so that they can continue the work he began: "But you will receive power," he says, "when the Holy Spirit has come upon you; and you will be my witnesses in Jerusalem, in all Judea and Samaria, and to the ends of the earth" (Acts 1:8). For Jesus' followers today, this promise guides our work as well. We, too, have been given power from on high, and the more we tap into that power, the more we will become the leaders God intends for us to be. The best leaders I know all take time to reflect, to pray, to listen for God's voice in their lives and in their organizations, and simply to know that they are loved and valued beyond what they do or how much they "produce." In my own life and leadership, as my life with Christ has grown over the years, I have been blessed by this life-giving relationship and by spending intimate time with God each day.

It is amazing what God can do when we simply take time to be with him. It can be through reading a passage of Scripture each day. It might be by journaling our prayers each morning. It could be through listening to worship music that enriches our heart with Jesus' own compassion. It could be a form of meditative or centring prayer, as we spend time listening for God in our busy lives. But however we do it, taking time with God will require intentionality. By means of such spiritual practices, many have experienced the inner movement from duty to discipline to delight, a movement I have heard Harold name many times. When we start out, it might feel like a duty, an obligation. Then it gradually becomes a discipline. Finally, it becomes a delight. We wake up in the morning and simply can't wait to spend some time with God. As we practise our own form of spiritual discipline, we ourselves are changed in this process. We are transformed by the renewing of our minds (Rom 12:1–2).

God is the source of all creativity. So as we spend time with God, we discover more ideas and visions of what God wants us to do. God is the source of our power, our strength, and our confidence. It is only as we spend time with God that we develop the "spirit of power" rather than the "spirit of cowardice" of which Scripture speaks (2 Tim 1:6–7). Again, God is the one who will give us peace and calm our hearts in the midst of any and all leadership challenges. As we lean into God, we discover an assurance and gratitude that changes how we respond to the needs and opportunities of ministry (Phil 4:6–7). All this and more is a direct result of spending time intentionally with God each day. As leaders, this is our greatest asset.

PERSONAL LEADERSHIP DEVELOPMENT

Although I believe it to be a leader's most important asset, a healthy spiritual life is only one aspect of personal leadership ability. Even though it is often neglected when leaders get busy, developing skills in other areas is also essential because, at the end of the day, the effectiveness of the organization and team will depend upon the effectiveness of their leader. John Maxwell calls this the law of the lid.[2] The leader represents "the lid" of the organization and will limit the success that is possible. According to a popular saying, "The speed of the leader equals the speed of the team." Despite what many believe, continued personal growth as a leader really isn't optional. It is significant not just for the leader but also for their entire team, project, or organization because as the leader grows, so does everyone else around them.

So how do good leaders help themselves to grow?

1. *Read as much as you can about leadership.* There are many excellent leadership books out there. *Courageous Leadership*, by Bill Hybels, is a classic and should be on every Christian

---

[2] John Maxwell, *The 21 Irrefutable Laws of Leadership: Follow Them and People Will Follow You* (Nashville: Thomas Nelson, 2007), 1–9.

leader's bookshelf.³ Any book by John Maxwell will bless you and your leadership, but I would particularly recommend *The 21 Irrefutable Laws of Leadership* and *The 15 Invaluable Laws of Growth*.⁴

There are many other good books on leadership, as well as excellent online resources and videos. The main point is that you must discipline and challenge yourself for continued growth in leadership. Again, as you grow, so will the people around you. Always share your new insights. Consider purchasing more than one copy of any book you like to give to the leaders around you, as a way of investing in them and encouraging their own growth.

2. *Attend one leadership conference each year.* There are many different conferences that will bless you in your role as a leader. The key is to recognize that part of your personal leadership growth involves regularly attending conferences that can develop your leadership skills. I am part of a group that has attended the Willow Creek Leadership Summit for over fifteen years, where we have been blessed to hear from some of the best leaders on the planet. Whatever conference you choose, you will be reminded and inspired each year about the significance of leadership and will pick up many helpful tips along the way.

3. *Find a mentor or coach.* I was blessed to spend the first fifteen years of my ministry life working with an amazing mentor named Norm Greene. Through sharing day-to-day life with him, sitting at the same table, praying with him, and simply watching his life and leadership, I grew in ways I didn't even realize at the time. We may not all have the luxury of a mentor in our actual day-to-day work in that way. However, we can all choose to meet with a mentor on a regular basis (I would suggest monthly). This is a time for you to ask questions, share challenges, and receive encouragement and wisdom as you make your way through life and leadership.

---

³ Bill Hybels, *Courageous Leadership: Field-Tested Strategy for the 360° Leader* (Grand Rapids: Zondervan, 2002, 2012).

⁴ John Maxwell, *The 15 Invaluable Laws of Growth: Live Them and Reach Your Potential* (New York: Center Street, 2012).

I want to close this section with one word that is of prime importance in each of the areas named. That word is "intentionality." None of the strategies that I have described will happen without your intentionally choosing to make them happen. When you do make that choice, I guarantee it will be worth it, because you will grow as a result. And when you grow, everyone around you will grow, too.

THE ROLE OF A LEADER = ULTIMATE RESPONSIBILITY

Different people have different definitions and ideas of what it means to be a leader. As far as I am concerned, leaders are people who make things happen. We could drill deeper into the way things get done or discuss guiding values and principles to ensure that the right things get done, but at the end of the day the leader is the one who makes things happen. Another way to think about the role of a leader comes from a phrase that I picked up at a conference many years ago, which described the role of a leader as taking "ultimate responsibility." In my mind, that makes sense: the leader is the one person who is ultimately responsible. Too often I see people who are in positions of leadership, at least in the sense that they have the title, but don't see ultimate responsibility as part of their role. I once heard a minister share the challenges of a congregation that was not very open to outsiders. In defeat, she complained, "They're just not that welcoming." Yet in my mind the question was obvious: "Whose job is it to help them *become* welcoming?" That is the role of the leader; *that* is ultimate responsibility.

Taking ultimate responsibility does not mean that leaders do everything themselves. Nor does it mean that everything always has to be perfect. It doesn't mean that other opinions are not valued or included as one leads collaboratively. It simply means that, at the end of the day, there is clarity about who takes ultimate responsibility for the outcome of the project: that person is the leader.

As the one who takes ultimate responsibility, there are a number of important ways that a leader can get his or her job done. Here are a few of them:

1. *Establish a vision.* Sometimes we get caught up in the task of defining a vision and never get past trying to find a good working definition for the ministry that needs to be done. A

vision doesn't have to be large and complicated. On the contrary, the more concrete the vision statement is, the more people will understand and be inspired by it. That, too, is part of the role of a leader—to inspire people with a vision.

It could be as simple as saying that we are going to have half of our people in small groups over the next three years. It could be that we are going to establish an outreach to a particular area of our community. It could be that we will work toward having 80 percent of our people pray and read Scripture on a daily (or almost daily) basis. It could be that we will send our welcome team into the parking lot so that every person who comes to our worship services will be greeted by someone even before they walk through our doors. Part of taking ultimate responsibility is taking responsibility for establishing a vision. And that points us back to why intentional time with God is so important—because God is always the ultimate source of every vision.

2. *Build a team.* Good leaders know instinctively that they cannot do it on their own. So a leader builds a team, which means getting other people involved so that they can be part of implementing the vision. Building a team also means allowing God to help leaders and their organizations reach their full potential.

In Exodus 18, Moses gets some great advice from his father-in-law: Jethro hears about all that Moses is doing and recognizes that the job is too much. He challenges Moses to get others involved, to break down his many responsibilities into manageable pieces in order to give some of the leadership responsibility away. Does this sound familiar? Do you ever feel like you're swamped or that there are just not enough hours in the day to accomplish everything that needs to get done? Sooner or later, every good leader reaches this point. But building a team and getting others on board does not mean that you are shrinking from your leadership responsibilities. On the contrary, sharing responsibility is one of the most important ways in which a good leader can fulfill their responsibilities. Involving others allows more of God's work to get done. Even more important, perhaps, is the fact that more people will get to participate in it.

More people will be inspired and grateful as they experience the blessing and privilege of being part of what God is doing in this place. They will be so glad you invited them in.

3. *Create a culture.* This is the behind-the-scenes work of a good leader. Although most people will hardly even notice, this dimension of leadership often takes the most time and has the greatest lasting impact. Every organization, family, team, or other group of people will have a "culture" of its own. That culture is more often experienced than named, more often felt than thought about. It is about behaviour as much as it is about results. One of the key responsibilities of a leader is to be intentional about what kind of culture the group will have and then to work towards creating that culture.

For example, if you coach a Little League baseball team, do you want team members to be encouraging of each other? If so, the culture must be created. You name it: we will be a team that encourages each other. You model it: even if there are areas in which a single player or the entire team needs to be challenged, you also include some encouragement every time you speak. You teach your team how to live like this: here is how to encourage each other. Over time, you will develop a team with a culture of encouragement. Parents, other players, and their coaches will all be asking why your team is so encouraging. The real answer (behind the scenes) is that the team is encouraging because you are a good leader and have worked to create a culture of encouragement.

If we translate this example into practical principles for our churches, we will begin to see how important it is to work at creating a particular culture. Within a community of Christian faith, a leader can work towards creating a culture with these characteristics:

- People pray.
- Leadership is encouraged.
- Reaching out to new people happens regularly.
- Generosity is normal.

- People are open and transparent and *still* get along.
- Hard work is expected.
- A sense of fun and positivity rule most days.
- Creativity and new initiatives are expected.

None of this happens by accident. But with intentionality and a leader who takes ultimate responsibility, these are just some of the ways in which a community or organization can be blessed as they live out the vision that God has given them.

THE COURAGE TO LEAD

Although it has not yet been mentioned specifically, there is a common element to everything that has been said so far: every single item requires courage.

- It takes courage to lead, to say, "I will take responsibility for this."
- It takes courage to consider a vision, let alone share it with others.
- It takes courage to invite someone else onto the leadership team and courage even to accept that invitation.
- It takes courage to grow in one's own leadership skills, to follow God's leading toward new vision and greater responsibility.

In short, leadership takes courage. I remember one of my first leadership assignments, which was to lead a children's ministry. At the time, I knew nothing about leading children's ministry, and looking back, I'm not even sure why they hired me. I was afraid I would fail, and at times the fear was almost overwhelming. I remember the first time I conducted a funeral: I was literally trembling in my boots. What if I said the wrong words or the family didn't like what I had to say? I remember taking a leadership initiative that would eventually lead to establishing The Journey,[5] a neighbourhood centre in an underprivileged area of Brampton. There were so many unknowns and so many people wanting to challenge the project. It was one of the scariest things I've ever done. All these initiatives (and many more!) required leadership. And they all required courage.

---

[5] Learn more about The Journey at http://www.thejourneyneighbourhoodcentre.ca.

God gives courage and strength, and Jesus promises that he will always be with us (Matt 28:20). This is especially precious for leaders who are trying to advance his work and presence in the world. Much earlier, Joshua faces an assignment that gives him great fear, keeps him awake at night, and overwhelms him almost to the point of paralyzing him. In the face of that fear, God provides Joshua with courage, saying, "Be strong and courageous; do not be frightened or dismayed, for the Lord your God is with you wherever you go" (Josh 1:9). The same promise remains true for us as well. God will give us courage to lead in times of need:

- When circumstances are difficult and it takes courage even to name the facts of the situation, God enables us to speak.
- When we face difficult decisions or are afraid to announce something that is unpopular or controversial, God gives both the words and the courage that we need.
- When it is time to have a difficult conversation that we have been avoiding for fear of the consequences, God will provide strength and courage to face the situation head on.
- When we have a new idea or project that could easily get left on the drawing table because it's a little scary and involves many unknowns, we can be assured (like Joshua) that God will be with us and give us courage to move ahead.

It takes courage to lead, yet the good news is that God will give us all the courage we need.

ONE STEP AT A TIME

Although the responsibilities of leadership can seem overwhelming, it is reassuring to know that every leader has felt this way from time to time. Yet it remains true that God will provide you with all that you need to fulfill the calling God has given you. It is important to remember that the skills, responsibilities, and plain hard work of leadership are not about being perfect or arriving at your final destination all at once. True leadership is more about taking one step at a time, which is the way even the largest projects and the most humanly impossible visions are ultimately accomplished.

Terry Fox began his Marathon of Hope back in 1980, running the equivalent of a marathon a day for 143 days. How did he do it? His brother Darrel reported, "If he thought about getting to Stanley Park [Vancouver] and finishing the marathon, that was too far out there. It was running to that next hill or that telephone pole, that's how he visualized and told himself he'd be seeing home."[6]

In fact, that is how any marathon has to be run, not just a Marathon of Hope. Leadership, too, is like running a marathon because leading church or other organizations simply requires us taking one step at a time. Even reading this book is taking another step towards becoming the leader that God is leading you to become.

Because it is God who leads us in leadership, we can hardly do better than to end with prayer:

Gracious and loving God,
> Thank you for the invitation to follow you and to become part of what you are doing in the world. Amidst all the challenges of leadership, I entrust my life and ministry to you. May your power, grace, confidence, humility, patience, courage, and joy fill me as I lead your people. May others be blessed by the person and leader that you enable me to be. Ultimately, may my will be one with yours; may my heart become more like yours; may my sphere of influence, however small, reflect your presence and power because of your work in my life. In Jesus' name and through his Spirit, amen.

---

[6] Dan Robson and Catherine McIntyre, "I Only Think about the Next Mile," *Maclean's*, June 29, 2017, http://www.macleans.ca/i-only-think-about-the-next-mile.

BEING INTENTIONAL IN LEADERSHIP
JUDY PAULSEN

ONE OF THE MOST INSTRUCTIVE EVENTS EVER TO SHAPE MY MINISTRY OCCURRED WITHIN the first fifteen minutes of the first day that I was in charge of a parish. I had been ordained only a few weeks before, and the senior pastor had left on vacation. As I entered my office I eagerly anticipated my first day in leadership. What significant theological tasks would I engage in? Would I help someone to know God more deeply? What would be my part in the growth of the kingdom of God?

My office phone rang just as I was taking off my coat. It was a call from a church member annoyed that the planters they had donated to the church were not being watered properly. As I hung up the phone, I realized that my grandiose ideas about parish ministry had been dismantled swiftly and thoroughly. (As you might have guessed, the flowers weren't this person's only complaint!) There were, apparently, forces at play in the day-to-day life of a pastor of which I had been blissfully unaware. I realized that my entire ministry could easily be spent in reaction to church members' felt needs.

Of course, seminary had prepared me for the fact that at least part of my work would focus on responding to those needs. After all, that is what it means to be a community of faith. We love each other. We listen to and care for each other, and the pastor or priest is fully engaged in that dynamic. As a pastor, you expect that people will share their needs, worries, and opinions with you. But I saw that without a more intentional focus on other priorities, my days could easily be spent completely in reactive mode, resulting in an internally driven vortex that would suck up every ounce of my energy. I began to see that a more balanced approach was needed.

One of the seasoned clergy who helped me flesh out a different approach to ministry was Harold Percy. Two of the most important pieces of advice I received from him were as follows: first, in order to cultivate churches that are engaged in the mission of God, church leaders need to be intentional about that task, as opposed to reactive. Second, Scripture needs to be the touchstone that defines what such a church is and does.

Intentional ministry, grounded in Scripture, lives itself out in numerous different aspects of ministry and involves assessment, exploration, experimentation, and development in each area. Church structures, discipleship training, preaching, finances, pastoral care, worship, and leadership development are just a few of the areas of parish life that we can examine in terms of an *intentional* approach to ministry that is focused on mission.

INTENTIONAL CHURCH STRUCTURES

One of the biggest surprises for me when I first began my role as senior pastor of a church was just how often church structures operate apart from any intentional assessment or development. Quite simply, we don't ask frequently enough why we organize ourselves the way we do. Whether we are talking about leadership structures, meeting formats, or even long-standing ministries, too often they are regarded as being set in stone and unchangeable.

Towards the end of my first month in a new church, the monthly leadership team (the "parish advisory" group) gathered. I already knew from the previous year's minutes that attendance at these meetings was less than stellar. I soon discovered the reason. Few people had a clear sense of why they were there. Who was "advising" whom? Few people were sure. Over the years, these meetings had essentially become reporting sessions in which every ministry group offered up a thorough (often *very* thorough) report of all they'd been doing. No one wanted to look lazy, so no detail was too small to be included. Apart from a short opening prayer, there was little time allotted for really engaging with God or considering where God might be leading us next. These meetings seemed primarily to be about *maintaining* what was already in place.

Subsequent meetings were quite different. We began by studying a passage of Scripture together, focusing on some aspect of mission and leadership. We then broke into smaller groups to pray specifically for our respective areas of ministry, both giving thanks and bringing needs to God. We then shared and discussed information that was pertinent to the whole group, with more general ministry updates submitted in point form and disseminated to the whole group via email. We reduced these large group meetings from twelve to five times a year, with each meeting having a specific focus (e.g., September: ministry start-up review; November: ministry budget building; January: preparation for the annual meeting; April: annual ministry assessment review; June: fall ministry planning). Not surprisingly, attendance flourished.

Other structures in the parish also needed to engage in self-assessment with respect to purpose, configuration, and format. For example, it became clear that the senior pastor wasn't needed at every meeting of all the various standing committees (e.g., the property and building committee or the chancel guild). Leaders of these groups were well able to direct these ministries, and I could be kept informed by receiving minutes of their meetings and by meeting with their leaders on a regular basis. This approach allowed lay leaders to actually lead these groups. It also freed me to focus more intentionally on leadership development for other ministries and to cultivate missional engagement with our neighbourhood—building partnerships with local schools and developing a new catechetical tool for people with little to no church background.

Other examples of changes in structure included the dropping of at least one standing committee, the formation of time-limited working groups to tackle specific projects, and changes to how new ministry leaders were developed and equipped. In every case, our meetings began to be more grounded in Scripture and prayer, especially as we considered how all that we were doing was to further the spread of the gospel.

Within a year or so, we had learned to view our church structures more intentionally. We asked all our committees, groups, and ministries to examine and develop their work according to four main criteria:

1. *Intentionally place God's mission at the centre as they defined their purpose.* Each group and ministry was asked to articulate clearly the purpose for which they existed.
2. *Intentionally assess their present configuration and practices in terms of engagement and efficacy in accomplishing their purpose.* Were the people engaged in that ministry the most passionate about and gifted for that work, or did some people need to be freed to engage in other ministries?
3. *Intentionally explore other structures as needed to better fulfill their purpose.* Where were the gaps? What new groups, ministries, or processes could fill these gaps?
4. *Intentionally rely upon God's gifting and timing to advance their purpose.* Each group started with the assumption that God would place in their midst everything that was needed to accomplish whatever it was he wanted done.

Why this approach? Because no group, ministry, or church is called to do everything. Discern where and to what you are called so as to join in God's own mission and ministry in that place; then watch for his provision and timing to accomplish it.

INTENTIONAL DISCIPLESHIP

Christian formation is one of the most pressing challenges facing leaders in the church today. It is challenging because we now live in a society in which few people have any knowledge of even the most basic Christian teaching. We need tools and processes that help introduce unchurched people to the faith. Christian formation is also challenging because many of the long-time church members, though better grounded in Scripture and Christian practice, still do not feel equipped (or compelled) to share their faith with others. We need tools and processes that help Christians to share the gospel and to mature in the practice of their faith.

Yet in many churches across North America, little attention is given to the intentional development and use of such tools and processes. Many congregations remain primarily focused on their Sunday (or other weekly) worship services as the core of "what they do," hoping that by getting better at worship they will attract people back to church. This is misguided thinking. Worship itself should not be focused on attracting the unchurched (or even on ourselves, for that matter). Worship must always focus squarely on God. It should be both about God and directed to God. This does not rule out the possibility of people being drawn to God through worship; quite the contrary. Conviction, conversion, and transformation may all take place in the course of worship. But these are not the true *purpose* of worship.

How, then, do we intentionally develop people as disciples, which is to say, as apprentices of the Saviour and Lord Jesus Christ? I suggest that churches need to take initiative in four ways:

1. *Intentionally recognize that because people are at different places in the journey of discipleship, they need different resources.* I distinctly remember a young woman asking, "Did you really mean what you said about people not needing to know *anything* before coming to that group? Because I don't want to embarrass myself." Offer discipleship training for people who are starting from scratch, for those who are returning to faith with some basic background in Christianity, and for long-time Christians seeking more in-depth learning and practice. This assumes, of course, that your church intends to engage and develop a range of people in the task of growing disciples.

2. *Intentionally present a simple account of the gospel, while offering opportunities for people to respond.* Remember to offer opportunities for repentance and acceptance of Jesus as Lord and Saviour. Provide clear next steps people can take. At the conclusion of a course for those exploring Christianity, for example, offer to those who want to become followers of Jesus a second course in preparation for adult baptism. Hold an annual adult confirmation or reaffirmation of faith service for those who are already baptized but have recently taken a significant new step in their walk with God. From time to time during Sunday worship services, invite people to respond to God by committing (or renewing their commitment) to Christ when they gather at the Lord's Table.

3. *Intentionally teach and preach that becoming more like Christ is a process that extends throughout our whole lives.* For instance, be intentional about teaching about the fruit of the Spirit (Gal 5:22–23) as a helpful measure of Christlikeness and a key indicator of spiritual growth. At least once a year, engage your congregation in a self-assessment exercise that asks which fruit they most need God to bring forth in them, whether love, joy, peace, patience, kindness, goodness, faithfulness, gentleness, or self-control.
4. *Intentionally attend to your own growth as a disciple of Jesus.* Set aside time and space to read Scripture, pray, receive spiritual direction and mentoring, and practise spiritual disciplines. You cannot give others what you yourself do not already have; only disciples can make disciples. So be intentional about your own relationship with God, and teach other teachers and mentors in your church to do the same.

INTENTIONAL PREACHING

Preaching may seem like an odd thing to include on a list of things that leaders need to be more intentional about. After all, isn't preaching one of the primary tasks of priests and pastors? Of course. Preparation of sermons, whether for Sundays, funerals, weddings, or other special services, often consumes a significant proportion of the week for any church leader. Even so, it is remarkably easy to fall into patterns and habits that remain unexamined (and therefore unremedied), sometimes for years.

This is why it is particularly important for preachers to assess and develop their preaching very intentionally. Four questions have helped me in this task:

1. *Do my sermons intentionally reflect the significance of the preaching task?* During my seminary training, a senior pastor circled all the qualifiers and passive verb forms in one of my sermons. Then he asked me why I didn't hold the task of preaching in more reverence. I was shocked; I hadn't realized how hesitant and uncertain I sounded as a preacher. This, then, is the challenge: to root out all the qualifiers and passive verb forms that undermine the authority of the pulpit. Preachers

should say what God gives them to say from Scripture. They should declare it plainly and directly and be unafraid to challenge people to respond with action.
2. *Am I intentionally sharing the good news of the gospel in my sermons?* Again, this seems like a given. Yet it is easy to "major on the minors," forgetting that some of those listening may be there for the first time. (This is especially the case if your sermons are recorded and made available online.) It takes very little effort to acknowledge and include those who are just starting to explore Christianity. Recognize them, and show them the next steps they can take on the journey of faith. Be explicit in acknowledging their different points of departure: use phrases like "Perhaps this is all new to you" or "Many people in our society today have never heard this before" or even "If this all sounds strange to you, you're not alone." It may also be helpful to acknowledge, through the careful use of rhetorical questions, what people may be experiencing as they listen: "Despite the questions you have, do you have a sense that Jesus is inviting you to respond to him?"
3. *Do my sermons intentionally teach the truths found in Scripture about God, about ourselves, and about the world God loves?* Again, this may sound obvious, but such a question can provide a simple "check and balance" that guards against the tendency for preachers to neglect the importance of sound theological instruction. In our rush to application, we can easily end up focusing on human beings instead of on God and our relationship with him.
4. *What does the sermon (reflecting the particular text or texts of Scripture) want listeners to know, feel, and do?* This question intentionally builds into a sermon some clear goals for growth and response, but it also makes certain that Scripture itself determines these goals. Some texts call us to be thankful, and others call us to repentance. Some should lead people into deeper joy, while others lead to renewed commitment. Be intentional about allowing the text to lead both the sermon and the hearers alike.

INTENTIONAL BUDGETING AND FINANCES

Many church budgets are more a reflection of tradition than of intentional planning. In other words, this year's budget is simply last year's budget with a few adjustments to the figures, depending on how optimistic the financial planning team feels at the moment. Have our insurance rates or utility costs gone up? If so, let's just plug in a higher (completely unrealistic) number on the "offerings" line to produce a balanced budget! Did we automatically disperse our "outreach budget" to all eighteen projects that the outreach team chose a decade ago? Great! They're all worthwhile agencies, so let's just do that again.

It is incredibly easy to fall into patterns of behaviour that do not require us to change. So a balanced budget is passed, even though an unbalanced budget might have signalled a deeper truth that the church would prefer to avoid. Questions of efficacy and effectiveness are ignored. Or perhaps the "sympathy hiring" of someone unqualified or dysfunctional is shored up for another year. Have we traditionally been a congregation that never talks about money? Best not to ruffle feathers.

In fact, budgets can be one of the best indicators of the internally focused vortex that controls many church organizations. Churches rarely develop self-absorption intentionally. They fall into a self-centred focus over a period of several years; it simply becomes a habit. Changing this perspective requires intentionality on the part of church leaders. Here are three ways for leaders to become more intentional regarding budgets and finances:

1. *Intentionally place the formation of disciples (the clearest command Jesus gave the church before his ascension) as the driving force behind the selection of projects and expenditure of funds.* If building repairs are necessary, spend the money they require so as to increase your hospitality toward strangers and better engage the surrounding neighbourhood. Buy new audiovisual equipment or furniture in order to help you offer a new course for people exploring Christian faith or to provide space to nurture children in discipleship. Find out how the church can join in and support the work of a local school with the kids they teach, or of the local hospice or shelter, and intentionally increase your

church's outreach budget. Whatever you do, examine it from the perspective of joining in the mission of God.
2. *Intentionally talk about money.* Jesus was never afraid to do this. Have your leaders examine the church budget for what it says about you as a church. What does your church budget say about your church's priorities, your church's heart? What has been hidden, emphasized, or forgotten?
3. *Intentionally challenge church members to give sacrificially.* Since there ought to be visible differences in the way that Christians live, the way in which we spend money should definitely reflect our priorities. Plainly put, Christians ought to live simply and share. This means that most of us ought to be living on 90 percent or less of our net income and giving away at least 10 percent. Although this undoubtedly appears more challenging on a smaller income than on a larger one, that is often not how things play out. For instance, several churches in the more depressed areas of the Greater Toronto Area have significantly higher per member donations than those in wealthier neighbourhoods. Sometimes a larger income just goes toward a larger house, newer cars, more elaborate vacations, and more stuff in general. Help your church see that growing as disciples means growing in giving to others in need.

INTENTIONAL PASTORAL CARE

During my first week as a senior pastor, I was presented with a list of "shut-ins"— members of the church who could no longer join us for Sunday worship or other parish events due to age or illness. There were thirty names on the list. When I asked how they were normally cared for, I was told that they generally received Christmas and Easter Communion from the priest in their home, as well as home visits whenever the priest's schedule allowed. They also received Christmas baskets containing handmade jams, baked goods, crafts, and cards from the church's women's group.

As I thought about these people, many of whom had been in the parish their whole lives, I felt uneasy. Surely we could do more to maintain an ongoing, lively connection between these faithful folk and the church as a whole. In addition to what was already in place, how would we structure things so that they received Communion at least every other week; were sent birthday, Christmas, and Easter cards; and received regular monthly visits updating them on the news of the parish so they could be joining in the ministry of prayer?

It was not all that difficult. We simply needed to be more intentional about the pastoral care of these wonderful people. The parish designated a small honorarium for a pastoral visiting coordinator, established a "friendly visitors team," and trained people to take Communion to congregants unable to attend church on Sunday. The list of thirty shut-ins was divided up in such a way that regular visits became the norm. It really wasn't rocket science; it simply required a little conscious intentionality.

Whenever systems change (even for the better), there will always be some adjustment and discomfort. Initially, people found it strange to be taking Communion brought by someone other than the pastor. But the strangeness soon wore off, and the recipients enjoyed joining in the worship of the church more regularly as they shared the bread and wine of the previous Sunday's Communion service.

Pastors will (I hope) always provide sound pastoral care. But it has often been assumed that they do this best as those who take primary responsibility for hospital and home visits, home Communions, marriage counselling, grief care, and the like. In my view, this is not only inefficient; it is theologically wrong. As the church, we are to *love one another*. Every congregation is blessed to have people with caring hearts, those who are well able to pray and read Scriptures with someone, to share Communion with them, to write a note of encouragement or make a phone call. Pastors need to identify such people intentionally and then equip them to use their God-given gifts.

Many hospitals offer training programs for hospital visitors, and several great programs are available to train pastoral care teams.[7] Clergy are generally well equipped to develop grief or divorce support groups, marriage mentor teams, or young parent coaching groups. Yet there is no need to "recreate the wheel," as there are already plenty of excellent resources on the market to help in these and other areas. Caring for people in all the pivotal moments, stages, and challenges of life can be both exhilarating and exhausting

---

[7] For example, at Trinity Streetsville we used materials from Stephen Ministries (www.stephenministries.org).

ministry. Pastors should definitely be involved in this caring work, in terms of both hands-on personal engagement and general oversight. Each church will require a somewhat different combination of these, depending on size, makeup, and context. However, here are two guidelines that will encourage the intentional development of healthy pastoral care that utilizes all the gifts God has given to the congregation in question:

1. *Intentionally care for people of different ages and needs.* Assess the needs of your church as well as the needs of its neighbourhood context. What is needed to care for people well: a parenting course for first-time parents, a parents and tots group, a parenting teenagers course, an after-school homework ministry, a youth or senior drop-in social time, a retirement-planning course, a "Dealing with Depression" group? Or something else entirely?
2. *Intentionally challenge and equip people to care for each other.* Help people discern and use their gifts, talents, and passions to care for others. This might mean training Communion, hospital, or home visitation teams. It could mean developing leaders for parenting courses or grief support groups. It could mean challenging your church to offer a weekly day program for seniors or an after-school reading club for kids. It could mean forming a team to plan a special "Blue Christmas" or "Prayer for Healing" service. It all depends on matching up the gifted people God has already provided with the needs that you discover around you.

INTENTIONAL WORSHIP

As an Anglican, I love worship that is rooted in the ancient rhythms of the Christian year, a three-year lectionary, and a fourfold pattern to the weekly worship service that includes gathering, ministry of Word, ministry of sacrament, and sending forth. Surely, we qualify as among the most intentional of denominations when it comes to worship. Yet these same ancient rhythms, rich as they are, can also be a source of complacency and even neglect. The words of the liturgy, written with such care, can be rhymed off as if completely devoid of meaning or mystery. Beautiful hymns can be sung without feeling or attention to the meaning contained in them. Bread and wine can be received without a second thought for their significance.

This can also be true of worship in nonliturgical traditions. No matter what form your tradition uses, it can become a lovely but empty lamp in desperate need of oil. Often the first step in rectifying the situation is to notice that the oil has, in fact, run out. As always, intentionality begins with assessment, continues with planning and implementation, and involves ongoing review and evaluation:

1. *Attend more intentionally to your own worship of God.* It has been said that those who lead congregational worship need to find other times and places to worship God for themselves, but that makes no sense to me. In fact, I could not disagree more. If the people leading worship (including the pastor, choir or music team, readers, and Communion assistants) are not worshipping God, then what exactly are they doing? Performing for the congregation? We need to resist such an outlook strongly, starting with the pastor. As you lead in worship, be sure that your heart and mind are focused on God and on the wonder of being invited into his presence. Especially in a liturgical setting, discipline yourself not to read the liturgy but to pray it instead.
2. *Assess whether the worship of your church helps people to engage with the Living God, who is present in their midst.* Authentic worship has been defined as worship in which God is both the object and subject;[8] God is both its primary audience and its primary topic. In other words, worship involves *talking to God* as well as *talking about God.* Do our prayers and hymns pass this most basic assessment? Is God at the centre of all we are doing and saying? Additionally, worship ought to be a time when we celebrate actually being invited into God's presence, and indeed, celebrate his presence with us. Is the congregation behaving in a way consistent with God's presence among them? Whether it is liturgical or nonliturgical in form, this is the oil that will light the lamp of worship.
3. *Plan and implement changes that will allow your worship to meet the criteria of placing God at the centre and engaging the*

---

[8] Marva Dawn, *Reaching Out Without Dumbing Down: A Theology of Worship for This Urgent Time* (Grand Rapids: Eerdmans, 1995), 75–104.

entire congregation. Offer a sermon series on worship; lead a workshop for the musicians, choir, or other worship leaders; together with the music director review the theology of the songs used in worship; recruit and equip a team of readers or Bible storytellers; invite craftspeople to use their talents to enrich the worship space; involve children as readers, choir members, or Communion assistants; or plan for older members to share lessons of faith or lead the prayers. Again, the list of possibilities depends entirely on the current worship of your church and the gifts God has already given you.

INTENTIONAL LEADERSHIP DEVELOPMENT

By the end of my first week in the role of senior pastor, I realized that there was a whole layer of leadership missing from my new church. Although people were serving in a wide variety of ministries, many of those ministries lacked a designated leader who could coordinate the training of new volunteers, budget planning, or reporting to the core leadership group. I realized that I needed to identify and equip an entire cohort of new leaders.

For example, we had a fine team of committed Scripture readers but no one designated to orient new volunteers to this ministry or to recognize those who wanted to step aside for a time. Perhaps this was one of the reasons the same group of about ten people had served as readers for more than a decade. Over that time, a couple of the older volunteers had begun to experience problems with their eyesight. Although they now found public reading both challenging and stressful, they were reluctant to let the church down in the absence of any obvious replacements. One factor limiting the effectiveness of this ministry was a leadership vacuum.

Indeed, intentionality in ministry involves the development and equipping of people to use their gifts, talents, and passions as servants and citizens of the kingdom of God. To this end, I suggest three guidelines that help in the task of intentional leadership development:

1. *Intentionally assess who God has brought here and who among us is not represented in ministry leadership.* Sometimes subtle cultural expectations can affect our choice of who to invite into leadership roles or the willingness of others to offer themselves

in this capacity. Look intentionally for the gaps in age, gender, ethnic background, or length of membership, and seek to bridge them so as to engage the full breadth of the congregation in leadership roles within the church.

2. *Intentionally employ diverse gifts, talents, passions, and perspectives.* That is, intentionally seek difference and diversity, being open and welcoming of people who use gifts of music, technology, dance, visual arts, administration, teaching, and poetry. Attend to causes that inspire your people to action. Cultivate opportunities for discussion in which a variety of perspectives can be encouraged. Tap into the various past experiences of the people who make up the congregation.

3. *Intentionally make the discernment and development of gifts an ongoing activity.* Develop tools and processes to discover people's diverse gifts, talents, and passions. Sometimes this can be accomplished with the help of specific tools like Lifekeys[9] or other gift-identification resources. But often it requires simply getting to know people well enough (whether via church social events or in the context of a small group) to discern their areas of interest and gifting. This holds true for newcomers and long-time members alike. Develop both in yourself and your leaders the discipline of listening for the talents, passions, and interests that members of the congregation express. These are gifts that God has already placed in your midst.

The powerful inward pull that operates in many congregations can lead pastors and other leaders to focus *primarily* on responding to the needs and demands of their own church members. To cultivate a community of faith that focuses instead on making new disciples, leaders must deliberately develop an outward focus in all the various communication, programming, and organizational structures of the church. The rewards of such intentional leadership and ministry will be healthier congregations, better able to join in the mission of God in this world that he loves so deeply.

---

[9] Jane Kise, David Stark, and Sandra Krebs Hirsh, *Lifekeys: Discover Who You Are*, 2nd ed. (Minneapolis: Bethany House, 2005).

THE PASTOR AS CONDUCTOR
DAVE TOYCEN

IN THIS CHAPTER, I ATTEMPT TO REVIEW SOME OF THE ELEMENTS OF HAROLD PERCY'S leadership over the past twenty-four years at Trinity Streetsville. Because I served in numerous volunteer positions and my wife, Diane, was part of the senior leadership team, I am not able to give an objective view. But what I do know is that over those twenty-four years, Trinity grew dramatically in attendance, participation, discipleship, evangelism, and outreach. Harold would be the first to say that success was more about his staff team and the congregation than about him. Certainly, there is truth in that assessment, but it would be misleading to diminish the essential role of the leader in this process. I am also suggesting that much of what we experienced at Trinity is confirmed by observing the role of leadership in other flourishing churches across North America. I am honoured to offer this modest effort to a man who is my close friend, one who consistently proved courageous in the time of trial, and the pastor who was my greatest spiritual influence for twenty-four years. Harold Percy is one of the greatest gifts I received by immigrating to Canada.

The pastor of a church can be defined as the leader whom people in the congregation will follow. If no one is prepared to follow you, then you will not be the pastor for very long. In our challenging times, that is not an easy task. For hundreds of years, the pastor or priest was often the most educated person in a community, so there was automatic respect and deference. Today it is very different. In many cases, there will be lay people who have more advanced degrees and greater technical skills than the pastor. Regardless of the pastor's training, parishioners expect a level of maturity, knowledge in serving them, and the ability to meet their spiritual needs as well as to create a positive, healthy community. The demands of the "customers" can be unrealistic, provocative, and even toxic.

When Harold arrived at Trinity in 1987, attendance was fewer than one hundred parishioners. There was tension between the more traditional Anglicans and those from a more evangelical or charismatic background. Harold's task was to stabilize and grow the church. Trinity was one of many churches facing a generational change that wanted more twentieth-century authenticity, less ritual, more informal worship, and a shift in leadership style.

THE CHURCH AS ORCHESTRA

What developed at Trinity is an organizational model that can be compared to that of an orchestra. The pastor takes the role as conductor of the staff team as well as of the entire congregation. The staff leaders and empowered volunteers serve in key roles—worship and music, parish life and connections, youth and Sunday school, discipleship and small groups, outreach and administration. The leaders in these areas serve as the first instruments in the orchestra: not only do they play well, but they also have the training and mindset to recruit and develop parishioners who will join them in making music. This model defines roles, ensures accountability, gives permission, and—most importantly—builds a culture of teamwork and co-operation. The pastor-as-conductor guides a community of Christian faith, sharing in the defeats and triumphs of daily life as God nurtures and grows the church.

Depending on the polity of the denomination and the operative culture of the local church, the pastor-as-conductor has to manage the organization as well. While this responsibility may be shared with a deacon's board or parish leadership committee, the pastor is in a unique position to monitor and fine-tune the energies and strategies of a church community. The pastor's voice is essential in "defining reality" for the congregation, taking the initiative to help them move from Egypt to the Promised Land.

An orchestra is incomplete without music, and so is a church without a clear vision, mission, and implementation strategy. As the book of

Proverbs says, "Where there is no vision the people perish" (Prov 29:18, KJV). This component of pastoral leadership is equivalent to choosing the music for an orchestra and then deciding how to perform it, what instruments are required, who will play each of them, and whether an audience is there who will listen to your music once you begin to play. Vision, mission, and strategy are critical for a church, providing the sheet music for the orchestra and the map for a congregation to find their way forward.

The pastor-as-conductor has a primary responsibility to see that team members and volunteers have opportunities to develop their technical skills and their capacity for leadership, as well as their own spiritual formation. Identifying the gifts that everyone brings to the table of ministry is a priority. A flourishing church depends on contributions from every member of the leadership team, the involvement of the entire congregation, and the empowering of the Holy Spirit. The apostle Paul puts it this way:

> There are different types of spiritual gifts, but the same spirit; there are different types of service, but the same Lord; and there are different types of activity, but it is the same God who operates all of them in everyone. The point of the spirit being revealed in each one is so that all may benefit. (1 Cor 12:4–7, NTE)

For this reason, an effective pastor-as-conductor also needs to be curious. At Trinity Church, it was a common practice to survey the opinions of the parish on a regular basis. Similarly, understanding why other churches and denominations are growing is important when a pastor is moving to expand the vision and leadership strategy for his or her own church. Unfortunately, doing the necessary homework to look at other denominations that are experiencing success can give rise to resentment, jealousy, and even resistance on the part of church leaders. I remember Harold attending numerous conferences on church growth, leadership, and community outreach in Canada and the US. Some were Anglican, but many were sponsored by other denominations and Christian organizations. Trinity staff and lay leaders were included on many occasions. As a leader, Harold was not threatened by talented lay people; on the contrary, his desire was to increase our knowledge and expand our capacity to be an effective congregation.

The pastor-as-conductor helps to create an environment of accountability and transparency. The commitment to grow disciples and engage those outside the church requires a rigorous and disciplined review of the key activities within the congregation. This includes a disciplined review of worship, liturgy, structure, curriculum, music, and preaching as well as of procedures for welcoming new members, building community, and engaging in outreach. Is there a healthy balance between meeting the needs of the current followers of Jesus and paying strong attention to the visitors and the unreached? Of course, no church (or orchestra!) can do everything. Since choices always have to be made, the congregational vision, mission, and implementation strategy provide the guidance and the discipline to make these often difficult decisions.

HONOURING THE TRADITIONAL CONGREGATION

As an example, Trinity's numerical growth was driven by expanding a single contemporary worship service into two services each week. Yet a small but important part of the congregation still treasured a *Book of Common Prayer* service every Sunday, even though their numbers were not increasing.

Many churches face the same dilemma with a specific part of the constituency that remains stable, loyal, and committed. At Trinity, the decision was made to offer an 8:00 a.m. *Book of Common Prayer* service rather than force this group to join one of the later services or take over one of the later services to serve their interests. This is an apparently small but actually significant challenge for leaders who are serving an intergenerational church—how do you make compromises that support smaller interest groups while maintaining the major focus that is more relevant to the growth and vitality of the church as a whole? This is a test for any pastor-as-conductor. Getting it right is really important, yet the leader, staff, and volunteers will have to take risks in order to find the right solution.

THE SENSITIVE TOPIC OF MONEY

In the last chapter of *Following Jesus: First Steps on the Way*, which addresses stewardship and money, Harold writes, "People who are serious about spiritual growth have to think about their money."[10] Every pastor-as-conductor needs to take this seriously. The power of money in our culture ranges from subtle to overwhelming. Jesus makes it clear that loving God and loving money are a contradiction; it's just not possible to love both equally: "Nobody can serve two masters. Otherwise they will either hate the first and love the second, or be devoted to the first and despise the second. You can't serve both God and wealth" (Matt 6:24, NTE).

Many pastors are reluctant to address the topic of money because it makes them appear to be fundraising for themselves. In contrast, the Bible establishes that we are stewards of all the things that God gives us. Everything belongs to God, but God trusts us as stewards to use our possessions in the best way possible to fulfill God's redemptive plan for the world. Coming to terms with this reality provides an invitation for us to give back to God generously with time, money, expertise, and influence. Stewardship is meant to be a celebration, not a guilt-laden duty pressed upon us. Of course, it is easier to give money away when it doesn't belong to you in the first place! The question, as Harold has said, is not "How much do I have to give?" Rather, it's "How much do I need to give in order to break the power of money in my life?"

Under Harold's leadership, Trinity budgeted 10 percent or more for global and local outreach. Getting outside the church and into the community is also an essential part of living out the gospel. The pastor-as-conductor ensures that the team and volunteers research their local context before planning and taking action. On many occasions, it means leaving the church premises and going into the community or utilizing your facilities to host local community activities for service and outreach. Over the years, Trinity has found a number of ways to be involved in the community:

- Trinity provided support for a staff member and volunteers to establish The Dam, an organization focused on the needs of at-risk youth in the Mississauga area. The concept was to reduce the exodus of struggling youth to Toronto and provide outreach for them in their home community. The Dam remains

---

[10] Harold Percy, *Following Jesus: First Steps on the Way* (Toronto: Anglican Book Centre, 1993), 107.

a flourishing organization, addressing the critical needs of youth in Mississauga.
- Trinity has also been a site for a community Bible study,[11] offering a weekly Bible study program for more than thirty-five women from across the community and a range of churches for the past twenty years.
- Over many years, Trinity parishioners have served as staff and volunteers on a regular basis at The Open Door. This outreach of the Christian churches in Mississauga is located at a major shopping centre and serves families and individuals in situations of poverty and distress.
- For fourteen years, Trinity has offered free conversational English as a second language classes to immigrants in the community.
- At a global level, Trinity supported World Vision Canada through child sponsorship, including making a number of visits to community development projects in Honduras and the Dominican Republic.
- Members of Trinity also participate annually in the Samaritan's Purse Operation Christmas Child initiative, another opportunity to engage overseas.

Most importantly, Harold encouraged the Trinity congregation to support parishioners who were serving, professionally or as volunteers, in Christian organizations addressing the needs of the local community and beyond.

THE TEST

What does the conductor do when a tragedy happens? On April 26, 1996, in the midst of a large building and renovation project, our 150-year-old church was largely destroyed by fire, the result of arson. In the midst of the heartbreak, Harold saw an opportunity for Trinity to stand for what really matters. In his discussions with the parish executive committee, the decision was made to give forty thousand dollars from our precious building fund to provide nine homes for families who had recently lost theirs in a hurricane in Honduras. Harold believed that while we were

---

[11] See www.communitybiblestudy.ca.

building our new church home, we should also help poor people who had lost their homes in a disaster.

In addition, Harold led the church to forgive the lad who set the fire. Everyone who was there will always remember the poignant service of giving and forgiving when the young lad tearfully apologized to the congregation. His community service was to set up and take down chairs for us in the school auditorium that was our temporary church home and to give 10 percent of his income from his part-time job to the building fund. The Trinity vision of "coming in, growing up, and reaching out" rose to a new level.

BUILDING IN ACCOUNTABILITY

Finally, every pastor-as-conductor is accountable not only to Christ but also to the authority structure of the particular organization, which for most churches operates primarily at the local or parish level. Even the conductor of an orchestra is accountable to a board or executive body. The pastor-as-conductor will only be successful if there is a healthy partnership with the church board, built upon a common objective: fulfilling the church's mission. Yet it is extremely important for the unique roles of the pastor, the board, and the congregation to be clearly defined. There needs to be a commitment to transparency so that none of the partners has to become a detective in order to know what is really happening in the church. Frank conversation is important so that different views can be discussed, after which everyone is able to embrace and own whatever decision or conclusion they eventually come to.

Of course, it is essential that the pastor-as-conductor refrain from trying to do everything. Micromanaging will lead to mediocrity rather than excellence. It is essential that the pastor only does those things that no one else can do. The rest of the tasks should be delegated to either staff or volunteers, depending on the size of the congregation. Again, it is important that the board be there to support the pastor and also to ensure that the mission of the church is being implemented. This agreed-upon mission holds both the pastor and the board accountable, whatever tasks they undertake. What makes all this possible is a pastor-as-conductor with a God-driven imagination that invigorates the same element in the people in the congregation. It is a passion generated by the gospel to take decisive action when human need is urgent. This in turn inspires risk-taking and creativity.

WHAT DOES THIS MEAN FOR TODAY?

It is my firm conviction that most growth in mainline churches depends on three areas: orthodox theology, contemporary worship, and vital youth programs. Under Harold's leadership, Trinity demonstrated success in all three areas. These emphases are likely to remain important for the foreseeable future.

The Angus Reid Institute recently shared research that identifies four Canadian mindsets on religion: non-believers (19 percent), spiritually uncertain (30 percent), privately faithful (30 percent), and religiously committed (21 percent).[12] The religiously committed regularly attend religious services and strongly identify with their faith and the various practices that it involves. The privately faithful do not attend religious services, but they nonetheless believe in God or a higher power; many of them pray, read the Bible or another sacred text, and feel God's presence. In contrast, the spiritually uncertain and non-believers have little connection to God or religion.

Perhaps the most obvious commonality here is the significant percentage of those identified as the privately faithful. They believe in God and share in many of the observances of the religiously committed, but they do not attend church or other religious services regularly. There is a great opportunity for further analysis to identify innovative ways for us to connect with people who have this mindset outside the context of regular church attendance. At Trinity, Harold's preaching was progressive and certainly less judgmental or dogmatic than in many churches. The focus of his sermons was on the good news of a loving God who rescues a broken world and on God's invitation to us to receive this wonderful gift. In addition, Trinity was an oasis for those who felt restricted by the anti-intellectualism and opposition to women in leadership that they had experienced in other churches.

Harold's winsome mission statement was clear and simple: "We are a community of ordinary people learning to follow Jesus in our time—

---

[12] "A Spectrum of Spirituality: Canadians Keep the Faith to Varying Degrees, but Few Reject It Entirely," Angus Reid Institute, April 13, 2017, http://angusreid.org/religion-in-canada-150.

coming in, growing up, and reaching out." This approach may resonate with the privately faithful because it is less judgmental, more relational, and more culturally relevant than seems to be the case with some other churches. At Trinity Streetsville, the motto was "We are fuzzy at the edges, but solid at the core." We wanted to make it easy for newcomers to get inside and then walk together with us in the adventure of discovering Jesus at work in our journey.

THE FINEST TRIBUTE

The finest tribute we can offer Harold Percy will be for others to match his passion for the gospel of Jesus Christ and, through God's grace, have the audacity to lean into this culture and gain a hearing for another way to live. Much of what he practised is still relevant, but the future will require new leaders, other pastors-as-conductors, who want to make great music to set the world on fire for Jesus.

GIVING IT ALL AWAY: EMPOWERING OTHERS FOR MINISTRY
WALLY VOGEL[13]

ALL CHURCHES REQUIRE LEADERSHIP: ST. PAUL WRITES, "WHOEVER ASPIRES TO BE AN overseer desires a noble task" (1 Tim 3:1, NIV). More specifically, healthy churches require strong leaders, and growing churches require leaders who understand how to grow an organization, including the infrastructure of leadership provided by lay people. Harold proved effective in growing Trinity Streetsville from a small congregation to one of the largest Anglican churches in Ontario, with its impact felt in the surrounding community, across the country, and internationally. What was the leadership style that he employed to enable this growth?

There are many different styles of leadership, ranging from an authoritarian top-down approach to a *laissez-faire* approach where little supervision or feedback is provided. The first ensures the leader's strict control but can limit or even stifle contributions from members of an organization. The second provides freedom and independence for the members and allows their creative input but also risks the organization straying off focus and failing to fulfill its intended mission. One of the keys to the rapid and sustained growth seen at Trinity during Harold's tenure was his ability to multiply the impact of his ministry by giving power and responsibility to lay members while still maintaining a shared vision and mission.

---

[13] With thanks to Jane Vogel, Patricia Wood, Bob Motz, and Peter Neufeld.

Harold's approach began with setting and communicating a clear vision, sharing a high-level strategy that explained how to achieve it, and conveying core values for how we should conduct ourselves in pursuit of this vision. This framework enabled people with various different gifts, interests, and abilities to come together with a shared vision of Trinity as "a community of ordinary people learning to follow Jesus in our time." Many of the people drawn to this vision already held prominent positions in society, among them the mayor of Mississauga, a national hockey legend, and CEOs of successful corporations and not-for-profit organizations. Harold was able not only to attract them to the church community but also to harness their gifts in building the community and multiplying its impact. Of course, his empowerment for ministry was not limited to high-profile individuals with gifts for leadership. Many others were less well-known, coming with gifts such as hospitality or care. Harold valued the contributions of all lay members and often professed his love for those who, in his words, "work quietly in the corners."

The present chapter describes how Harold "gave it all away" in order to empower others for ministry. One of his catch phrases was that he wanted Trinity to be "fuzzy at the edges, but solid at the core." In terms of organizational leadership, "solid at the core" refers to mission, shared vision, and shared values. Being "fuzzy at the edges" (that is, flexible at the point of implementation) enables the organization to attract people and identify new leaders. Between the core and the margins is where an organization grows by equipping those leaders, empowering them to fulfill the core principles while encouraging them to make creative contributions that expand the fuzzy edges. The focus of this chapter is primarily on empowering lay leadership, as distinct from staff development, a somewhat related but separate topic that is thoroughly covered in secular writings on leadership and organizational development.

MISSION

Organizational leadership, whether for a church or secular organization, begins with a clearly defined mission. Since this emphasis must be at the very centre of an organization's vision, strategy, and practice, defining that mission must be the leader's first and foremost task. In the Great Commission—"Go therefore and make disciples of all nations, baptizing them in the name of the Father and of the Son and of the Holy Spirit, and teaching them to obey everything that I have commanded you" (Matt 28:19–20)—Jesus himself establishes the church's mission. As its true leader, Jesus sets a clear and universal mission for his church in every time and place, a mandate that still applies today for local churches around the world. It now falls to the leaders of those local churches, each in the context of their own circumstances, to take up the role of helping to carry out the Great Commission, and this task begins with defining their local church's mission statement.

A mission statement defines the core purpose of an organization, answering such questions as "Who are we?" "What do we do?" and "How will we do it?" It should be concise, clear, and memorable and yet be rich enough that it can be unpacked into specific principles and values that enable the actual pursuit of that mission.

Just so, Harold's mission statement for Trinity was for us to be "a community of ordinary people learning to follow Jesus in our time." First, this short phrase described who Trinity was: that it was a community (in which case community-building activities furthered its mission) and that the members were ordinary people (so that new members were welcome without having to meet some prior standard). Second, it described what Trinity did: learning (to be achieved though sermons, small groups, and courses) and following Jesus (that is, growing as disciples in missional service). Third, it described both when and how this would be done: "in our time," which situated us in the context of our present day and informed Trinity's casual worship style, contemporary music, and use of technology.

Once defined, a mission statement needs to be shared broadly, consistently, and frequently. At Trinity, the mission statement was on the cover of the weekly bulletin, on the website, and on the church's letterhead. The name of Trinity Anglican Church, Streetsville was almost always accompanied by the subtitle "A community of ordinary people learning to follow Jesus in our time." The mission statement was mentioned in almost every sermon and was frequently included as a focus of the sermon as a whole. It would not be an exaggeration to say that virtually every member of the church had memorized the mission statement and could recite it on demand—it became an ingrained and innate part of how people perceived the church. It provided the solid core that was the foundational first step to enabling the effective sharing of leadership with lay members.

SHARED VISION AND STRATEGY

Whereas a mission statement describes what an organization does, the vision statement describes what success looks like. If the mission is the journey, the vision is a snapshot of the destination. It is arguable that Jesus' vision for the church is summed up in three words from the Lord's prayer: "Your kingdom come." When the universal church carries out its mission to make disciples of all nations, baptizing and teaching them to do all that Jesus has commanded, the church itself embodies God's kingdom and reign here on earth.

In the case of a local church, the vision statement should describe what success looks like in the context of that particular congregation and its particular circumstances. It may describe a specific goal or goals; at Trinity, we formulated specific vision-related goals to be implemented over different periods of time—for example, to welcome one hundred new members or to have 80 percent of the congregation join a small group. Early in Harold's ministry at Trinity, the vision goals were set annually by Harold and the staff, then shared and discussed at the annual congregational meeting. One year, the vision goals were printed on small laminated cards and given to every member of the congregation to carry through the year—to pray over, to participate in, and to hold ourselves accountable so that we could review our progress at the next meeting.

As the church developed lay leadership in various areas, the visioning process became a more broadly shared activity that included small-group discussion, congregational surveys, brainstorming, and a weekly prayer focus. The amount of time and effort involved necessitated a longer time frame for the visioning process itself, and the goals that resulted likewise expanded in scope, becoming more of a qualitative framework over a five-year timespan to which more specific annual goals could be attached.

Of course, the visioning model that evolved at Trinity was only one of many ways in which it is possible to define and communicate vision. As a different example, National Community Church (NCC) in Washington, DC, expresses their vision as one of "God-given dreams":

NCC is a community of people that believes in the power of God-given dreams. We believe that NCC is a dream-factory where people get a vision from God and go for it! We want to be a part of the personal dream God has given you, and we invite you to be a part of the corporate dreams God has given us . . .
We dream of a day when . . .
Every NCCer is making disciples in their sphere of influence
We open the doors of a second dream center in DC
Ebenezers [coffeehouse] expands in the city and across the country
An NCC Mission team is deployed 52 weeks of the year
We are giving $2 million to missions every year
We baptize 500 people in one day[14]

Whatever the visioning process, and whatever form the vision statement takes, it should be appropriate to the opportunities and resources of the local church, and it must be in perfect alignment with the congregational mission statement. It is the role of the pastor to ensure this alignment and to communicate and share the vision throughout the entire church community, making certain that it is understood and becomes the focal point at which all the activities of the church come together as the mission is carried out.

In order for a vision to be achieved, each specific goal or aspect of that vision will require a supporting strategy. How would Trinity go about attracting and retaining one hundred new members from the Streetsville area? What steps would NCC take to open the doors of a second dream centre in Washington, DC? Development of strategies will break down the goal into a series of concrete steps that will take the congregation from where it is now to the destination defined in the larger vision. Sharing this process with lay leadership will, in fact, make strategy development more effective. Each lay leader brings a particular perspective, along with areas of strength and weakness when it comes to implementation. Engaging with a broader group provides opportunity for much more input and additional expertise in specific areas of strategic implementation.

---

[14] From the NCC website: http://theaterchurch.com/about/our-dream. Reproduced with permission.

For example, aside from the aspects of worship and congregational development, opening a second mission centre may require expertise in assessing area demographics, surveying and pricing available real estate, assessing renovations, fundraising, and advertising. Bringing lay leaders with experience in these areas to the planning table ensures the formulation of strategies that are more complete and more likely to result in effective progress towards achieving the vision goal.

At Trinity, Harold always engaged the expertise of lay leaders who had relevant experience in their roles outside of the church so that they could bring their talents to bear in helping to contribute to the church's mission and vision. He had a tremendous respect for their abilities and would seek out and trust their opinions within their respective fields of expertise. Yet while bringing together diverse abilities and perspectives, he avoided unhealthy conflict by ensuring that the context of the collaboration was always based on shared values—another area where the church was "solid at the core."

SHARED VALUES

As the mission statement expresses what the church does and the vision statement describes what success looks like, shared values describe how the church acts as it carries out its mission. Whereas the mission is definitive and the vision is descriptive—often quantitative—the shared values are qualitative.

At Trinity, shared values were encapsulated in six key purposes, defined as follows:

1. To share the good news of what God has done in Jesus with everyone we possibly can.
2. To worship in such a way that people experience God's presence and respond with adoration, praise, and thanksgiving.
3. To bring people into vital relationship with Jesus Christ and disciple them to wholeness and spiritual maturity.
4. To be a genuine community that welcomes all people—children, youth, and adults—in which we love and care for one another and that provides a safe environment for learning to follow Jesus and experiencing God's grace.

5. To serve our local community and beyond in the name of Jesus with ministries of mercy, compassion, and justice in order to relieve suffering and bring glory to God.
6. To help other churches become more effective in their ministry of sharing and living the good news of Jesus.

Shared values need to be clearly communicated and available for people to refer to, since they are not as concise or memorable as the mission statement. At Trinity, the key purposes were not only posted on the church website but also printed on cards that were available in the seat backs of every pew in the church, every Sunday, all the time. Of course, in addition to verbal and written communication, shared values must also be modelled by congregational leaders. Otherwise the message lacks credibility.

For example, in the context of a board discussion regarding the approach to take on a certain decision, one board member suggested a course of action that, while not improper, might have been perceived as lacking the degree of integrity and transparency to which board members had all committed themselves. Harold commented, in effect, that "if there is a line between right and wrong, we don't want to see how close we can come to the line without crossing to the wrong side; we want to stay on the right side and as far away from that line as possible."

ATTRACTING AND IDENTIFYING LEADERS

Before equipping and empowering people for lay leadership, the pastor will need a pool of people from which to recruit the leaders. Although this chapter does not attempt to address the manifold aspects of fostering church growth, it may nonetheless be helpful by way of illustration to share the perspective of one person who came to Trinity and, over time, became a key leader in the congregation:

> In May of 1994, I moved into the Streetsville area. One of the first things a good Streetsville resident does is to attend the Bread and Honey Festival and Parade. So my family and I went on a sunny Saturday morning to attend the parade. About halfway through the parade we noticed this flatbed truck with crazy musicians and

singers, and they all seemed happy! Then I saw the sign, "Trinity Anglican Church," and I realized that any church that can put a float in a community parade is pretty good in my books.

Our first arrival later that year was very welcoming and casual. It was probably the first and only time I've worn a suit to a church service at Trinity! We were greeted by Harold, who wasn't wearing any vestments, and it took me a while to realize that he was the rector of the church.

I was blown away by his speaking style and his ability to relate to issues that affected me and my family and relate them back to the gospel message. As the months and years went by, we became more engaged with church life and activity. But Harold continued to develop the Christian man in me in so many ways—through courses, reading the Bible, small groups, sermons, prayer, and men's ministry. As a chartered accountant, it was a simple transition to take on financial responsibilities at Trinity, joining the board as the treasurer and then later serving as rector's warden.

Yes, my relationship with Jesus and the working of the Holy Spirit in me have made me who I am today, a follower of Jesus. However, if it were not for Harold, I'm not sure I would have followed that path. Harold guided me there and showed me the way. The Bible may be the "lamp to my feet and a light to my path" (Ps 119:105), but Harold was the one that showed me that there was a path in the first place.

Harold was able to attract people to the church, and as they became part of the community he was able to identify those who were ready to step into leadership—committed Christians with a strong sense of self as well as an ability to work with others. He would get to know them personally, then help them to see where their passions intersected with their skills, identifying the areas where they were truly gifted for ministry. Their experience in the secular world would often be an indication of where they could play a role in the church—the CFO of a large telecom firm in the role of treasurer, the CEO of a not-for-profit organization to lead a stewardship committee, or a caterer to organize dinner events.

It may seem that these choices are obvious, but far too often churches will accept volunteers into roles for which they would not likely qualify if they were applying in the secular world. Further, the lay volunteer will have a limited number of hours per week to devote to a volunteer role. If, for example, the volunteer treasurer is asked to manage a budget of a million dollars, he or she should already be accustomed to dealing with larger budgets at work. Harold was unapologetic in being very selective about who was chosen for leadership responsibility at Trinity, as these were the people in whom he himself would invest his time, equipping and enabling them to share in carrying out the vision and mission of the church.

EQUIPPING LEADERS

Harold took the task of equipping lay leaders very seriously. When Trinity was a smaller church, he would spend much of his personal time with the lay leadership—communicating the mission, sharing the vision, and teaching the faith as well as the shared values of Trinity as an organization. Leadership retreats provided formal teaching both from Harold and from guest speakers, including some who had had a formative influence on Harold himself. These retreats—usually off-site and over a weekend—also provided the time for participants to bond over shared values and to discuss ways of working together in order to make progress on the specific goals of the church.

As the church grew and the task of equipping leaders grew with it, Harold assembled a few senior leaders with experience in education, human resources, communications, and strategic growth to form a leadership development team. This team was entrusted with the responsibility of the equipping of future leaders for the church. Along with helping to organize the annual retreats, they also arranged leader training days as further development for those already in leadership roles. In addition, they presented seminars on topics such as communications, conflict resolution, and team building, which were open to the congregation but tended to attract those who were already serving or who had potential as leaders.

The leadership development team provided specific training courses for small-group leaders and was available for individual coaching if any lay leader sought support for challenges or obstacles they were facing.

This focused training was important, since, even for those with relevant experience in a secular work environment, the mission, vision, and values of the church are different from those of the business world. You could have leaders who were very comfortable with the functional aspects of their roles but out of their comfort zone in terms of providing ministry leadership that entailed a deep spiritual dimension.

One important aspect of empowering lay leadership is not only to share a vision but also to define boundaries. These boundaries help the organization maintain an effective structure by avoiding overlap or conflict in ministry roles, and they also help to protect the lay leader from taking on too much responsibility. As a former chair of the board at Trinity commented,

> With Harold, I was able to understand the limits of authority and responsibility. He made it clear that it was the staff who were to do the work, and we were there to provide governance and decision making. I think this is why I was able to participate for close to five years without getting burned out. I have been asked to be on the board (and chair) at our new church in Europe, and my experience at Trinity under Harold has prepared me to lead. Having done some work with the church already, the comment from the pastor is that I seem to understand what the board is to do and what it isn't. Some boards get caught up in "running the church" and some in "being the pastor's friend." Both are less effective and abdicate the key role of helping the church make wise decisions to move forward. With Harold, I felt empowered to play this role.

Another important aspect of equipping leaders and helping them to grow in their role is providing honest and direct feedback on their performance. Harold was not hesitant to speak if someone was not delivering on a specific task and at the level required. The criticism was delivered privately and respectfully, directed to the performance and not the person. It was framed in the context of a mutual trust relationship that had been built over time. Even so, the identification of a performance problem was not softened or downplayed for the sake of harmony or personal comfort. Being entrusted with a leadership role was so critical that avoiding a difficult conversation or ignoring a problem would only lead to more significant problems down the road. Another beneficial outcome of this forthrightness is that when Harold praised someone's work, the recipient knew that the praise was genuine and unreserved. And while criticism was always delivered privately, praise was shared publicly.

Thoroughly equipping and supporting lay leaders—defining boundaries and providing them with direct feedback—meant that their ability to excel in their respective areas was maximized so that they could be further empowered to participate in carrying out the mission of the church.

EMPOWERING LEADERS

Jesus himself provides an example of empowering leaders when he dispatches the disciples to go from village to village: "Then Jesus called the twelve together and gave them power and authority over all demons and to cure diseases, and he sent them out to proclaim the kingdom of God and to heal" (Luke 9:1–2). He equips them through his teaching and his presence; then he entrusts them to act independently so as to carry out the mission that he has shared with them.

In the context of the local church, once potential leaders have been identified and equipped, and once they have a clear sense of the shared mission, vision, and values of the congregation, they can be trusted and empowered to act independently within their areas of strength and with minimal direct involvement from the pastor. Ultimately, they are of course accountable to the pastor for their performance in their respective areas of responsibility and for strategic alignment with the core direction of the church, but they do not need to be micromanaged in terms of day-to-day activities. Monthly or even quarterly meetings with the pastor may be sufficient to ensure continued communications and coordination.

Having a number of capable lay leaders working in their areas of experience, passion, and giftedness allows the church to grow much more quickly than does a top-down authoritarian style of leadership. It multiplies the effectiveness of the pastor, more than recouping the time invested in sharing core principles and identifying and equipping leaders. Furthermore, the leaders will have specific experience and skills that the pastor will not, as a result of which they will be more effective if they are able to take initiative and make decisions. And finally, each of these leaders has their own personal spheres of influence, consisting of people outside the church with whom they come in contact, making them effective ambassadors for the church and its vision to many more people than one pastor could ever hope to reach. Capable, effective, well-connected lay leaders raise the profile and influence of the church in the surrounding community, helping it to attract more new members and continuing the cycle of growth as more leaders are identified, equipped, and empowered.

GIVING IT ALL AWAY

Perhaps the best way to illustrate the principle of carrying out the mission of the church by empowering others is to consider a specific example of how Harold gave away the power in an area that by its very name implies it is the role of the pastor: pastoral care.

Almost twenty years into Harold's ministry in Streetsville, Trinity had grown into a corporate-sized church with thriving ministries in many areas. At that time, a collaborative visioning process within the congregation identified pastoral care as an area in which the church had outgrown the model of having the clergy lead in providing pastoral care to its membership. Even though much of the "pastoral" care was being delivered through small groups, as well as prayer and healing ministries, the coordination and leadership of these ministries required more than the part-time attention that the clergy were able to provide. Although one option would have been to hire additional clergy to lead pastoral care, Harold chose to take a different approach and empower lay leadership for this important part of the church's mission.

Harold identified a long-standing member of the congregation who had already played numerous key leadership roles in the church and, in consultation with the board, approached her with an invitation to consider what it would mean to refashion what had previously been "pastoral care" into a new "congregational care" model. Having just stepped away from an executive role with a firm that assists employees in career transition, she found that this opportunity engaged every aspect of her professional background and ministry passion, weaving everything together into an exciting ministry opportunity.

Using her knowledge of organizational and strategic planning, she created a five-year plan for congregational care. The completed document was twenty pages long, modelled and written just as a professional business plan or proposal would be. It began by defining the overall philosophy of congregational care, linking it directly to the mission, vision, and key purposes of the church and showing how each aspect would be supported by this new model. It went on to outline what specifically would be required to deliver congregational care, including resources and time. It set specific activities and goals for each of the following five years in terms of programs, staffing, volunteers, training, and leadership.

When Harold received the proposal, he was impressed and commented that he had never seen such a thoroughly thought-out strategic plan for a care ministry. He immediately accepted the plan and extended an offer for this leader to move into a lay staff role as director of congregational care, creating a framework to bring together the existing care ministries under her direction and allow her to create the new ministries she had proposed. Having been given the freedom and authority to develop congregational care while being supported both by Harold and by a board member who served as her liaison to the larger leadership team, she said that she felt "energized and in [her] element."

She commented, "Harold has tremendous gifts for preaching, leading, and visioning. He knows what is in his wheelhouse and what is not—and he respects others for what they know." She also noted that he sometimes entrusted her with roles that she may not have previously imagined taking on. One example was when a long-time parishioner passed away at a time when Harold was out of the country. When she phoned him to let him know, he asked her to visit the family and help them begin making plans so that when he returned he could conduct the funeral. Harold would still be in charge of the service, but she would work out the planning and details beforehand. This was not something she had done before, but he expressed his confidence in her, and she was able to help the family figure out what was important for the service and to select readings, songs, and so forth. In fact, this one conversation was the beginning of a new lay ministry that saw her meet with families to plan funeral arrangements. She realized that he could have done this himself, yet he entrusted her with the sensitive task of helping people through this most difficult of times.

Harold also helped to elevate the profile of the director of congregational care by having her provide regular updates to the congregation and even sharing the pulpit by asking her to offer a Sunday sermon on her role and the work she was doing. The care ministry grew not only within the congregation but also out into the surrounding community, and it became recognized as an effective model for delivering care. The director was subsequently invited to be a guest speaker at a large Christian organization, sharing what was being achieved through this new approach at Trinity.

In a role and area of ministry that had traditionally belonged exclusively to the pastor, a new model emerged that created more effective ministry simply by empowering lay leadership and "giving it all away."

FOLLOWING JESUS

The growth of Trinity Streetsville, whether measured in terms of numerical growth, growth in discipleship and spiritual maturity, growth of new ministries, or growth of public profile and community impact, was enabled by Harold's leadership style. By creating a "fuzzy at the edges, but solid at the core" organization, he was able to establish and communicate shared mission, vision, and values; attract people to the church; and identify leaders, empowering them to help carry out this shared ministry. Rather than holding the leadership power closely to himself, he was prepared, with the right leaders and under the appropriate conditions, to "give it all away." In doing so, he himself became a tremendously effective leader, and Trinity Streetsville became an effective local church, enabled and equipped to carry out its mission in the name of Christ.

Harold did this by following the model of Jesus himself, who empowers his disciples and establishes the mission of the universal church: "All authority in heaven and on earth has been given to me. Go therefore and make disciples of all nations, baptizing them in the name of the Father and of the Son and of the Holy Spirit, and teaching them to obey everything that I have commanded you" (Matt 28:18–20). May we do the same, for his glory.

NEW WINE IN NEW WINESKINS: DENOMINATIONAL LEADERSHIP AND NEW FORMS OF MINISTRY
LINDA C. NICHOLLS

> It was the best of times, it was the worst of times, it was the age of wisdom, it was the age of foolishness, it was the epoch of belief, it was the epoch of incredulity, it was the season of Light, it was the season of Darkness, it was the spring of hope, it was the winter of despair, we had everything before us, we had nothing before us, we were all going direct to Heaven, we were all going direct the other way . . .
> —Charles Dickens, *A Tale of Two Cities*

THIS QUOTATION FROM THE OPENING OF *A TALE OF TWO CITIES* COULD EASILY DESCRIBE THE current reality for many churches today. It is the best of times and it is the worst of times as we seek to find the ways to be vibrant, thriving, sustainable church communities in the midst of a world that longs for the succour of faith while often rejecting the institutional vehicle through which the invitation is given.

It is the best of times, as we are given the opportunity to explore creative expressions of our faith; to try new ideas; to be nimble, flexible, and responsive; to ask new questions and discover new answers. These opportunities excite the imagination and fling open the doors of tradition.

It is the worst of times, as the ways in which we have always "done church" no longer speak to our day. Many churches with aging congregations find strength and meaning in traditional expressions of faith, yet those familiar traditions no longer attract younger generations. Clergy and congregations feel the stress as they look around and know that what has sustained them in the past is not meeting the spiritual hunger of those younger than themselves. Financial pressures continue to increase, while aging buildings vacuum up limited resources. Fear and desperation lead to unhealthy congregational behaviours, including conflict. Although anxieties—and expectations of clergy—are high, there are no quick fixes.

Into the midst of this exciting, agonizing time, the church is taking the plunge into new forms of ministry for which neither the minister nor the denominational leader has been prepared. It is invigorating and scary for both! In this chapter, I reflect on the role of the denominational or judicatory leader in the oversight and support of new forms of ministry. Although I write from within a mainline church tradition with deep historical roots (the Anglican Church of Canada), I believe that my experience and reflections resonate with many traditions, as each of us have expectations and commitments that are being challenged by the needs of ministry today.

Apart from traditions that are exclusively congregational, most churches have some form of denominational leadership structure that invests an individual or group with authority for exercising ministry in the name of that tradition. That level of leadership sets boundaries for ministry, holds it accountable, and has the power to support and encourage—or the potential to present a roadblock to—the healthy development of that ministry. It is essential to reflect on how we exercise this ministry of oversight in light of emerging needs.

Let me begin with personal reflections and then identify key areas for consideration. When I began my ministry as a parish priest, Harold Percy was a well-known voice in the Diocese of Toronto, calling for renewed evangelism. During my early years, he began his ministry at Trinity Streetsville, and I began to hear about the ways in which he was making changes. Some complained that he was jettisoning our tradition, while others were eager to hear more. I was struck by the fact that his area bishop stood by him and supported his ministry, even in the face of much opposition—the first inkling for me of the role a denominational leader can play in emerging ministry.

In my time as area bishop of Trent-Durham in the Anglican Diocese of Toronto, I had the joy and privilege of accompanying the Rev. Ryan Sim as he developed a new ministry in our area. From the very first steps we took in establishing this ministry, I was aware of my capacity to nurture, support, and protect it—as well as the potential for me to be a stumbling block and detractor. I was also aware of the risks for us both, as I was being invited to accompany this pastor into a form of ministry about which I knew little or nothing. This was not the traditional parish-based ministry for which I had been trained. Ryan was establishing a ministry that began with a vision for a digital platform for evangelism and discipleship, which would lead in time to the establishment of a gathered church.

Ryan was seeking to reach double-income young families in a satellite community of Toronto, people who spent much of their day commuting. He envisioned and designed a platform for evangelism in the form of a downloadable app for Apple and Android that he entitled "Redeem the Commute." He developed online content, videos, and daily challenges in order to engage commuters. His larger hope was that people using this material on the commuter train would find one another and build relationships and even small groups that could then develop further in the context of a gathered community. He often worked in isolation and in ways that were not well understood by ministry colleagues. The usual parameters and guidelines set by the diocesan system would not necessarily be helpful. So we were both setting out on a journey that involved many uncertainties and much unknown territory.

From the outset, Ryan was clear about the kind of support he needed as he began working in a new form of ministry. He knew that he needed an advocate within the diocesan system to ensure that the policies and procedures required by the traditional parish model of ministry did not unduly penalize him. He also needed ongoing personal support. I was clear that this ministry offered an exciting opportunity to try something new that would challenge me as a leader, as well as our tradition, as we explored its implications. It would stretch us all.

From that experience, and from watching other ministries and fresh expressions of church seek to grow, I became aware of the implications for those of us who share administrative responsibilities. We stand alongside these new ministries as those who have the capacity either to nurture and encourage or to block and dissuade. At times, we stand on the same threshold as the Pharisees and Sadducees of Jesus' day, watching something new emerge that challenges our long-established expectations and commitments. Like Gamaliel (Acts 5:33–39), we are challenged to discern whether to hinder these new expressions or wait to see in what way God may be working in and through them.

I explore three key areas of consideration for denominational leaders on this journey with forms of ministry that are different from the usual patterns dictated by our respective traditions: understanding our own role in ministry, developing a relationship with the new ministry and pastor, and maintaining continuity with the wider ecclesiastical systems of our own tradition. Reflecting on each of these is critical in assisting the success of new or emerging ministries.

THE ROLE OF DENOMINATIONAL LEADERS

The first area of consideration is that of the leader's own role and self-reflection. Denominational leaders are usually chosen for their gifts in ministry as it has been understood in the past, for their loyalty to that tradition, and for their ability to work within its systems. Rarely are we the risk-taking entrepreneurs of mission and ministry. So when we find ourselves confronted with the need for these new and different forms of ministry, we are asked to nurture and sustain ministries for which we have had little or no preparation or personal gifts. We no longer occupy the role of experienced expert or gifted leader. We are as new to it as those whom we seek to supervise and support.

The training we received (sometimes many years prior) was geared to established, stable church communities that required of us skills in preaching, teaching, pastoral care, and parish administration, alongside gifts for leadership and volunteer management. Today, we face radically different needs, for which social analysis, evangelism, church planting, and rebooting are primary skills.

Entering this territory is uncertain, scary, and destabilizing for us, both personally and corporately. Looking for a biblical analogy, I developed empathy for Moses, who found himself called to take on a leadership role in the Exodus with no experience for the work that lay ahead. Like Moses, we require the maturity to acknowledge our own fears and inexperience and to test our capacity to take new risks. We must also be deeply rooted in our own journeys of faith and willing to confront our personal weaknesses and biases. Honest, reflective prayer is an essential tool.

For me, this has also required a continued reiteration of the purpose of ministry. It has been essential to remember that we are called primarily to share the Good News of God in Jesus Christ. We are not called simply to preserve the past but to ask, in each generation, how to share the gospel in ways that can be heard and received, drawing on the gifts that the past can offer while remaining open to new ideas. There is a degree of sacrifice and of laying down our lives in this process, given that we were formed and nurtured in our faith through the church and have deep roots in the traditions of our communities. The tension between those traditions and what may be needed now requires a painful relinquishment. Grief becomes part of our journey as we let go of aspects of ministry that once formed and nurtured us—but may not be needed on the onward journey.

There will be new opportunities for theological reflection as we wrestle with ideas that stretch the tradition, at times seemingly too far. How much similarity is needed for continuity? How much difference will be life-giving? When might it be destructive? There will be no single answer to these questions. We are in a time of transition and testing in which denominational leaders will be constantly evaluating the effectiveness of emerging ministries, and the answers will depend on personal comfort with particular changes, denominational loyalties, and the need for others to support and commit to the new ministry. There must be a steady practice of testing and discernment by each participant or component of the system: the denominational leader, the new ministry and pastor, and the wider church. This testing requires consistent, clear communication between the different stakeholders.

The tension between tradition and emerging needs is particularly strong in identifying and affirming individuals for these new ministries. Denominational leaders, both individuals and groups, often have critical oversight for the process of approving and authorizing ministry leaders. Whether for ordination or licensing, our traditions set out expectations for ministry, including the gifts and skills needed—based almost exclusively on past experience. Our systems of discernment for ministry are established in such a way that, paradoxically, the very creative, different kinds of ministry leaders we need most may be screened out by the expectations we have set. The gifts needed to take risks, to share the gospel in new ways, and to nurture community outside the supports of a traditional administrative or ecclesiastical structure are the very gifts that may clash with established policies and procedures.

Just as different gifts are needed for urban ministry and rural ministry, so specific gifts are required for a fresh expression of ministry, a congregational reboot, and a church plant. The denominational leader needs to be able to see how the gifts of each candidate can fit within the full range of ministry settings that include long-established congregations, new church plants, entrepreneurial evangelism and discipleship, and quirky "fresh expressions" of Christian community.

Rather than looking for ministry leaders who mirror our own gifts and expectations, we must ask, Do we see gifts of faith, leadership, and calling in this candidate? Do we see the light of Christ in their life and ministry?

But we also need to recognize the limitations and gifts of our traditional structures in order to know whether we are able to nurture and support a particular ministry or candidate. Sharing ministry is a two-way street that must be life-giving for pastors and supervisors alike. Can our organizational structure embrace their gifts for ministry, both now and in the future? Will this ministry and leader be beneficial at this point in the life of our tradition? At times, the answer may well be no, as we reach the limit of our tradition to embrace a form of change that would stretch us beyond our present capacity to adapt.

Exercising leadership for emerging alternative forms of ministry will quickly push us back to the essentials—and to the core questions of the purposes of Christian ministry. It will take us out of our comfort zone of certainty about ministry and lead us into the uncertainties of exploring new models and ways of sharing the good news. We will be humbled and pruned (John 15:1–5) in order that we may share in the greater fruitfulness that God desires for the church.

THE RELATIONSHIP WITH A NEW MINISTER OR MINISTRY

Every new minister and every new ministry needs a Barnabas.[15] New ministry, for all the excitement and potential it offers, is lonely for the one who pioneers it and, at times, highly anxious. Its leaders require encouragement. Other clergy will be skeptical or possibly envious of this opportunity and have difficulty knowing how to offer support. The emerging ministry will not meet all expectations, and failure will be part of the experience. Financial pressures will be constant, with no certainty as to when or even if the new ministry will become self-sustaining. Because their gifts for this new ministry are different from those that suit more traditional forms of ministry, new leaders will not always fit the expectations of other clergy or leaders. Their entrepreneurial spirit and willingness to think and act outside the box will often clash with denominational guidelines or rules.

For all of these reasons, the denominational leader needs to be a key personal supporter of the ministry leader. There must be a commitment to publicly defend and support both the leader and the new ministry initiative. The pastor needs a public advocate who can help situate this initiative within the history of the tradition and interpret its contribution in the context of the denominational system. For Ryan and me, this meant being sure that the diocesan council received regular updates describing progress, challenges, and financial accountability. At least once a year, we provided a thorough review of the ministry. This had the benefit of forestalling rumours as well as, more generally, educating council members as they grew in their capacity to embrace newer forms of ministry and understand the dynamics involved.

With the ministry itself, the denominational leader is a key mediator between systemic requirements and ministry capacity. The usual markers of congregational success, such as average Sunday attendance or self-sustainability, will not be readily applicable. Tentative benchmarks for success will need to be discerned together. There will also need to be constant analysis of emerging difficulties and renegotiation of benchmarks as new information emerges. Discernment of appropriate risks, as well as of supports for risk-taking, will also be required.

Together with risk assessment, discernment of boundaries will be necessary. Sometimes those boundaries are important for theological

---

[15] Barnabas is first mentioned in Acts 4:36.

or pastoral reasons. Sometimes they are pragmatic boundaries for the sake of the common good. For Anglicans with a deeply rooted liturgical tradition, this has included discerning the essential elements of liturgy that must be present: All of the lectionary? Parts of it? If so, which parts? And what about clerical vestments? Never? Sometimes? Which ones? What of Eucharist? Every Sunday? Most Sundays? What defines this ministry as *Anglican*? And is that identity important as long as the gospel is reaching more unchurched people?

For example, Anglican tradition most often has clergy vested in clergy shirts and collars, robes, and seasonal stoles, with the bishop additionally carrying a staff and wearing a mitre. Are robes necessary at all? Helpful in some instances? Before my first visit as a bishop to the new gathered community of Redeemer Church, meeting in a school gymnasium, Ryan and I discussed what would be appropriate. The decision included what I was personally comfortable with alongside the understanding of the community. I chose to wear an episcopal shirt and collar with the stole (but no additional robes) and to carry my staff, with an opportunity to explain its significance. We also discussed what was essential for the shape of the liturgy and what traditional aspects could be changed, deleted, or offered in different ways. For Anglicans, the shape of the Eucharistic prayer has a necessary pattern but does not, in every instance, have to be only what is in the authorized prayer books. The bishop can give permission for other texts or adaptations that fit the same pattern. Although these are specifically Anglican examples, they highlight the need to consider those aspects of the particular denominational traditions that shape identity and how far they can be changed.

To provide the support Ryan needed, he and I met about once a month. The agenda of the meeting lay with Ryan to share progress, outline challenges, or seek assistance. For me, this was the opportunity to accompany Ryan, listening, learning, asking questions, and praying together. There were opportunities for affirmation of his ministry, of seeing where I or others could come alongside with assistance, or sometimes of seeking to connect his ministry with other colleagues or resources. There were opportunities to discuss where boundaries needed to be maintained, as we discerned the limits of liturgical revision and assessed how best to handle the necessary administrative tasks required by a ministry that was still accountable to an institutional structure.

Our denominational traditions have grown out of specific historical and theological commitments that reflect wisdom borne of long experience. So we need to examine that tradition together to discern the core values that are essential to our ministry and identity. Doing so requires careful reflection, as well as willingness on the part of co-workers for the purpose of the gospel to listen together to the voices of past and present alike.

RELATIONSHIPS WITHIN THE TRADITION

Closely linked to direct and personal support of both pastor and ministry is the task of supporting them in the midst of the wider systems of the tradition. The new ministry will not fit the existing categories, policies, and rules in every aspect. Since this initiative needs a champion within the system, the task falls to those with responsibility for its oversight—in a word, to us!

As denominational leaders, we sit in the wider councils of the church, where we can advocate for, support, and encourage new ministries, ensuring that their goals and principles are well understood and widely supported. This requires us to communicate clearly the nature of the ministries in question, how they connect with our tradition, and how we support them. We may also need to defend and protect them when others do not see the potential and are critical of the resources being given to a ministry that is so fragile. We must also be prepared to answer questions and concerns that are raised for consideration.

At times, the system or tradition will set up roadblocks, usually unintentionally, simply by virtue of the way the institution normally operates. For Ryan and me, the first challenge was finding a way to manage the finances of the fledgling ministry within the expectations of a larger, corporate system. Accountability needed to be maintained, but flexibility was required so as not to overburden the new ministry with paperwork. We were able to work out a plan of action within the corporate system that satisfied both needs, but clear communication and commitments were required at every level. My role was to negotiate the plan and keep our communications clear.

Discerning appropriate benchmarks that are comprehensible to leaders with a more traditional focus is a new and challenging task. When a new ministry is still emerging, it will not meet the usual benchmarks of average attendance or membership, the number of participants at the Lord's Supper, baptisms, or financial stability. Helpful information may be available from similar ministries in other places, but it will not always be clear how such information can be applied or compared to the present context. Both the ministry leader and the denominational leader will need to discuss, discern, and agree upon benchmarks that fit the ministry, its unique context, and its particular goals. Articulating these standards will be important for encouraging wider support from within the tradition. Yet they will always be tentative, as the fragility and fluidity of an emerging ministry mean that unforeseen challenges will require frequent communication and renegotiation.

As Ryan developed the plan for Redeem the Commute, we knew we needed to set benchmarks that would be helpful, both for us and for those watching this ministry emerge. Since there was no comparable ministry to investigate, we needed to examine the tasks themselves and ask what kind of measures would be appropriate. For an online resource, this meant setting some quantitative benchmarks based on social media statistics—the number of users and repeat users, the locations of the users, some financial benchmarks based on best guesses—as well as qualitative benchmarks, such as the nature of the online contacts Ryan was able to establish and signs of growth and commitment demonstrated through online communications. At several points in the year, we would discuss progress towards these benchmarks, then re-evaluate whether they were still the best and most appropriate measures given emerging challenges or lack of progress towards particular standards.

Here as well, keeping the ministry accountable both to its own goals and to those who support it will at times require the naming of appropriate boundaries and restraints. This, too, will be the task of the denominational leader, requiring more frequent and regular oversight than is customary for traditional ministries. Ryan and I met monthly and, between meetings, made contact via email whenever necessary. He was careful to check with me when considering ideas that represented departures from our tradition, and I in turn needed to consider what customs or practices were essential to hold on to and which we could relinquish. Because we are Anglicans, once the gathered community began to meet, these questions often concerned worship style. We often discussed progress towards benchmarks and shared our analysis of emerging challenges.

The applicable biblical image is that of the body of Christ, in which there is a variety of gifts for ministry, yet all of which serve the common good (1 Cor 12). The denominational leader is responsible for helping discern these gifts, for engaging them appropriately, and for holding every member of the body accountable to every other one for the sake of the gospel.

There will also be times of failure, when initial goals and plans fail to fulfill their promise. This outcome is difficult for all involved, particularly since we are not a culture that copes well with failure. Yet in this process, we will come to learn that failure is essential to growth; that risk-taking will include times when we do not succeed; and that failure can be a source of fresh insight for discipleship, leadership, and ministry alike. The ministry and denominational leaders will need to spend time reviewing, analyzing, and reflecting on goals and activities with honesty about where expectations were unrealistic and where actions were inappropriate. At that point, goals, actions, and benchmarks will need to be reset. This process is like a long journey in which the destination cannot yet be seen. The path requires faith and patience to plan and travel in one direction until a new vantage point shows the need to change course. It is rarely a journey as the crow flies and much more like that of crossing a mountain range. Course corrections are necessary at many points. Flexibility is an essential value at all times.

At a certain point, Ryan began to realize that although many people were using the online application and were engaged in the discipleship program, he had not been able to translate the online relationships into a gathered community. Despite using several different approaches, we needed to acknowledge that the transition we had anticipated was not happening—yet we were still committed to the goal of establishing a gathered church community in the area. We were also aware that the resources set aside for this new ministry were being depleted and, though benchmarks were being met, it was happening more slowly than expected. For all of these reasons, we needed to make a course correction.

Redeem the Commute had a life of its own as an evangelistic tool and needed to continue in some other form. So in order to establish a gathered worshipping community, we went back to more traditional church planting methods and began Redeemer Church, focusing specifically on young families while drawing on relationships that Ryan and his family were building in the community through neighbourhood activities. We also recognized the wisdom in Ryan's ministry becoming bi-vocational, with secular employment providing support and thereby relieving financial pressures. These were significant shifts in direction, yet, by discussing them together, weighing pros and cons, and keeping our eyes on the goal, they bore fruit, at least initially. In the longer term, the gathered community did not grow in the way expected and sustainability did not emerge, and Redeemer finally closed.

Communicating this process to the wider community, with all of its ups and downs, is not only necessary but can also provide encouragement to other ministries. Rather than being paralyzed by fear of failure, we can honour and encourage risk-taking by the ways in which innovative ministries find support, even from those who are not immediate stakeholders, even in the midst of renegotiation.

THE CHALLENGE OF A FRESH APPROACH

In our current social and cultural context, as many aging congregations face significant decline, we need to consider fresh approaches to mission and ministry. Yet as these new initiatives emerge, they challenge our established ways of doing ministry and disrupt the systems that maintain the traditions that we cherish. It is an exciting time of new possibilities for Christ's church yet challenging for denominational leaders who have been nurtured in tried-and-true ways from the past.

Harold Percy initiated conversations and actions in ministry that continue to reverberate within the Diocese of Toronto and beyond. In my own work as an Anglican bishop, it was a joy and privilege to accompany an emerging new ministry. For me, my meetings with Ryan were times of learning, of having my assumptions challenged, and of being invited to consider new and different expectations of what ministry can and should look like. The process was at times scary, as I knew that I myself did not have any of the skills required for this ministry, even while I needed to affirm institutional expectations and boundaries. Accompanying this ministry opened my heart and mind as I saw God at work in new ways.

This is a journey that I believe every denominational leader will encounter in the near future as we seek new ways to be faithful to the call to share the good news in our communities. It will be exhilarating, demanding, and filled with joy. May God grant us courage for the task ahead!

SECTION B
DISCIPLESHIP AND SPIRITUALITY

MAKING DISCIPLES: AN URGENT NECESSITY
TIM DOBBIN

WHEN JAMES MALLON MAKES PRESENTATIONS ON PARISH RENEWAL, HE GIVES PARTICIPANTS an eye-opening exercise.[16] He identifies the four tasks that Jesus gives the early church in the passage known as the Great Commission. Jesus charges his followers, "Go therefore and make disciples of all nations, baptizing them in the name of the Father and of the Son and of the Holy Spirit, and teaching them to obey everything that I have commanded you" (Matt 28:19–20). Of the four commands (go, make, baptize, and teach), one is a finite (or main) verb in the original Greek, and the other three are participles. Mallon reminds his audience that the finite verb is what anchors a sentence and what the participles depend on for their meaning. He then invites the audience members to identify which is the finite verb— the fulcrum—around which the other verbs revolve. Is it to go, to make, to baptize, or to teach? Apparently, of the thousands of participants he has instructed, only a handful have ever chosen the correct answer.

The answer? That which lies at the heart of the Great Commission is not the going, not the teaching, and not the baptizing. The finite verb is "make disciples" (*mathēteusate*). In other words, it is the making of disciples that provides the focus of the church's mission.

The Greek word for "disciple" is *mathētēs,* derived from the verb *manthanein,* meaning "to learn." As Mallon reminds us, to be a disciple

---

[16] James Mallon, *Divine Renovation: Bringing Your Parish from Maintenance to Mission* (New London: Twenty-Third Publications, 2014), 19–22.

is to be a learner. A disciple of Jesus Christ is one who is committed to a lifelong process of learning, of instruction, of apprenticeship from the teacher and master, Jesus Christ. The Latin term *discipulus* ("learner") gives us the English word "disciple" and with it the dimension of intentionality and discipline in the process of formation and growth.

While many churchgoers are familiar with this term, the question remains of whether and to what extent those same people would describe themselves as "disciples" or "followers" or "apprentices" of Jesus. It remains a challenge in many churches to spark interest in adult faith formation. Couple this with the rate at which the cultural tides are shifting from a Christendom to a post-Christendom mindset, when we can no longer expect to have our faith stance reinforced by structures around us, and the church finds itself asking deep questions about its identity and vocation.

HAROLD'S UNDERSTANDING OF DISCIPLESHIP

One of the hallmarks of the life and ministry of Harold Percy is an arresting clarity concerning who we are and what we are about as a people of God. The mission statement he crafted for the people of Trinity Streetsville was deceptively simple: "We are a community of ordinary people learning to follow Jesus in our time." It is unpretentious and has a singular focus—learning to follow Jesus, growing as his disciples, being formed as his apprentices.

It was Avery Dulles, in his seminal work *Models of the Church*, who initially proposed five models of church: as institution, as mystical communion, as sacrament, as herald, and as servant.[17] He later added a sixth model: "the church as school of discipleship."[18] In his later years, Dulles clarified that his "preferred model" was the church as "The Community of Disciples."[19] I am not sure whether church as a "school of discipleship" was a term Harold employed. John Bowen uses the term "the

---

[17] Avery Dulles, *Models of the Church*, expanded edition (New York: Doubleday, 2002). This reference and the two following were cited in a presentation by Dr. Lizette Larsen-Miller at the annual Diocese of Huron Clergy Conference on September 28, 2016, at Mount Carmel Spiritual Retreat Centre in Niagara Falls, Ontario.

[18] Avery Dulles, *A Church to Believe In: Discipleship and the Dynamics of Freedom* (New York: Crossroads, 1984).

[19] Drew Christiansen, "Drew Christiansen on Avery Dulles," *America*, December 13, 2008, https://www.americamagazine.org/content/all-things/drew-christiansen-avery-dulles.

trade school of Jesus."[20] Nonetheless, Harold regards making disciples as the primary task of the church, and he has set out his understanding of discipleship in two books: *Following Jesus: First Steps on the Way* and *Your Church Can Thrive: Making the Connections That Build Healthy Congregations.*[21]

FOLLOWING JESUS: FIRST STEPS ON THE WAY

Trinity strived to live into its mission statement in a number of different ways. Harold developed a six-week course entitled "Following Jesus: First Steps" in the 1980s, guiding participants through the fundamentals of faith development and spiritual growth. The goal of the course was clear: "to help you grow in your ability to live out your decision to be a follower of Jesus with a sense of confidence, joy, and expectation." The book *Following Jesus: First Steps on the Way* expands upon the content of the course. To date, it has sold over twelve thousand copies, which is remarkable for a Canadian book!

Harold developed an organizing metaphor for his understanding of our growth in Jesus' likeness. Premised upon our need of both food and exercise for healthy physical growth, Harold posited a similar need for spiritual food and exercise in order to mature in Christ. Balanced spiritual development flows from careful attention to the elements he identifies in the following table:[22]

FOOD	EXERCISE
Scripture	Prayer
Community	Ministry
Worship	Stewardship

The book devotes a chapter to each of these sources, giving biblical background and providing practical tips on how to grow in the practice of

---

[20] John Bowen, *Making Disciples Today: What, Why and How . . . on Earth?* (Richmond: Digory, 2013), 5.
[21] Percy, *Following Jesus*; Harold Percy, *Your Church Can Thrive: Making the Connections that Build Healthy Congregations* (Toronto: Anglican Book Centre; Nashville: Abingdon, 2003).
[22] Percy, *Following Jesus*, 8.

these habits. Harold's writing is accessible and practical, likely responding to questions he encountered in the course from which the book arose. He presents the material with simplicity and in a way that is easy to remember. A good example of his manner of instruction is the acrostic he provides for "disciple":

> **D** stands for our dream of the person God is calling us to become.
> **I** stands for the regular inventory we take of our growth in Christ.
> **S** stands for our need to start immediately.
> **C** stands for the importance of counting the cost of our commitment to follow Jesus.
> **I** stands for our informing others of our decision to live as a disciple of Christ.
> **P** stands for our need of patience in the lifelong journey of faith.
> **L** stands for learning to laugh at ourselves.
> **E** stands for our expectancy of the great, although not necessarily spectacular, things that will happen in us and through us by God's grace.[23]

YOUR CHURCH CAN THRIVE: MAKING THE CONNECTIONS THAT BUILD HEALTHY CONGREGATIONS

Harold revisits and expands on the topic of discipleship in *Your Church Can Thrive*, published in 2003. In the foreword, well-known church growth consultant Thomas Bandy captures well one of Harold's charisms: "Harold has the ability to be frighteningly optimistic without scaring people to death."[24] Bandy goes on to identify the shifts in attitude among leaders that are necessary for church growth to occur: a focus on missiology before ecclesiology, a focus on making disciples rather than preserving church harmony, and a focus on process before programs.

In framing his reflection on discipleship, Harold proposes two fundamental questions that congregations need to ask themselves. The first is "Why are we doing what we are doing?" The second is "Why are we doing it the way we are doing it?" Harold describes the church as a community of people learning to live to the glory of God. Living

---

[23] Percy, *Following Jesus*, 125–28.
[24] Thomas Bandy, foreword to *Your Church Can Thrive*, by Harold Percy, 10.

to the glory of God means living in such a way that we enhance God's reputation in the world, an idea he attributes to Leith Anderson.[25] The leader's primary responsibility is to envision what such a congregation might look like in its own setting and time and then to nurture the congregation into being as it seeks to penetrate its surrounding community with the gospel.

The congregation wants to help those whom they intend to reach to become "committed and enthusiastic followers of Jesus learning to live the new life of the kingdom."[26] Harold recognizes that before congregations can desire this for those they are seeking to reach, they need to desire it for themselves. Discipleship is about helping members of a congregation grow in spiritual maturity so that they themselves can live increasingly to the glory of God:

> Disciples are learners. As disciples of Jesus we are called to the lifelong adventure of learning to follow him closely and faithfully. In learning to live to the glory of God, our desire is to become more like Jesus in thought, character, attitude, behavior, and purpose; to live lives that are pleasing to him in every way.[27]

For this reason, Harold regards making disciples as "the first and most important task of the church. . . . Everything else we do—from worship to witness to service—depends on this and cannot grow beyond it."[28] The true measure of a congregation's effectiveness is its ability to make disciples and to send them out into the world. To this end, a strong discipleship training process must become a core feature of congregational ministry. "It is growth in discipleship—developing a deeper understanding of the faith, nurturing a more intimate relationship with God, and learning to make the connections between faith and everyday life—that constitutes the real adventure and excitement of the Christian life."[29]

---

[25] Leith Anderson, *A Church for the 21st Century* (Minneapolis: Bethany House, 1992), 129.
[26] Percy, *Your Church Can Thrive*, 23.
[27] Percy, *Your Church Can Thrive*, 26.
[28] Percy, *Your Church Can Thrive*, 28.
[29] Percy, *Your Church Can Thrive*, 32–33.

Conversely, the failure of North American mainline denominations to make disciple-making a priority is a primary cause for the decline we are currently experiencing and for the frequent lack of vitality in local congregations. Harold acknowledges that congregational leaders do not often receive practical instruction in their seminary training to help them design and offer discipleship programs. Yet he believes that the key to transformation in local congregations is reclaiming disciple-making as our number one priority.

Harold is a teacher. He recognizes that for disciple-making to be a priority, an emphasis on discipleship needs to impact all the various dimensions of our lives. He acknowledges that discipleship is a lifelong process—a direction and a way of life rather than a destination—that consists of four main aspects:

- Our relationship with God through Bible reading, prayer, and worship.
- Information received through instruction in the Christian faith.
- Transformation in our thoughts, attitudes, and behaviour through spiritual growth.
- Application, as we make connections between our faith and daily lives.

A healthy and balanced discipleship process will provide nourishment and nurturing for the head, heart, and hands of disciples, irrespective of where they are on their journey with Jesus.

Harold also describes three dimensions of our lives as disciples which the four subject areas described above will inform.[30] When we say yes to Jesus, first we are saying yes to becoming a child of God—a personal response. Second, we are saying yes to becoming part of Jesus' community—a corporate response. And, third, we are saying yes to becoming part of the reign of God, to living the new life in the world—a public response.

Given these four main subject areas and three key dimensions, Harold goes on to identify his top-ten topics in a balanced discipleship curriculum:

---

[30] Harold clarified these dimensions in a personal interview (August 23, 2016).

1. Gospel
2. Church
3. Scripture
4. Prayer
5. Reconciliation
6. Worship
7. Financial stewardship
8. Christian mindset
9. Daily witness
10. The Holy Spirit

Again, however, he emphasizes that discipleship is a process before it is a program, as a result of which the topics he has identified will be expressed in different ways for different congregations. The guiding question is "What is most appropriate and effective for the particular congregation?" A culture of growth is paramount: "The single most important aspect of this whole process is creating within the congregation the expectation of growth and nurturing a congregational climate within which growth can occur."[31] In this way, the church as a whole and the individual disciples within it grow together.

IN CONVERSATION

This, then, is a brief summary of some of the contours of Harold's writing on discipleship. In the course of my conversation with him, Harold underscored the importance of "intentionality"—that a disciple is someone who has made an *intentional* decision to follow Jesus and, in Lesslie Newbigin's terms, is learning to live a new life as a sign of God's reign in the midst of a broken world.[32] Harold described for me a visual metaphor that he once saw leadership expert John Maxwell employ. Maxwell held one arm elevated at a 45-degree angle. Everything that is worthwhile in life is uphill, said Maxwell, including learning to follow Jesus. The other arm he held at a 45-degree decline. Maxwell's point was that we can't move uphill with downhill habits. What is important, therefore, is commitment to the uphill process, not how far we get.

---

[31] Percy, *Your Church Can Thrive*, 44.

[32] Lesslie Newbigin, *The Gospel in a Pluralist Society* (Grand Rapids: Eerdmans, 1989).

Along the same lines, Harold emphasized that discipleship is more about becoming the kind of person who represents Jesus well and lives a certain kind of life than it is about simply assenting to a set of doctrines. He referred to Darrell Johnson's concept of "kingdomized" people—those who have heard Jesus' vision through the Beatitudes and whose hearts and lives have been grasped by God's reign.[33]

Harold also reiterated the corporate dimensions of discipleship. Discipleship involves learning to live in community. Our common life together is a sign of the new life of God's reign, not because we are perfect but because we are being formed as apprentices of Jesus. Reflecting on his time at Trinity, he celebrated not so much the change he witnessed in the lives of specific individuals as the change in the life of the congregation as a whole. People were able, willing, and excited to talk about following Jesus and to pray with and for their fellow travellers. Many of them remarked how being part of Trinity had helped them to become more committed Christians. On newcomers' nights, Harold would assure those gathered that the congregation would meet them wherever they presently were in order to help them to grow and move forward as followers of Jesus.

HAROLD'S LIFE AND TEACHING

I have tried in the foregoing sections of this chapter to outline some of the dominant strands in Harold's understanding of discipleship. As is probably evident, he is simply espousing principles and priorities that faithful Christians have understood and promulgated over the whole history of the church. What justifies exploration of his particular model of discipleship is its success in practice. In particular, it is a model of discipleship in which the gospel takes precedence over all else. Harold has always been determined not to allow anything to stand between the gospel and the average inhabitant of Streetsville. If it meant hosting a Valentine's Day dance in the ballroom of a major hotel with a bar and giving a short "commercial" about God's love with an invitation to check out the church, rather than gathering in the parish hall, then that is what Harold would do. He knew, too, how to persuade Christians to invite non-Christians to these events. If the gospel needed to be

---

[33] Darrell Johnson, *The Beatitudes: Living in Sync with the Reign of God* (Vancouver: Regent College, 2015).

disentangled from its Anglican dress, then again Harold would do it. Many of us aspire to adapt our liturgical offering to engage better with our surrounding communities. Shocking though it seemed to some of his clerical colleagues, Harold was not averse to making substantive changes to Anglican liturgy in order to achieve this goal. In many ways, he modelled a way forward.

While Harold has set out a compelling and comprehensive model of discipleship by identifying crucial areas, dimensions, and topics, it remains a challenge for us to separate what Harold taught from who he is as a person. He is endowed with personal charisma, a winsome smile, an engaging chuckle, and a playful humour that tends to win people over, whether or not they agree with him. He is plugged into life in a real way and asks good questions. He has a deep and abiding passion for mentoring others and is very generous with his time. He has a wonderful way of inviting people into the life of Jesus, much of which has to do with the particular gifts he incarnates.

THE DIOCESE OF HURON

Colleagues from the Anglican Diocese of Huron, where I serve as a pastor, still recall a workshop that Harold facilitated more than twenty years ago, at the invitation of the evangelism task force of the day. Harold was able to talk to the church about evangelism at a time when Anglicans were experiencing considerable anxiety about the word and were hard-pressed to recognize it as part of their denominational identity.

He has always regarded evangelism as a necessary corollary of following Jesus. At the same time, he is aware that Christians need some sense of their own relationship with God before they are able to share it with others. The need for a sense of the breadth and length and height and depth of God's personal love precedes the need for a working knowledge of the fundamental doctrines of the Christian faith.

He therefore invited participants to construct a timeline for their lives, marking out milestones and significant events along the way. He then asked them to indicate times when they had a sense of God's intervention in their lives. Deep-seated memories surfaced for many folk, some painful and others joyful. Participants recall that it was a sacred and deeply personal time, which Harold himself acknowledged by reminding those present that they stood on holy ground. As one participant remarked, Harold had (and he still has) a gift for identifying a sense of God's presence in the everyday lives of people, reflecting his own belief in God's prevenient grace at work even when people are not aware of it. He has sought to put people in touch with God's relationship with them before seeking to instill in them the confidence to talk about that relationship. This is evidence not simply of Harold's passion for the gospel but also of his conviction that formation in the gospel should be enfolded in pastoral sensitivity, especially for those with whom he did not always see eye to eye.

HAROLD'S INFLUENCE IN OUR OWN PARISH

The question remains as to what extent it is possible to replicate what Harold accomplished at Trinity. He inherited a church in decline and set about changing it. It required vision and courage, faith and focus, self-confidence and determination, to say, "By the grace of God, I am going to reconstruct this congregation." There are likely few others who could accomplish what Harold has achieved.

At the same time, however, Harold's understanding of congregational life, and of the role of disciple-making in particular, has been profoundly helpful in shaping the vision and self-understanding of the church in which I currently serve. One of the challenges I find in parish ministry is that of balancing priorities, of knowing how to adjudicate between the various priorities and commitments that make demands on the congregation's time and resources. Yet as "apprenticing with Jesus" has become the focus and heart of our life together, we have gained a clearer sense of our identity in God together with the mission and ministry to which God calls us.

LEARNING TO LIVE THE LIFE JESUS WOULD LIVE IF JESUS WERE LIVING MY LIFE[34]

We have found it helpful to express our focus on discipleship in this simple graphic.

---

[34] Adapted from Dallas Willard, *The Divine Conspiracy: Rediscovering Our Hidden Life in God* (New York: HarperCollins, 1997), 283: "I am learning from Jesus to live my life as he would live my life if he were I."

Section B: Discipleship and Spirituality

At St. Mark's Brantford, this graphic has become the lens through which we view our life together as (to adapt Harold's motto) a community of everyday folk who are learning to walk with Jesus in our time. We have a clearer sense of ourselves as apprentices who bear witness to the new way of being that God is creating in our midst. We are learning to live as a sign, an instrument, a foretaste of God's reign in the midst of a broken world here in our neighbourhood. We are better able to greet people wherever they presently find themselves in their walk with Jesus as we help them by God's grace to walk further.

More specifically, we have been able to identify and embrace six different practices or habits or patterns of life that the Holy Spirit uses to draw us more deeply into God's life and love, thereby forming us as apprentices of his Son:[35]

---

[35] These principles are adapted from Robert Schnase, *Five Practices for Fruitful Congregations* (Nashville: Abingdon, 2007).

- Welcoming others—as we provide social opportunities that build and strengthen our life together and invite others into that life.
- Celebrating God—as we hear and respond to God's Word and celebrate God's presence through traditional and contemporary worship.
- Growing spiritually—as we offer opportunities to deepen our faith and equip people to live Jesus' life in the world.
- Caring for each other—as we share Jesus' compassion with those in need among our parish family.
- Engaging the community—as we extend helping hands and respond to need in our neighbourhood and beyond.
- Cherishing our resources—as we care responsibly for all the gifts God has entrusted to us.

We recognize the reciprocal relationship between these practices and our being formed as disciples. As the Spirit inspires and empowers us to give our best attention to each of these areas of our lives, we grow as Jesus' apprentices; as we grow as Jesus' apprentices, we find that we want to invest more of our time and energy in these practices.

A THEOLOGICAL ACCOUNT OF DISCIPLESHIP

In this concluding section, I wish simply to explore a temptation for any model of discipleship, a temptation that becomes clear when we consider discipleship through a theological lens. First, it is important to locate discipleship within the spectrum of what can be said theologically about the Christian life, "that form of human existence which is brought into being and upheld by the saving work of God," as John Webster describes it.[36] Discipleship is an exploration of what happens when that which God has accomplished in the life, death, and resurrection of his Son is unleashed in human history through the work of the Holy Spirit, as fallen creatures are made children of God.

---

[36] "Discipleship and Calling," *Scottish Bulletin of Evangelical Theology* 23 (2005): 133. Note: some of the thoughts expressed in this section come from two papers by John Webster presented at the Refresh Conference, Wycliffe College, Toronto, in May 2004: "Discipleship and Calling," *Scottish Bulletin of Evangelical Theology* 23 (2005): 133–37; and "Discipleship and Obedience," *Scottish Bulletin of Evangelical Theology* 24 (2006): 4–18.

Often theologians highlight "moments"—adoption, regeneration, conversion, faith, justification, sanctification—as a way of tracing how the Holy Spirit is at work, shaping our human life. There is usually recourse to a theology of the church as the communion of saints within which our life in Christ plays out, concluding with a theology of glorification, when God brings our life in Christ to its eschatological fulfillment.

With only a few exceptions, the topic of discipleship has not enjoyed much attention in these contexts. However, as John Webster notes, the theme of discipleship actually directs our attention to the eschatological character of the Christian life and what is distinctive about the lives of those called to follow Jesus.[37]

The temptation in proposing any model of discipleship, or indeed in reflecting upon any of the motifs in a theology of the Christian life such as those here mentioned, is to privilege the human role in our being restored and made whole over God's action in enacting the new life now operating in the disciple. Our growth as followers of Jesus is not sourced in us, as though becoming an apprentice is akin to taking out a gym membership. It is God's call on our lives and God's decision enacted within us that establish us as Jesus' apprentices and situate us under God's intended conclusion for our lives.

To this end, we can say that the church does not make disciples; that work belongs to God. In any conversation about making disciples, we need to begin by speaking about God—God's election and God's grace, God's intervention in human history in his Son, and Jesus' call on our lives to follow him. In other words, when we talk about discipleship, we not only begin by talking about God, but we also need to *continue* by talking about God. Otherwise, we can find ourselves viewing the church in naturalistic terms—making the church in and of itself responsible for the gospel. That places an impossible burden on the church and risks becoming a counsel of despair. The church then becomes no different from any other voluntary organization, doing whatever it takes to persuade new members that their association is the best option among the host of others on offer. Again, as John Webster reminds us, this is not how disciples are made. Rather, it is the risen Jesus who still calls people to follow him and, in so doing, to

---

[37] See also Dietrich Bonhoeffer, *The Cost of Discipleship* (1937; New York: Touchstone, 1995).

discover the abundance of life that God extends to us all. "Disciples are made as he strides through the world which he has reconciled to himself and does his own work among his creatures."[38]

What, then, is the church's role in the work of discipleship? First, God calls the church simply to testify or bear witness to the call of Christ. We bear witness to Jesus' presence, allowing our living Lord, as best we can by God's grace, to speak to us. The church simply attests to what Jesus has already said—and still says—with his characteristic clarity, passion, and authority. Second, the church obeys Jesus' call by following the example of Simon and Andrew and James and John of leaving their nets and following him (Mark 1:16–20). We testify to God's power to transform lives as the Spirit empowers us to lay down what is life-denying in order to take up and receive what is life-giving—dying that we might live. It is here that the food and the exercise of spiritual growth, the areas and dimensions and topics of discipleship that Harold presents so compellingly, take their rightful place. We acknowledge that, left to our own devices, we would stumble over the most elementary of practices. Our learning as followers, our growth as disciples, our formation as apprentices, is from beginning to end the grace of the Holy Spirit at work in our lives.

LIVING THE MESSAGE

Harold can write and speak so convincingly on discipleship because he lives it. What he says issues out of who he is. He both bears witness and obeys. At a time when many churches are struggling with issues of identity and mission amidst a culture in significant transition, the need for prophetic voices to remind us of who we are and what we are called to do has never been greater. Harold's clear, winsome, and hope-filled voice remains a precious gift in the life of the church and in the lives of those called to share in Jesus' ministry of making disciples.

---

[38] Webster, "Discipleship and Obedience," 18.

THE BUSINESS WE'RE IN: PRAYER AND THE SPIRITUAL LIFE OF THE PASTOR
KELLY BAETZ

But he would withdraw to deserted places and pray.
—Luke 5:16

First, a confession. Prayer does not come easily to me. You would think that for an Anglican priest, prayer would come with the territory. And it does (as for any Christian), but I still find it difficult. Coming up with words is easy. It is the faith part that takes work. If you believe, as I do, that prayer is about talking to God and listening to God, then it follows that the stakes could not be higher.

It did not take me long in congregational ministry, however, to learn that when it comes to prayer, many of the folks in my congregation do not share this core belief. A member of our congregational leadership team once told me that he values prayer because it helps him focus, but not because he believes anyone is actually listening. My hunch is that if we were to press people for their honest opinions, many of them would say something similar. Prayer feels good, they might say, but does not make a difference in the real world. At the opposite end of the spectrum might be those who regard prayer as a type of magic. They believe that God is listening but that the goal of prayer is to convince God to do our bidding. This description sounds crass, but I have heard so many claims to "successful" prayer formulas or styles that the label of "magic" seems, regrettably, to be apt.

Of course, as leaders of congregations we will not want to settle for either of these extremes. The reason prayer is so difficult for me is because that middle ground is such a challenging space in which to dwell. How can I cultivate a life of prayer that bridges the gap between people who hold such profoundly different beliefs? And am I willing to go, daily, to this vulnerable place of believing that God is alive and active and may have an agenda for me beyond granting or not granting my petitions?

Prayer is tough, personal work, because every time we pray, we act on our faith. And to act on our faith is to confront the content of our faith. Every day. Every time. Every prayer. But while this is true for all Christians, Christian leaders must also make decisions aimed at cultivating the relationship between ministry and the life of prayer. This essay seeks to encourage such reflection. Of course, prayer is a huge topic, so I have limited myself to reflecting on three of my favourite "Haroldisms"—things said by Harold Percy that have stuck with me and made a difference in my daily life and work.

"GO TO THE WELL"—THE PRAYER LIFE OF THE LEADER

Harold Percy prays. As far as I know, he prays at least every morning. He calls it "going to the well." I like this description because it speaks of a daily need for spiritual nourishment rather than that legalistic duty many of us grew up with, often known as "quiet time" or "devotions." These descriptions are fine, but "going to the well" sounds much more inviting to me, a reminder that we pray first of all not because we have to but because it is going to be worthwhile. I know that Harold prays, not only because he has told me he does but also because he regularly passes on the learning gleaned from his time at the well. For all his smarts and all his charisma, I believe Harold's wisdom comes from the time he spends with God. And it makes me want to pray, too.

The effectiveness of a leader, Harold taught me, is directly related to how often that leader chooses to draw on the deep and reliable well of prayer and Bible reading. Leaders of congregations need to take control of their schedules in such a way that prayer and Bible reading become daily nonnegotiables. This is not always easy, and sometimes (as Harold also once said) it is a matter of beginning with duty, moving to discipline, and only then "going to the well" as a matter of delight. The goal is to pray daily and so to increase our ability to hear and respond to God. How can we get there?

First, we need to admit that prayer can be awkward. Whether it is praying with a group of people who have different beliefs about prayer (for example, those who enthusiastically add "Yes, Jesus!" to the prayers of others, and those others who are inwardly rolling their eyes the whole time because they are sure we are speaking to an imaginary friend) or praying on your own when you are not sure of your own beliefs, I think it is helpful to admit it: prayer is odd. That doesn't mean prayer is bad, only that it is distinctly peculiar! Even liturgy, which is comfortable for those steeped in its rhythms, can be awkward. How often have I marvelled at the scripted words we have just prayed, wondering how many in the congregation were metaphorically crossing their fingers behind their backs as we said them? It is important to make peace with that awkwardness so that it does not become an obstacle to making our daily trip to the well.

The way I make and remake my own peace with the oddness of prayer is to imagine that I am drowning in deep water. In that circumstance, I am not going to care how foolish I might look as I thrash my arms and scream for help. I am not going to care, because I know it is a matter of life and death. For the follower of Jesus, prayer is likewise a matter of spiritual life or death. It does not have to be perfect, but it has to be done, no matter how awkward or foolish we might feel about it on a given day.

Second, we need to give ourselves permission to allow our prayer time to "count" as work time. I recall an old *Leadership Journal* cartoon in which a pastor is on his knees in his study when a woman barges in, sees him praying, and says, "Oh good, you're not busy."

Sometimes we, too, are tempted to compartmentalize our personal devotion from our public vocation, our private prayers from our so-called professional ones. Certainly, boundaries of every kind matter in ministry, and where we set those boundaries is a matter of constant discernment. But taking a half-hour a day to pray for your people and your congregation's mission can always be afforded. Instead of starting your day by checking email, start your day by checking in with God. Not only is this legitimate work, but it is the most important work you will do all day.

"Oh, good . . . you're not busy."
Reproduced with permission of the artist.

Third, figure out what works for you. It matters more *that* you pray than where, what time, or in what posture you pray. For Harold, it's first thing in the morning with a cup of coffee. I cannot do that at this stage in my life because, for me, first thing in the morning is all about making breakfast for two little children and getting them safely to school. So my time of going to the well has become the first twenty minutes in my office. Or, if I know the office is going to be a nightmare that morning, I will take twenty minutes in my car! Before I talk to anyone, or check the computer, or even double-check my calendar, I pray. For me, this includes reading the Bible because that is how I feel most able to listen to God's voice. Do I succeed at this every day? No, but it happens a lot more than it used to, in large part because I admitted it was nonnegotiable and because I gave myself permission to see it as part of my job.

How we pray has to match our personalities if we want to be successful at it over the long haul. In *Courageous Leadership*, Bill Hybels advises leaders to develop whatever habits help us resist the temptation to wander away from a focus on God. He also points out that these habits will vary from person to person: "Every leader must figure out what rigors, practices, and spiritual disciplines are necessary for overcoming his or her proneness to wandering. And it's a waste of time for leaders to compare their spiritual regimens with anyone else's. Every leader's routine needs to be custom designed."[39] Maybe your hang-ups with prayer are different from mine. Or maybe you are not convinced that you have any hang-ups at all! What we have in common is that we can all improve and so begin more and more to pattern our own spiritual leadership after that of Christ's, who regularly withdrew from the most important work imaginable in order to visit the deep well of his Father's empowering presence and love. Personal prayer is not an optional extra, something we engage with if and when we have time. It is, as Harold says, "the business we're in."

"PRAY LIKE A TROOPER, AND HAVE YOUR PEOPLE PRAY LIKE TROOPERS"—THE PRAYERS OF THE CONGREGATION

As important as it is for us as leaders to "go to the well" ourselves, this is not our only prayer-related responsibility. We also need to teach our congregations to pray. In this section, I explore how we can lead our congregations in the ways they pray *together*. In the next section, we think more about teaching prayer to individuals as a matter of discipleship. (As in the whole chapter, the focus is on prayer that happens outside of the Sunday hour of worship.)

Harold Percy once said to me, "Pray like a trooper, and have your people pray like troopers." Now, I know the word "trooper" is not one that inspires everyone. War images can be problematic, and my guess is that if Harold knew I would be quoting him for this book, he might have chosen a different word. But we know what he means. Pray with purpose. Pray like you mean it. Pray big. And, somehow, get your congregation to do this too. Harold advised me to find people who will pray together for the mission of the church and for the needs of the community around the church.

My own advice to current or prospective leaders, or to anyone who feels called to improve the prayer lives of congregations, is to begin with a prayer audit. Every congregation prays together on Sundays, and hopefully those prayers are purposeful and big. But when else do they pray

---

[39] Hybels, *Courageous Leadership*, 204.

together, and what kinds of prayers do they say? Many congregations (in my experience) have what they call a prayer chain, a list of people who can be called on to pray for urgent requests or for those who are chronically ill or dealing with another long-term challenge. Some congregations have a small group of people that meets weekly, face-to-face, to pray. Still others might be blessed with a network of small groups that pray with and for one another on a regular basis. Probably, the more prayer going on, the better![40]

But what are they praying about? Again, I can only speak from my own experience, and sadly, based on much of that experience I have to conclude that many Christians pray small. We will gladly pray that Aunt Doris's broken ankle heals soon or that the pregnant granddaughter of a parishioner will safely deliver her baby. There is nothing wrong with such prayers; God knows and cares about the smallest details of our lives (see Matt 10:29–31). But if we only pray for our inner circles or only pray about health and getting back to health (as soon as possible, please) or restrict our prayers to a list of anonymous, disembodied first names read out on a Sunday morning, we will not be praying like troopers. Conducting an informal "prayer audit" (noting how, when, and where the congregation prays, as well as the content of those prayers) is a helpful start.

After you know where you are, you can take another step. Ask God to lead you to people who will pray (together, whenever possible) for the mission of the church and for your community at large. They do not have to agree on every detail of theology, but they should be open to the possibility that God desires to work in and through them to better the lives of others in godly ways. In *Becoming a Blessed Church*, Graham Standish defines "blessed" in part as follows: "*The blessed church is a church filled with God's purpose, presence, and power.* I believe that we *experience* the Trinitarian God as purpose, presence, and power."[41] Standish has a lot to say in this engrossing work on the spiritual theology and practice of prayer about why prayer matters. But purpose, presence, and power—

---

[40] The qualifier of "probably" is only inserted here to acknowledge that there can be dysfunctional patterns of prayer in congregations (i.e., prayer chains that function as gossip chains) that are doing more damage than good.

[41] N. Graham Standish, *Becoming a Blessed Church: Forming a Church of Spiritual Purpose, Presence, and Power*, 2nd ed. (Lanham: Rowman & Littlefield, 2016; first published 2005), 25, emphasis original.

which figure prominently throughout the early chapters of the book—are three compelling themes that everyone can understand. They offer a helpful measuring stick for groups that want to pray together effectively.

Again, we want to be careful not to wander into any understanding of prayer that even dances on the edge of magical thinking. We cannot measure God's power and how it is experienced in a quantifiable way. But we can certainly pray that our prayers will reflect God's very nature in that they will (a) be purposeful, (b) will ask for and receive the presence of Christ, and (c) will find Spirit-empowered answers of one sort or another. Prayers that are completely divorced from any relationship in space or circumstance (i.e., praying for Bob when you have no idea who Bob is or why he needs prayer) would likely have difficulty meeting these criteria. I am not saying that such prayers are altogether useless. I am not the judge of that. But it is difficult to pray with purpose when we do not know any details. It is difficult to seek the presence of Christ or the healing power of the Spirit on behalf of someone else when we have zero chance of becoming part of the answer to our own prayers. How can we be the hands and feet of Christ to an anonymous, unreachable person? Of course, I understand why people sometimes want public prayers to be anonymous. And I am confident in God's ability to sort it all out, despite our imperfect prayers. But I am also confident that we can do better.

James 5 offers a few significant principles for those who want to do better:

> Are any of you suffering hardships? You should pray. Are any of you happy? You should sing praises. Are any of you sick? You should call for the elders of the church to come and pray over you, anointing you with oil in the name of the Lord. Such a prayer offered in faith will heal the sick, and the Lord will make you well. And if you have committed any sins, you will be forgiven.
>
> Confess your sins to each other and pray for each other so that you may be healed. The earnest prayer of a righteous person has great power and produces wonderful results. Elijah was as human as we are, and yet when he prayed earnestly that no rain would fall, none fell for three and a half years! Then, when he

prayed again, the sky sent down rain and the earth began to yield its crops. (Jas 5:13–18, NLT)

In some ways, this is a difficult passage, requiring a fuller exegesis than is possible here. It is difficult for a number of reasons. First, it seems to link healing to a certain measure of faith, an idea that has famously been used to abuse people spiritually and cause them to believe that any lack of healing is their own fault. James also, more subtly, links physical healing with the forgiveness of sins, an idea that can and has likewise done damage. And I chuckle about James holding up Elijah as being "as human as we are," as if we could easily relate to the likes of one of the Old Testament's greatest prophets!

Even so, the key concepts of purpose, presence, and power are all over and in between James' words. As to purpose, James is intentional. Prayer and praise are the appropriate response to all of life's circumstances, good and bad. Nothing is left outside of God's care, and we can bring it all to God's throne. He also speaks of earnestness. The righteous person (whether Elijah or an ordinary joe) who prays earnestly can produce wonderful results. We might rephrase that to say that sincere and heartfelt prayers go a long way. When we pray with purpose, we have an agenda. We do not expect God to do what we say, but we come with an opening pitch. That is purposeful prayer.

As to presence, James says that God will show up. Whether God brings healing or forgiveness or a combination of the two, God shows up. James also commands his readers to be present not only to God but to one another as well. "Are any of you sick? You should call for the elders of the church to come and pray over you, anointing you with oil in the name of the Lord." That is much more personal and tactile than calling the elders of the church and asking them to add your name to the prayer list! James assumes the presence of Christian community as he exhorts the people to confess their sins "to each other" and to pray "for each other" so that they will be healed. Solitary prayer (and praise) of course has its place, and we must be mindful of the ministry of so many shut-ins who effectively offer intercessory prayer in quiet faithfulness. But we are also called to gather and to be present to one another as we seek the presence of Christ in our midst.

Finally, as to power, it does not get much more dramatic than the example of Elijah and the weather! Whatever you make of that prophetic episode or of James' assurances about healing and forgiveness, his point is that earnest prayer accomplishes great things. More properly put, God's power is made real in the world at least in part because we have prayed. That is a claim not everyone in your congregation will believe. In fact, we all have trouble believing it at times. But that is what James says, and it can contribute to a larger vision of prayer that will be large enough to inspire the life and work of your congregation.

When we pray "like troopers" we not only (by God's grace) enlarge our own capacity to glimpse the kingdom, but we also help to safeguard the long-term sustainability of our parishes. That cannot be our only reason for praying, of course, but it is nonetheless a wonderful spinoff. That is not to say that a given congregation will *never* close its doors, but as we earnestly seek God's will and direction, we will be in a better position to do all God has for us to do within a congregation's lifetime. Standish points out several times that many churches die spiritually before they die physically (he calls this "respiratory failure") and that the key to vibrancy (or blessedness) is prayerfully seeking the wisdom and power of God the Holy Spirit.[42] As we die to what we want and become alive to what God wants, the congregation will be faithful and, if God wills it, will grow.

"PEOPLE NEED TO BE TAUGHT TO PRAY, AND PEOPLE ENJOY LEARNING HOW TO PRAY"—PRAYER AS DISCIPLESHIP

To this point, we have considered the personal prayer life of the leader/pastor and the ways people pray together as congregations (or as smaller groups within congregations). The third arena requiring our consideration is teaching people how to work prayer more consistently into their own lives. This is a matter of discipleship, and what I most appreciate about this last "Harold-ism" is that he acknowledges prayer as a practice to be learned, not a natural ability that somehow comes to life on its own at the moment of conversion. Outside of a formal liturgy (which is itself a school of prayer, even if some sleep through class), do we teach people to pray? There is a reason that pastors are most often called upon to say grace or to open meetings in prayer, and the cultural norms of Christendom are

---

[42] Standish, *Becoming a Blessed Church*, 33–44.

only part of the explanation. The bigger reason, or the reason *now*, is that most of the people in established congregations are terrified to pray out loud. If I am going to ask someone else to say grace or open a meeting or Bible study in prayer, *I ask them ahead of time* as a matter of pastoral sensitivity. Not everyone is terrified, of course—there are exceptions to the rule. But the rule is pervasive enough that intentional teaching on prayer now needs to be on every pastor's radar. People need to be taught to pray.

Harold's second claim is that people enjoy learning how to pray. I have to admit that I have not seen enough evidence of this in my own ministry to say a hearty "Amen," but Harold has seen it in his own ministry, which is good enough for me! Whether through his books or his Christianity 101 courses or other forms of discipleship, Harold has taught many people to pray, and if he says that they enjoy it, I believe him. What I *have* seen for myself is that if people are given a safe space and patience and some encouragement, many of them will indeed get over that terror of praying out loud. And as we equip people to pray in their daily lives, whether on their own or with their partners or families or friends or co-workers, it will enrich their relationship with God and with God's world, and they will find deeper joy and satisfaction along the way.

So how can we teach people to pray? I want to suggest four ways.

The first way is more than a suggestion. It is a prerequisite: model prayer in your own life and in your interactions with people. As Harold has told me more than once, "You can't take people where you haven't been yourself." That is not to say that our own prayer life has to be perfect, or even especially inspiring. It simply means that the people we seek to lead need to know that we are on the same journey and that we will not ask them to do what we ourselves have been unable to accomplish. If we fail in this, we may find ourselves under the same indictment as the scribes and Pharisees, of whom Jesus says, "They tie up heavy burdens, hard to bear, and lay them on the shoulders of others; but they themselves are unwilling to lift a finger to move them" (Matt 23:4).

Now the grace in this is that even when we are hypocrites, what we teach may still bear fruit (see Matt 23:1–3), but our teaching will surely bear more fruit if we ourselves are doing our best to follow it. So, in order to teach prayer, become a leader who prays. Go to the well. Pray for the mission of your congregation and for the people in your congregation. Let your congregation see that you respond to difficult situations by praying, and nurture an impulse toward prayer as part of the congregational DNA. Pray for others not only on your own but also, when appropriate, on the spot. As a clergy colleague, the Rev. Bob Elkin of Thessalon, Ontario, once commented, "Don't say, 'I'll pray for you' when you can say, 'Let's pray now!'"

Another way to model prayer is to take opportunities to be appropriately transparent about your own victories and struggles. In their book *Bullseye: Aiming to Follow Jesus*, United Church ministers Jamie Holtom and Debbie Johnson begin each chapter by sharing their own experiences in various aspects of discipleship. On prayer, Holtom writes, "I . . . certainly didn't become a prayer expert by any means. I would have a stretch where I would do okay. I might be fairly regular for a month or even two months, and then I'd get bored of that routine or my schedule would change for some reason and I would get out of the habit."[43] He continues to share his story, both what works for him and what does not, and ends with this: "Over time I got to a point where prayer and time with God were an absolute delight. These days I can't wait to get up, put the coffee on, open up my Bible, and spend some time with God, being completely open to whatever God might have in store for me that day."[44]

In the same spirit, Johnson writes, "It's taken many years and many attempts at different practices to find what consistently works for me,"[45] and then she lists eight practical ideas for prayer and nurturing a vital relationship with God. Holtom and Johnson offer great examples about how to appropriately model a life of prayer to those you seek to lead. (Their book is a treasure house of ideas on prayer and other marks of discipleship that are biblical, practical, and accessible. I find it to be a great teaching tool.)

Second, preach about prayer. This could be done whenever passages come up (for instance, in the lectionary, if your church uses one) that naturally lend themselves to the topic (for instance, the Lord's Prayer or Paul's many exhortations on the subject), or it could be the topic of a

---

[43] Jamie Holtom and Debbie Johnson, *Bullseye: Aiming to Follow Jesus* (Toronto: United Church Publishing House, 2015), 14.
[44] Holtom and Johnson, *Bullseye*, 15.
[45] Holtom and Johnson, *Bullseye*, 17.

preaching series. Let your congregation see how those in the Bible have prayed. Teach people about the prayer of Daniel, the song of Mary, and the gratitude of Paul. This, importantly, will give them more models than just you! If you preach about prayer or any other spiritual practice, Standish offers a wise caution, reminding us that our job is primarily not to prove a theological point but to help our hearers to experience Christ: "The problem in so many churches is that the practitioners of much . . . preaching have forgotten to balance the theological with the spiritual, or even more important, to ground theological thinking and teaching in spiritual practice and experience."[46] So if you preach about prayer, aim for this balance. Teach what the Bible says, but proclaim how Christ is present as we live out (or struggle to live out) what we are learning.

Third, equip people with resources they can take home to aid them in learning about and practising prayer. This could be as simple as a bulletin insert[47] or as involved as stocking your church library with books about prayer (or books *of* prayers). Many people have appreciated Anne Lamott's *Help Thanks Wow: The Three Essential Prayers*,[48] and there are many others that could be made available to help people to get started or to go deeper. Blogs or daily emails from capable practitioners of prayer can also be recommended.

Fourth, offer a course on prayer outside of Sunday worship. This could be an evangelistic opportunity as well as a means of discipleship, since many people now outside the church are very open to and interested in prayer and already have their own practices of prayer. For teaching a course on prayer, Jamie Holtom and Debbie Johnson recommend Jane Vennard's *A Praying Congregation: The Art of Teaching Spiritual Practice*.[49]

Taken together, all of these means of teaching (modelling, preaching, and equipping people through resources or short courses) can help

---

[46] Standish, *Becoming a Blessed Church*, 90–91.

[47] Harold Percy often encourages people to begin with a form of prayer he calls "Fifteen minutes with Jesus." A bulletin insert could include a brief Scripture passage, two questions for reflection, and a way to pray through both the passage and the questions. In my own parish, I have done this during Advent and Lent, as people seem more open in my context to seasonal studies and practices. At least it is a start!

[48] Anne Lamott, *Help Thanks Wow: The Three Essential Prayers* (New York: Random House, 2012).

[49] Jane Vennard, *A Praying Congregation: The Art of Teaching Spiritual Practice* (Herndon: Alban Institute, 2005).

individuals take steps in their growth to spiritual maturity. Teaching someone to pray, whether a member of your congregation or your own child, is one of the best gifts you could ever give to them.

A PRAYER FOR MY MENTOR

In this chapter I attempt, imperfectly, to pass on some of what I have learned from Harold Percy. I was very blessed to have been part of a small group that Harold formally mentored from 2012 to 2015. I know that Harold does not seek honour for himself, so I will let my words be few. My prayer is that God will continue to bless Harold with wisdom, clarity, and laughter and that many more leaders in the body of Christ will follow his example of passing on what they have learned from their own years in ministry and in relationship with Jesus. Harold's gifts to me of perspective, interest, and steady faith came at a time in my ministry when I badly needed all of those things; they will continue to inspire me for many years, and I am grateful.

FIVE KINDS OF MENTORS: THE FIVE PEOPLE PRINCIPLE
BILL FIETJE

IN WESTERN SOCIETIES, WE HAVE AN INCREASING TENDENCY TO PATTERN OUR LIVES IN terms of what sociologists call "cocooning." Cocooning refers to our preference for social independence, even isolation, and for compartmentalizing our lives. Too often, we live autonomously, disastrously disconnected from people and society around us. But living well and leading well require just the opposite of this, with a purpose that intentionally contradicts this social trend. To succeed over a lifetime, effective leaders must build a circle of close friends and mentors who will influence their personal and professional lives toward effectiveness and fruitfulness. If, as the saying goes, "It takes a village to raise a child," it will also take a village—a supportive community—to form a leader.

My wife, Lois, and I had the pleasure of attending Trinity Streetsville for several years while we jointly served as Canadian national directors for Overseas Missionary Fellowship (OMF) International. Having previously heard of Harold Percy, I welcomed the opportunity to get to know him personally. I soon discovered that he is what I call "a man for all seasons." As a leader and mentor, Harold showed that he knew not only how to work effectively in community but also how to serve that community well. Above and beyond doing all that is required of a pastor, he has been a developer of people.

Harold has always understood the need to invest in others and to let others invest in him. He understands what it means both to be mentored and to mentor others. He has consistently maintained an openness to others who impact him in such a way that he can in turn have an effective impact on those around him. In short, Harold Percy has understood and lived out the secret to serving well, leaving a positive legacy for those who follow in his footsteps. He exemplifies what I call the "Five People Principle," which focuses on five kinds of people that all leaders need to know in order to succeed in Christian ministry and in life generally.

If we desire to be effective leaders for the kingdom of God, we need to build into our lives five key relationships that will see us through to the end. We need all five relationships over the course of a lifetime, but we will develop each of them more intensively at different times throughout our ministry. Most writers on the subject of mentoring emphasize these relationships; Clinton and Stanley, in their book *Connecting*, speak of a "constellation model" (by which they mean a relational network of upward, downward, and lateral mentoring),[50] while John Maxwell, in his book *Winning with People*, makes reference to the importance of key friend relationships.[51] Regardless of what terms we use, we can all benefit from these simple yet complex relationships, especially so if we have been given responsibility for leading others.

1. A MENTOR TEACHER: EVERY MOSES NEEDS A JETHRO (EXODUS 18:15-24)

Every leader needs a Jethro who is not afraid to bring correction at the right time. Even though Jethro loved and admired Moses, he wouldn't let him destroy his life and ministry; Jethro tells him directly, "You will surely wear yourself out, both you and these people with you. For the task is too heavy for you; you cannot do it alone" (Exod 18:18).

Moses is ordained of God, commissioned to the daunting task of challenging Pharaoh to let the Hebrew people leave their slavery behind and worship the one true God. Yet this is only the beginning, for Moses soon learns that securing freedom is one thing, whereas leading an entire nation through the desert is an entirely new game. Still, God has uniquely called and qualified Moses to lead. Over the course of forty long years (so Acts 7:30 tells us), Moses learns to submit to Jethro, the father of his wife,

---

[50] J. Robert Clinton and Paul Stanley, *Connecting: The Mentoring Relationships You Need to Succeed in Life* (Carol Stream: NavPress, 1992), 157.
[51] John Maxwell, *Winning with People: Discover the People Principles that Work for You Every Time* (Nashville: Thomas Nelson, 2007), 177.

Zipporah, while tending his father-in-law's flocks. Only then does Moses receive his commission from the burning bush (see Exod 3:1–12), so that even though they are both in their eighties, he and Aaron can succeed in challenging the leadership and the gods of Egypt.

Once they have escaped into the wilderness of Sinai, in Exodus 18, Jethro comes to visit Moses, accompanied by his daughter and grandchildren—Moses' own wife and sons. Jethro honours his son-in-law and rejoices at how the Lord has brought the Hebrews out of Egypt. Still, all is not well. Jethro watches while Moses sits as judge over the people, who inquire of their leader as to the mind of God. As a priest in Midian, Jethro must already know what it takes to serve people who rely on his judgment. So, as we read in Exodus 18:13–26, Jethro challenges his son-in-law's leadership style. He tells him, "You will surely wear yourself out, both you and these people with you. For the task is too heavy for you; you cannot do it alone" (Exod 18:18). Moses responds wisely, choosing reputable men as heads over the people in groups of thousands, hundreds, and tens. Guided by Jethro, Moses learns to delegate. By stewarding his own abilities and energy and by employing the gifts of others, Moses sets in place a system of governance that contributes to forming the wandering group of slaves and exiles into a nation.

What future would Moses and the nation have had without this divine intervention? How would they have survived had Moses not been willing to listen to his mentor, one who had already travelled the same path on which Moses now found himself? Like Moses, we, too, need to cultivate "Jethro" relationships with mentors who have travelled the same path ahead of us. These are the people who will guide us along the way. From when I was seventeen to the present day, my own life mentor has been a "Jethro" to me. In everything I did throughout my life and ministry career, I would ask myself, "What would Ernest do?"—and I have often told him that I would not be where I am today without his faithful mentoring of me.

The Role of a Jethro:
- To offer more experience and maturity than we possess.
- To love us enough to confront our inexperience.
- To see the road ahead because they have travelled it already.

- To rebuke and instruct wisely . . . and leave detailed instructions.
- To earn respect, so that we trust and follow their advice.

Another such mentor in my own life was David, who had been the senior pastor of a large, growing church for thirty years. He and I served together in a busy, demanding ministry setting. One day, David came into my office and gently yet firmly confronted me with some negative tendencies that he perceived in me. Frankly and lovingly, he showed me that I was developing a messiah complex: I believed being a leader meant thinking I could solve everyone else's problems. He correctly saw this as a weakness in me as a younger leader, one who wanted to be seen as indispensable. He showed me clearly that I was on a collision course with failure if I continued in the leadership style that I had adopted. I abruptly stopped, and I believe that doing so saved my ministry. Thank the Lord for all those like David who are true Jethros in our lives.

2. A MENTOR FRIEND: EVERY DAVID NEEDS A JONATHAN (1 SAMUEL 20:1-42)

No one can go it alone. Even though David is a mighty "man of valour" (1 Sam 16:18), he weeps when he sees the depth of Jonathan's love for him (1 Sam 20:41).

As was the case with Moses, so again we see God's clear call and commission in the life of David, son of Jesse. Yet David, too, is called to a difficult role. Yes, David is the giant slayer; David is the man of valour; and his popularity is growing. Saul essentially welcomes David into his own family so that David enjoys the status and privilege of being in the king's inner circle. Yet David does not forget that God alone has called him. Yet trouble arises because Saul wants to retain his hold on the kingship in order to pass it along to his own son, Jonathan. Saul must be aware that the prophet Samuel has already anointed David, a relatively young and obscure figure in Israel. Certainly, by 1 Samuel 20, it is clear that Jonathan has befriended David against the wishes of his father.

By now Jonathan and David are the best of friends; in fact, they love each other as brothers, with Jonathan deferring to David. First Samuel 20:12–23 records the oath of covenant that David and Jonathan swear to one another. The depth of their friendship is so profound that we see here that Jonathan chooses fidelity to David not only over the wishes of his father Saul but even over his own wishes as the eldest son and immediate heir of Israel's first king. Theirs is a peer friendship that goes well beyond the level of acquaintance, of simple co-operation, or even of dedicated partnership in ministry.

This is the type of relationship that makes a person grounded and centred. Because it is built on trust, respect, and mutual understanding, it brings hope and insight into otherwise confusing situations. In human terms, it could even be said that if God had not used Jonathan to rescue David from the king's mortal anger, he would have been dead long before. Their friendship explains why David's loyalty extends to the family of Jonathan and lineage of Saul even after Jonathan has been killed in battle. By bonding David's life with that of Jonathan, God proves that he himself is David's ultimate and true protector.

I am blessed by having had many men and women as close friends and fellow ministers, but only one fits the role of a Jonathan. My own David-Jonathan peer-mentor relationship keeps me grounded and centred. In the same way, all leaders need at least one person who is on their side in the battle, someone who always has their back. At the present time, my wife and I are part of a group of five couples who meet monthly to speak into each other's lives. Since each of these couples leads a growing, demanding ministry, we share a great deal in common. This mutual accountability and encouragement are important because Christian leadership is often a lonely experience. In our peer group, we are learning to be ourselves, yet with the knowledge that we stand together as we face the challenges of ministry. These types of friendship are rare, but by God's grace they can be available to us if we take the time and energy to cultivate them.

The Role of a Jonathan:
- To share life experiences together with us in real time.
- To be loyal to us in difficult times and adversity.
- To understand and embrace the deepest feelings that arise out of our experiences.
- To demonstrate unconditional love; to think the best of us and for us.
- To risk for the sake of the relationship.

3. A SPONSOR MENTOR: EVERY SAUL NEEDS A BARNABAS (ACTS 9:26-28)

We all need people in our lives to lend us credibility—their own credibility offered on our behalf and for our benefit.

Acts 9 introduces us to what turns out to be a long, close, and at times rocky relationship between two strong leaders in the early church. The New Testament Saul is noted for his persecution of Christian disciples. He says of himself in Philippians 3:6 that he had been full of zeal and a persecutor of the church. As we read in Acts, Saul obtains letters from the Sanhedrin to be able to arrest and bring to Jerusalem the followers of the Christian Way who have gone to Damascus in Syria (Acts 9:2). While on the road, he is blinded by a vision and visitation of Jesus Christ and has to be led by the hand into Damascus. For three days, Luke tells us, he is without sight, neither eating nor drinking, until he is healed by the Lord Jesus through the ministry of Ananias (Acts 9:8–9, 17–19). Immediately thereafter, Saul begins a ministry of proclamation in Damascus, which quickly threatens his own life even as he has threatened the lives of others.

Indeed, such is the danger that he is forced to flee from Damascus to Jerusalem. Although he wants to introduce himself to the apostles, they are justifiably afraid of him, not believing that he is truly a disciple of Christ. Barnabas (which according to Acts 4:36 means "son of encouragement") puts his own credibility on the line in order to convince the other apostles to accept Paul as a true believer. Quite simply, the others accept Saul because they trust Barnabas. This creates such a bond between them that by the time we see them again in Acts 13, Paul and Barnabas are already a well-accepted ministry team. With Barnabas as his sponsor, Saul (now called Paul) launches out into further ministry; in fact, they go on to serve in partnership together. God uses Barnabas to advance Paul's ministry, and even though he is a leader in his own right, Barnabas takes a back seat to Paul for the sake of the kingdom.

God uses mentors of this kind in two ways: for opening doors and for encouraging growth. First, a sponsor sees our gifts for ministry and trusts God's work in us. They convince others to trust God's work in us. Finally, they step back and let our work grow beyond their own. In this way, sponsor mentors cause others to accelerate into ministry, delighting when they see others succeed.

The Role of a Barnabas:
- To demonstrate credibility in their life and ministry position.
- To maintain great faith in God's ability to change lives and to see God's best in others.
- To offer the gift of encouragement, advancing other ministries ahead of their own.
- Over the long term, to model wisdom and faithfulness.

4. A MENTEE: EVERY PAUL NEEDS A TIMOTHY (2 TIMOTHY 1:1-2; 3:10-11)

To this point, we've concentrated on how others can build into our lives. As we learn from those mentors, we in turn can and must build into the lives of others whom God brings near—men and women who come along with us in the journey of faith. These folks may not necessarily be younger than ourselves, nor do they need to be novices in what they are doing. Being mentors ourselves simply means that by carefully stewarding the gifts, insights, and people we have been given, we learn to empower others so that they can succeed in turn. The mark of true leadership lies in one generation's ability to raise up a generation of leaders to follow.

This is a giving and patient relationship of grace of the sort we see between Paul and Timothy, in particular. Paul is a spiritual father to Timothy (Phil 2:22) as well as to others, such as Titus, whom Paul calls "my loyal child in the faith we share" (Titus 1:4); Tychicus, "a dear brother and a faithful minister in the Lord" (Eph 6:21); Epaphroditus, "my brother and co-worker and fellow soldier" (Phil 2:25); and many more whose names we do not know. Paul pours himself into fellow disciples, who will in turn lead others into maturity in Christian life and ministry.

So this is at least a three-step process. First, Paul is careful to walk in faithfulness and to teach all the truths of Christian life and ministry. Second, Timothy watches and learns from the apostle, until Paul is confident that he has passed on to his mentee all that he is, all that he does, and all that he knows. As he tells Timothy, "Now you have observed my teaching, my conduct, my aim in life, my faith, my patience, my love, my steadfastness, my persecutions, and my suffering" (2 Tim 3:10–11). Then, third, Paul encourages Timothy to do the same for others: "You then, my child, be strong in the grace that is in Christ Jesus; and what you have heard from me through many witnesses entrust to faithful people who will be able to teach others as well" (2 Tim 2:1–2). In this passage, Paul is mainly referring to the gospel message itself but at the same time offers himself as a living example for Timothy to follow, so that Timothy can be an example to others in turn. This is exactly how things play out in the church at Corinth. Paul reminds the Corinthian believers that he is their spiritual father "in Christ Jesus . . . through the gospel" (1 Cor 4:15). Because of all that Timothy has learned from him, Paul has sent Timothy in person, bearing the letter, as a reminder and an example to the congregation: "I appeal to you, then, be imitators of me. For this reason I sent you Timothy, who is my beloved and faithful child in the Lord, to remind you of my ways in Christ Jesus, as I teach them everywhere in every church" (1 Cor 4:16–17).

In short, just as every Timothy needs a mentor, so every Paul needs a mentee. Educators tell us that the best way to stay sharp in one's field of knowledge is to continually teach others. To be a mentor, we must be aware of our own inevitable tendency toward entropy. Over time, we can slow down as leaders; we begin to take what we do for granted, at times running on fumes, as the saying goes. If we are going to be honest in our relationships, we need to remember that others look to us for guidance, teaching, and encouragement; this knowledge will keep us focused on Christ and clear in our ministry goals. But this is not just for our own sake. Every Paul needs a Timothy, not just to stay sharp but more importantly to ensure that the work of ministry continues. In order for values, mission, and vision to remain constant, leaders must empower and equip others who will continue on the same journey. Otherwise, the lessons we have learned will be lost for the generation that follows.

The Role of a Timothy:

- To be faithful to Christ and to their mentor (in that order!).
- To commit to the same vision and goals.
- To be always ready to listen, to learn, and to obey.
- To remain humble of heart, mind, and spirit.
- To be responsible, reliable, and hard working.

5. THE SPIRIT OF JESUS: EVERY SINNER NEEDS A SAVIOUR (PHILIPPIANS 3:7-14)

Of course, there is one mentoring relationship that takes precedence over all others, as much (maybe even more!) for leaders as for other disciples. That is our relationship with Christ himself, and here again the apostle Paul provides the best example we will find. Although Paul is rightly considered to have been the greatest missionary, teacher, and statesman of the early church, he is first and foremost a disciple of the Lord, one whose confidence lies in Christ alone. As he himself explains, Paul puts "no confidence in the flesh" (Phil 3:3), whether for salvation, for attaining maturity as a Christian believer, or for the work of ministry.

On the contrary, following Christ has cost him everything: "Yet whatever gains I had," he insists, whatever he previously relied on to provide a sense of personal identity and spiritual direction, "these I have come to regard as loss because of Christ . . . because of the surpassing value of knowing Christ Jesus my Lord" (Phil 3:7–8). To what exactly is he referring?

- Loss of ethnic pride and educational superiority for the sake of embracing mystery.
- Loss of confidence in his own righteousness, as he clings instead to the all-sufficient righteousness of Christ.
- Loss of assurance that he has obeyed God's will—the Law with its detailed commands—in favour of faith and grace.
- Loss of personal security, as he learns to embrace suffering—"living is Christ and dying is gain" (Phil 1:21).

In much the same way, 2 Peter 1:3–11 provides a manifesto for servant leadership, highlighting our absolute dependence on Christ. In case we are ever tempted to rely on our own strength, this passage reminds us that all we have is in and from Christ: "His divine power has given us everything needed for life and godliness, through the knowledge of him who called us by his own glory and goodness" (2 Pet 1:3). It reminds us of who we are. At the same time, however, we ourselves are responsible for nurturing and developing the gifts Christ gives us. So the passage states, "For this very reason, you must make every effort to support your faith with goodness, and goodness with knowledge, and knowledge with self-control, and self-control with endurance, and endurance with godliness, and godliness with mutual affection, and mutual affection with love" (2 Pet 1:5–7).

Still, all of our efforts to attain spiritual maturity are hollow if we pursue this grand goal by means of the "flesh." That is, no man-made program can make someone a Christian. Likewise, human efforts alone—whether our own or those of our mentoring companions—cannot ultimately help us mature as believers if we are not sealed with the indwelling power, sanctification, and person of the Holy Spirit. The Holy Spirit is Christ's own Spirit dwelling within us, resting upon us, and working through us. Unless we rely directly on Jesus in the power of the Spirit of God, we will be frustrated in all of our efforts. It is for this reason that Paul calls the Galatian believers "foolish," even telling them that they are "bewitched" (Gal 3:1) to think that they can attain sanctification and maturity as servants of Christ apart from the Spirit of God.

The Role of a Disciple:

- To be willing to bear the high cost of discipleship.
- To lack confidence in their own ability to serve and honour God.
- To have a deep trust in and reliance on the power of the Holy Spirit.
- To embrace the suffering and hardship that come with following Christ.
- To accept their responsibility to employ Christ's gifts to the full.

This, then, is the Five People Principle. As I see it, we need all five kinds of relationships in order to develop as faithful and effective leaders for the kingdom of God: as Moses needs Jethro, we need mentors who can teach us out of their experience; as David needs Jonathan, we need mentors who can stand with us as friends; as Saul needs Barnabas, we need sponsors who can open doors for us; and as Paul needs Timothy, we need to invest in the next generation of leaders. But more than any of these—in fact, for any of them to succeed —we ourselves need to be constantly mentored, directed, and sustained by Christ.

Both personally, as a disciple, and publicly, as a minister of the gospel, Harold Percy has always understood and taught the person and work of Christ and the Holy Spirit. The other four relationships are certainly vital, but here is the true secret of the Christian life and the secret of true servant leadership: Jesus Christ, raised in glory and alive in us.

GROWING THE GIFT OF GENEROSITY: HAROLD PERCY AND MONEY
PETER PATTERSON

MY FIRST EXPERIENCE OF HAROLD'S THEOLOGY OF MONEY WAS WHEN HE APPROACHED me, a young churchwarden, to see if I would align with his suggestion that we eliminate one of the parish's fundraising strategies—our semi-annual rummage sale. Since our parish was at that time "on the dole"—meaning that we always came up just short of budget and each year relied on the diocese to bail us out—this was the first time anyone had talked about cutting out something that generated money, even if was not a large amount.

I pointed out to Harold that rummage sales were easy to organize; the ladies involved enjoyed each other's company; and many of them were survivors of the Great Depression, so they were inveterate hoarders and, hence, had lots of cheap items to offer each year. The likely outcome of Harold's idea would be to upset the Anglican Church Women (ACW) and put the parish a little further into debt.

Harold's answer showed that he was less worried about hurting the feelings of the elderly stalwarts of the church and more concerned about how this form of fundraising might help or hurt the parish's mission to reach new followers of Christ. What kind of impression, he asked me, would the neighbourhood form of a church that filled their basement with musty old clothes and sold these for a few coins? Would it encourage a visitor to return on Sunday morning to learn more about the Lord and

Master of such a place? Put that way, of course, I couldn't honestly say that it would.

THE END OF THE CHRISTMAS BAZAAR

Anyone who knows Harold will not be surprised to learn that this conversation proved to be the thin edge of the wedge and that, not long afterwards, another—much larger—sacred cow came under attack. The ACW ran a very successful annual Christmas bazaar. The bazaar involved virtually every woman in the congregation in one way or another, whether that meant spending much of the year knitting, crocheting, or sewing to produce items for sale; baking, canning, or crafting Christmas specialties; or setting up and staffing booths at prearranged sites in local shopping centres.

Largely through the sheer volume of goods offered for sale, the Christmas bazaar was a financial bonanza that each year bridged whatever gap existed between funds arriving via the collection plate and what was needed to keep the parish on an even keel. The ACW knew that its chief raison d'être was this indispensable income. One can thus imagine the resulting consternation when Harold let it be known that, according to his understanding of church, whatever money was needed to cover expenses should be raised by the parishioners through their weekly giving. Harold told the women that they were now free to use their time to study the Scriptures together! If they simply had to spend their leisure time raising money, proceeds should be directed to the marginalized and needy in the community, whether locally or globally.

Although the focus of Harold's message was much wider than money alone, he clearly recognized that "where your treasure is, there your heart will be also" (Matt 6:21). As a result, he was in no doubt that the way church finances were handled mattered deeply to the spiritual health of the congregation.

Since this was Harold's first parish (prior to his tenure at Trinity Streetsville), it took him a little while longer to discover that the church, in fact, had a long-held philosophy of budgeting. This policy dictated that each year's budget should project just enough of a shortfall in giving that the parish would qualify for a supporting grant from the diocese. By this point, however, no one was surprised when Harold announced that the parish should henceforth expect to pay its own way.

Harold believes strongly that spiritual commitment means that a Christian can actually learn to enjoy giving generously. Indeed, he is one of a relatively select number of clergy who actively endeavour to remove any barriers to such generosity.

THE SPIRITUAL ROLE OF TREASURER

Very early in his ministry, Harold recognized the pivotal role that a church treasurer can play in building a healthy congregation. In terms of Anglican Church hierarchy, the treasurer comes under the authority of the churchwardens and, hence, is often chosen for the position based almost entirely on the professional qualifications he or she might possess, rather than on the basis of spiritual maturity.

When this happens, the treasurer can easily become a negative force, working against the growth of a parish, since they fulfill their expected role by protecting whatever assets the church may own while minimizing expenditures. Such goals are often relatively easy for a conservative treasurer to achieve.

The way it works is this: giving in most churches runs below average for months until a relatively sharp rise near the end of the calendar year as Christmas approaches, when many hearts open to helping others and more pragmatic donors realize that the opportunity for a charitable donation tax receipt is about to disappear at the end of December. The church is typically in a deficit situation throughout the earlier part of the year, as a result of which expenses must be curtailed. The problem can be compounded when the current shortfall is mentioned every week in the bulletin, thereby creating a sense of failure—which further inhibits giving on the grounds that there is no sense in throwing good money after bad.

Conversely, when treasurers are chosen for attributes other than financial acumen alone—such as exhibiting a passion for ministry and a desire to spread the gospel—they can often contribute greatly to the spiritual health of the church. Basic to this work is accurate reporting, which builds a congregation's confidence that they really can provide the resources needed to follow God's call. A treasurer can also facilitate opportunities for people to designate part of their offering for specific needs or programs that touch their own hearts. Providing such opportunities—whether for food banks; for sending kids to camp; for assisting in times of local, national, or global catastrophe; or for some other cause—can increase total giving by 30 or 40 percent. Harold's first parish moved from subsistence and dependence on diocesan charity to raising an additional fifty to one hundred thousand dollars each year for outreach projects and other designated purposes.

Of course, resistance to the notion of encouraging gifts for a specific purpose can come not only from the treasurer but sometimes from ministers themselves. Usually such objections will be justified by the argument that church members should give to the church with no strings attached. However, many Christians will give generously, even beyond their own perceived means, to help people worse off than themselves or to support a cause greater than themselves. As a result, it seems strange for the church to discourage opportunities for people to learn about the joy of giving. A godly person, ordained but skilled in the area of facilitating generosity, once said to me, "The church has perfected the art of blocking giving."

An accompanying worry about encouraging designated giving, often unspoken, is that if parishioners are left free to donate to specific purposes, the everyday needs of the parish—light and heat, personnel costs, insurance, and so on—risk not being met. This concern reflects very little faith in the common sense of ordinary people. Ministers and treasurers are not the only ones who recognize that heated buildings and competent leadership are necessary to facilitate the church's worship. What is more often true is that as people start giving generously to special needs, they learn that their lives are enriched rather than impoverished, and they begin to seize more such opportunities, usually even increasing what they put in their weekly offering envelope.

Harold has always understood the benefits of a philosophy that enables charitable giving, including reporting back on the good that has been accomplished, the example that has been set, and the love that has shone into the neighbourhood as a result. He often used the words "This parish punches above its weight" to encourage continued generosity.

THE STRATEGY OF THE OFFERING PLATE

Although prolific giving is a good indication of a committed parish, it is not reasonable or fair to expect someone coming to a church for the first time to respond similarly. In fact, newcomers can quickly form the opinion that the main reason they were encouraged to come to church in the first place was for their money. This impression is immediately reinforced when, partway through their first service, a collection plate suddenly materializes in front of them, and it is clear that they are not expected simply to ignore the plate as it passes by. What is more likely to happen is that the person beside them will wait with the plate while the newcomer quickly fumbles to produce a bill of some sort—anything that will allow the plate to continue on its path down the pew.

Although there may be a number of sensitive solutions to this situation, few seem to have been put into practice. Harold has always prioritized the welcoming of newcomers and the removal of barriers to their journey to faith, so it is not surprising to discover that in parishes where he has been the minister, collection plates are not often passed around during the worship service. Instead, they are placed at the back of the church, where regular parishioners know to deposit their givings. Newcomers, on the other hand, are not expected to contribute; they will likely not even notice the existence of the collection plates until they are brought forward to be blessed.

I know of one instance in which a teenager joined the youth group and began to attend church with them on Sunday mornings. As his parents belonged to another denomination, they duly sent along an envelope with some money for him to contribute. Each week, he returned home with the envelope, telling his parents that his new church did not pass the plate. When this had happened several times in a row, his parents instructed him to search more carefully for the plate, which must surely be there somewhere. He eventually found the collection plate at the back of the church, but by this time he (and his parents) clearly understood that his attendance at church did not carry with it any financial obligation to the parish.

This approach probably costs the church some open collection—largely coins and small bills—but in the long run, the congregation will benefit by not turning off visitors and newcomers, who will be invited to make a commitment to follow Jesus before they are asked to help pay the bills.

One of my most remarkable spiritual experiences concerning finances occurred early in my time as a churchwarden under Harold's auspices.

Before Harold had weaned us off habitual diocesan support, we were unexpectedly confronted with a request by the diocese to begin paying interest on a loan of thirty-five thousand dollars that had been outstanding since the construction of the church building many years before. Further, the diocese asked that we plan to repay the loan itself as soon as possible.

For a parish that was still on the dole, this seemed like an impossible request. There was no extra money to cover the interest, and we certainly did not have sufficient funds to pay off a debt of thirty-five thousand dollars. The leadership team went into session, and we began both to pray and to reflect on the situation. It occurred to us that what seemed like two problems was really only one, since the annual interest charges would disappear once the loan itself had been repaid. This, however, was no easy feat to accomplish. In what is now almost a forgotten era, interest rates were very high, with GICs returning 15 or 16 percent annually. We decided to ask the members of the congregation to consider "lending" the church money that they did not currently need. If we could borrow funds in this way, invest them at a high rate of interest, and return them after two or three years, we could use the interest earned in that period to reduce the thirty-five thousand dollar loan.

We offered to pay a modest interest rate—6 percent seemed fair—to compensate for what might have been earned in a regular bank account. We hoped that something like ten or twelve thousand dollars would be forthcoming. We were bowled over, however, when members ended up loaning the church forty-three thousand dollars! In addition, most of the parishioners put the 6 percent interest payments back in the offering plate, thus speeding up our debt reduction even further.

Meanwhile, the diocese was so impressed by our determination to repay the loan itself, and not just the interest, that they offered to credit the parish with double the amount repaid. It should be added that they quickly decided to limit this offer to the first two years, since the plan succeeded so spectacularly that twenty-five thousand dollars of the debt was wiped out during that period.

Some parishioners even decided to forgo our repayment of the money they had loaned us, and as a result the mortgage was fully retired within three years of the inception of the plan. While it was a cause for great rejoicing, and a subsequent mortgage-burning party in the parish hall, this result was not the important spiritual lesson to which I previously referred. That lesson was yet to come.

FINANCIAL PRIORITIES

Another of Harold's priorities was the care and spiritual nurture of children and young people. This was evidenced at one memorable worship service when he got up to say that we were short two church-school teachers that day and, if the situation could not be remedied by the following Sunday, Harold would himself go downstairs to take one of the classes, leaving the congregation to take care of the worship upstairs by themselves. Not surprisingly, that course of action did not prove necessary, as several volunteers soon came forward to help with the children's program.

Consistent with his interest in making children and families comfortable attending on Sunday mornings, Harold recognized the need for some new, brightly lit, and well-furnished classrooms, since it was not enough to provide for different classes simply by subdividing the parish hall with curtains. A professional quantity surveyor was engaged to estimate the cost of fitting a two-storey addition into the available space. The answer was at least one hundred thousand dollars. Although this was quite a sum for a congregation in our financial situation, there was great determination to make it happen, and a successful fundraising campaign, plus some assistance from the diocese, resulted in four lovely classrooms on the lower level and a new, expanded nursery on the upper floor.

The financial upshot was a new mortgage on the building for thirty-five thousand dollars—exactly the amount that had been retired a couple of years prior. Yet, whereas the older mortgage had felt crushing and onerous, the new mortgage, for the same amount, seemed almost inconsequential and easily managed. The difference was that the congregation now felt blessed and empowered by the Holy Spirit and was looking for new ways to do God's work in the world. What ensued were decades of outreach and evangelism.

What is true, I think, is that a fearless ordained leader, trusted and supported by lay leaders in the congregation, can take the parish on a spiritual journey of financial stewardship, although he or she may never even use that word. Harold certainly showed no fear as he took this church off the dole, showing us that understanding our true Christian calling could reframe our understanding of our financial situation and even transform apparent weakness into strength.

When a parish understands this principle, it will change the way that it views any problem. After Harold moved on to his next parish, the church building needed a new roof, which would cost forty thousand dollars to complete. The challenge before us was that of raising so much money from a congregation that was already carrying a sizable mortgage and not long before had been surviving only with diocesan assistance.

We announced to the congregation that we needed a new roof and that if we were going to spend forty thousand dollars on ourselves, we should spend the same amount blessing others. So the congregation was asked to donate eighty thousand dollars, half of which would be sent to World Vision for use in their microenterprise program in Kenya, geared to create small businesses that were necessary for families to survive. To some, it might have seemed that we had lost our minds. Yet the money both for the roof and for the microenterprise project was raised almost without effort as we paid more attention to assisting brothers and sisters in Africa than to ensuring our own comfort under a solid new roof.

WIDENING CIRCLES OF VISION

The journey into generosity can be seen as a process of raising the eyes of the congregation from self-preoccupation to seeing beyond themselves, looking toward the horizon of the needs of others. Harold recognized that this process requires deliberate intent, along with much persistence and patience.

Helping people become aware of the needs of the marginalized in their own neighbourhood and recognize the call for the church to make a difference in these lives is an important first step. Because most people readily accept that they have a civic responsibility to their neighbours, this first step is not difficult to achieve and usually leads to the members of a congregation becoming personally involved, perhaps assisting at a parish food bank, taking food to shut-ins, or providing a meal for those at a halfway house. Commitment to generosity begins to build, and often those involved find such actions give meaning to their own lives, as well. Engagement with the local community can broaden to include a national perspective, which in turn can lead to understanding that true Christian generosity includes helping people in some of the most distant and difficult parts of the world. This final step is a very challenging transition, however, and not easily achieved.

At Trinity, Harold was enormously successful in focusing the congregation on this more distant horizon, building this sort of global perspective into their worldview. For a time, the congregation focused on their own needs as they responded to a fire that had destroyed their nearly completed church building. Having recovered from that catastrophe, they began to rebuild once again. With a brand-new building and a growing congregation, Harold realized that he had at hand exactly what was needed to awaken a global worldview among members of the congregation. The national office of World Vision Canada was situated within his parish boundaries. Even better, their president and CEO, Dave Toycen, was a member of the congregation. A passionate Christian, a wonderful advocate for children all over the world, and a powerful speaker, Dave was a natural leader and a key motivator in establishing Trinity Streetsville's interest in fulfilling its Christian calling to the world outside its walls.

Over time, the church committed to supporting many of World Vision's programs for vulnerable children, especially those orphaned by the AIDS epidemic that was sweeping across the African continent. Without affecting their regular giving, they raised a great deal of money for those in need. They were able to engage the whole of Mississauga in this cause by running a program called Hazel's Hope (endorsed by then mayor Hazel McCallion), which by its goals and its accessibility attracted widespread support.

GROWING GENEROUS CHRISTIANS

A key element of Harold's success in inviting his congregations to join him on a spiritual journey of generosity has been his own willingness to accompany them in the process. He has always been willing to lead by example and reach deep into his own pockets. He has also invested considerable time and energy to demonstrate that the joy of generosity can be taught, nurtured, and grown in the same way as with other spiritual gifts.

More specifically, Harold has demonstrated his trust in non-ordained congregational leaders within all of his parishes. He has accepted the risk of failure. And he has been willing to leave the outcome in God's hands. These things have deeply enriched his ministry, as well as blessing those with whom he has travelled and (not least) those who have been the beneficiaries of his churches' generosity.

SECTION C
CONGREGATIONAL MINISTRY

WELCOMING AND INTEGRATING NEWCOMERS
DIANE TOYCEN

MY FIRST VISIT TO TRINITY STREETSVILLE WAS ON THE LAST SUNDAY OF DECEMBER 1987. MY husband, Dave, my eleven-year-old daughter, and I were all Americans who had recently arrived in Canada after living for six years in Melbourne, Australia. For us, this was a new country with a new job, and now we were looking for a new church. We had already experienced the importance of being part of a church community while living away from our original home, country, and family. We had been nurtured for more than twenty years in formative worshipping communities: in the large, dynamic Anglican church in Melbourne, and in the even larger Episcopal church in Pasadena, California. I had worked on staff for ten years as director of children's ministry, and Dave had served in various areas of leadership. So we knew what kind of a church we were looking for: one in which we could put down roots, make friends, and serve by using our gifts.

Trinity was the closest Anglican congregation, so we showed up that Sunday eager to determine if this could be our new church home. The almost 150-year-old building was small, well-worn, and to our eyes actually rather dumpy. There were fewer than a hundred worshippers, who sang hymns led by a robed choir that processed in to the accompaniment of organ music. This was not a good first impression. Yet the robed pastor stood in the centre aisle to deliver his sermon with passion, clarity, and intensity. We did not know at the time that he had only been in place since October and was currently in the middle of a congregational tug-of-war over worship style and leadership. However, something about this pastor engaged us and led us to stick around and see what would happen. We could sense that he had a vision and was a leader we ourselves might want to follow.

We had originally expected to check out other churches in the area, but we ended up staying at Trinity for twenty-nine years. What kept us there all that time? It started with conversations I began to have with Harold about his vision for this new church assignment. Those conversations led to my joining the staff within the first year, initially planning parish life events and leading the children's ministry. That job expanded into a newly created position as director of programming and parish life, in which I served for twenty-four years. Since my role included managing the process of welcoming and assimilating newcomers, I want to share what we learned and developed over the years as we worked to attract *and* keep the newcomers who showed up at our church. (Dave eventually served as rector's warden, chair of the stewardship campaign, and small-group leader, as well as taking charge of goal-setting for congregational vision and strategy.)

AFTER THEIR INITIAL VISIT, WHAT MAKES PEOPLE RETURN TO YOUR CHURCH AND STAY FOR YEARS?

In this way, our family became an example of people who check out a church and then find there are reasons to return, to stay long term, and to take on ministry responsibilities. This is what all church leaders hope to accomplish, yet we continue to hear unfortunate stories from people who complain that no one talked to them when they visited a church for the first time. That was not our experience. Already in his first months at Trinity, Harold had put in place a newcomers' program that linked us with another family, whose job was to mentor us. After a few weeks, this couple stood up in church and introduced us to the rest of the congregation. After the service, at coffee time, they introduced us personally to other members of the congregation. This simple process helped us to feel welcome as we started learning names and making friends.

However, even the best process doesn't always work out as planned: our mentor confidentially informed us that the new rector wasn't really a Christian at all! It turned out that the mentor was a major player in the tug-of-war over worship style and leadership that was underway in those early months. Fortunately, we already knew enough from what we had heard in Harold's sermons, as well as from our conversations with him, to understand what lay behind the man's comment. It certainly points out the importance of knowing who you choose to represent your church to newcomers.

Harold proved to be a creative communicator with a talent for expressing himself in ways that motivated the parish. He developed a new mission statement that captured our hearts and minds and motivated us to act: "We are a community of ordinary people learning to follow Jesus in our time—coming in, growing up, and reaching out." The "coming in" part was my area of responsibility, involving a thorough, disciplined, and well-organized process for welcoming first-time visitors and new members. Harold treasured community, so we developed a wide variety of activities to engage people in the spiritual life, on the one hand, as well as games, parties, retreats, and celebrations to recognize the joy of being together, on the other. Newcomers did not get lost, nor were they "tackled" too aggressively. We created newcomer dessert evenings, as well as a membership course to assimilate people into the life of the church community. The concept was simple enough: that it was important to develop friends in the church community who would be there for each other in the difficult times. Most importantly, it worked!

HOW TO DEVELOP A PROGRAM OF WELCOMING AND ASSIMILATING NEWCOMERS

Intentionally welcoming the newcomer is a crucial part of attracting and keeping them as involved and spiritually growing members of your congregation. Helping newcomers make friends, build relationships, and get more deeply involved needs to be a well-thought-out part of your church program. I have heard it said that people need to make friends with a minimum of six other people to feel that they are connected. Having friends in our church is one of the top reasons that we continue to attend Trinity, and having friends is what would make it virtually impossible to leave. So we spent a lot of time thinking through what we needed to do to make our church the kind of place where newcomers could make friends, learn about the faith, and use their gifts to reach others outside the church.

We developed a process of welcoming new members that (with some variations over time) basically consisted of the following multi-level steps and stages.

1. *Preparation*
    a. Facilities: Look at your facilities through the eyes of a newcomer. Are the outdoor signs easy to understand? Are the service times listed? Intriguing programs and events highlighted? Entry doors well marked, lit, and inviting? Are the internal signs easy to follow? (These should include the location of the nursery, washrooms, elevator, worship area, and children's program, to name only a few.) Just as you would prepare your home for company, does your facility say, "We are ready for guests"? Are the walls, floors, nursery, and washrooms clean and attractive? Is there a welcome or information desk with friendly staff, at which newcomers can seek information about your church and your programs?
    b. Parking: Is your parking area clearly marked? Are spaces close to the church allocated to visitor and accessible parking? Are there any directions for overflow parking should it be needed?
    c. Staffing: Recruit a team of friendly welcomers to greet people as they come in the main entrances to the building. A friendly face, handshake, and "Good morning!" set the tone. Ushers, too, posted at the doors to the worship area, must be ready to offer a friendly greeting. They will most often be aware if someone is new and in need of special attention to find a place to sit or directions to the children's programs. A training and appreciation event for all who serve in this capacity should be held periodically. Remind these front-line people to be on the lookout for newcomers, to engage them in conversation, to invite them to coffee after the service, and to introduce them to others in the congregation. This is important at all times, even when they are not officially on duty.

2. *Notice*
    a. Be aware of newcomers: Teach your congregation, leaders, and staff that they should be continually on the lookout for

newcomers, both on Sundays and at all church events. Once you have been a member of a congregation for a few years, you tend to notice new faces. People standing around alone at coffee time or reading the bulletin boards are often in need of friendly personal engagement. Anyone can be a welcome ambassador for your church by introducing themselves with a simple, "Hi, I'm Diane. I haven't met you yet. What's your name?" Conversation about the length of time they have been coming to the church or about family or work can easily follow. Once you have welcomed them, the next step is to introduce the newcomer to other friends or to someone else you know with whom they might have something in common.

b. Welcome as a part of worship: As creatures of habit, we all tend to sit in the same place every Sunday, so we notice if someone new is next to us or nearby. It is important to encourage members of the congregation to greet one another during the worship service and to seek out those whom they do not know.

c. Assign welcomers: It is worth repeating the point made earlier that a team of people can be trained or assigned the ministry of identifying and embracing newcomers. Choose naturally outgoing, friendly, and positive people who can patrol the church lobby, seeking out new faces, both before the service and during coffee time. Encourage team members to introduce themselves and welcome visitors to your church. Ask if they have filled out a newcomer form, signed up for a newcomer dessert, or attended a new member information class.

d. Name tags: Name tags are extremely helpful for everyone. We provided simple stick-on labels at two tables in the lobby, where everyone could identify themselves upon arrival—new visitors and regular attenders, adults and children alike. That way, newcomers were not embarrassed by being singled out. If this is part of your regular tradition, it also helps those serving Communion to be able to ==use a first name when offering the bread and wine==. Nothing is more personal than hearing "Susan, this is the body of Christ, broken for you."

3. *Follow Up*
   a. Get information: All of this friendly welcoming probably will not accomplish your goal of having the newcomers return unless you get personal information about them that will permit you to follow up afterwards. Having an easily accessible form to fill out with contact information for the newcomers is the next step in bringing them into the life of your congregation. The newcomer needs to be encouraged to fill out this form and turn it in (either in the offering plate or at your welcome desk) in order for someone from your congregation to be able to contact him or her later in the week.
   b. Make contact: Follow-up begins, at a minimum, with a welcome letter from the pastor within a couple of days of the visit. This not only acknowledges their presence in your service but also initiates a pastoral relationship. The letter can also inform newcomers that someone else from the congregation will be calling them or tell them of an upcoming newcomer dessert where they can meet the minister and staff, as well as other newcomers, to hear more about the life of the church.
   c. Person to person: Having a staff member or volunteer dedicated to looking after these newcomers is important for keeping track of them and helping them take the next steps toward fuller commitment and involvement in the life of the faith community if they so wish. At Trinity, our newcomer secretary called, made an appointment, and personally visited everyone who filled out a form. (At one point, she even brought muffins specially baked for the occasion by a group of ladies.) As the number of newcomers grew, a team of callers took on this ministry. They would ask if the visitors were willing to answer a few survey questions—for example, the names of family members, career or employment information, previous church involvement, personal interests, and the like—and this was later shared with the clergy and staff. An invitation to a newcomer dessert, held four times each year, followed. Of course, people are busy, and it is sometimes difficult to contact them, but in an era of impersonal communication it is worth the effort to make this

personal connection with someone whom God has brought into your church.

4. *The Newcomer Dessert*

Once there were at least four new couples or individuals, we held a newcomer dessert at the church on a Friday night (although Sunday after church or another convenient time would work too). Early on, we held these gatherings in the home of a volunteer, but later we moved to the church so as to provide a more neutral and accessible location. Church leaders and staff members were invited in order for the newcomers to meet more members and also because a larger group is less intimidating.

a. The evening also provided an opportunity for guests to hear from the pastor about our church's vision and programs. It was always inspiring to hear Harold explain what our mission statement meant and to know that this church was aware of who it was and where it was going. As our mission statement said, we were "a community of ordinary people learning to follow Jesus in our time." As a church, we explained that we were "fuzzy at the edges" (meaning that we were open to people, not dogmatic) but "solid at the core" (in our belief in and commitment to Jesus).

b. During the evening, we broke into small groups and asked our guests to discuss the following questions:

- Who is in your household?
- What keeps you busy?
- How did you hear about our church?
- What were your first impressions?

We were always amazed at what people were willing to share about themselves. We learned a lot about how we were perceived and how the church was doing, all of which helped us as we constantly tried to improve our ministry of welcoming.

5. *The Membership Class*

The next step was to welcome newcomers to a membership class. In addition to sending personal invitations, we made announcements after the Sunday worship service so as to catch those who had not yet indicated an interest in attending. We called the class "What Am I Getting Into?" We explained that what we had in mind was not a formal type of membership but rather (as with the newcomer dessert evening) another opportunity for folks to hear more about the church, our programs, and opportunities for involvement. We were inviting them to identify with us, rather than us choosing them because they passed some kind of test. These classes were held on a Saturday morning, ending with lunch, usually twice a year. Each class was led by a layperson, although it included presentations by the pastor and members of staff. Fill-in-the-blank handouts helped focus attention and provide additional information. This process helped newcomers understand the history of our church and our philosophy of ministry; how they could become involved in opportunities for ministry, learning, and financial support; and what next steps were available for their own spiritual growth.

6. *The Membership Conversation*

Once the newcomer decided that, yes, they wanted to become a participating member of our church, I followed up with a separate conversation and visit, usually at their home. For the purpose of discerning where they could best become involved, I used a standard series of questions to ask about their background and interests and to gain insight into their needs and gifts. If the individual was new to Christian faith, I encouraged them to attend a four-week course called Christianity 101, which explained the basics of Christian faith. Everyone was also invited to join a small group. Once I had a sense of where they might best learn, grow, and contribute to the life of the congregation, I recommended an area of service and connected them with the leaders. And I prayed with them. Perhaps I benefited from this process as much as anyone; with many, our time together created a special bond that we still enjoy today.

7. *Welcoming and Celebrating*
   a. New member Sunday: Following the membership class, and once all the personal membership conversations had been completed, we took time during the Sunday worship service to welcome our newest members. Each family (including the children), if they were willing (and most were), stood at the front and were introduced briefly to the congregation. We presented them with an inscribed Bible (in a modern translation) and prayed for them. After the service, we held a special reception at which church leaders again welcomed them, this time in person.
   b. New member photo display: If folks gave permission, we took photos of the family and then displayed these photos on a "Meet our New Members" bulletin board, complete with names and a brief bio. This helped other members of the congregation get to know them and fostered a sense of belonging. It helped new members understand that this was now *their* church, these were *their* friends, and they had *committed* to helping make our church thrive.

AFTERMATH: ASSESSING THE IMPACT

Over the years, I have seen the impact of this process in the lives of many people. They have told me of the wonderful friendships they have formed and the meaningful areas of ministry in which they have served. I have seen their lives change as they made a deep commitment to Jesus. Right now, people who were once newcomers are involved in leading worship, teaching children or youth, serving as ushers and welcomers, leading small discipleship groups, and serving on the church board. Youth and younger children who came along with these newcomer families have grown up in our church and are now entering into positions of leadership and further involvement in Christian ministry. That is something to celebrate.

These newcomers stayed because they found friends—people who welcomed them as God welcomes them—and a place to learn about Jesus and meaningful service for him. That is the kind of church where we all want to be.

WORSHIP THAT MAKES DISCIPLES
JUDITH M. MACDONALD

HAROLD PERCY HAD NOT BEEN RECTOR OF TRINITY STREETSVILLE LONG BEFORE JOHN AND I each found our way there. We were not a couple at that point (in fact we had not yet met), but we arrived around the same time. Harold was already responding to the "decade of evangelism" (an initiative of the worldwide Anglican Communion) by instituting some liturgical changes at Trinity, and he was looking for a new music leader for the church. John applied for the job. I had met Harold five years earlier and was pleasantly surprised that he remembered me. At that point, we had no idea that we were beginning the most exciting and fulfilling decade of our lives.

John and I are both children of Anglican clergy and grew up in households that valued and enjoyed participating in music and theatre. We followed our interests toward careers: John trained as an operatic baritone, and I trained as an actress. We had also both been involved with experimental liturgies at various points in our lives, and we were both looking for a church community with a sense of life and purpose, authenticity and joy. We were both dissatisfied with services that seemed formal and dry, and we longed for worship that lifted our spirits and celebrated God's goodness. Fortunately, Harold felt the same way. It was not long before he involved us in helping to develop the liturgy that eventually emerged at Trinity and helped grow the church from eighty to five hundred people.

The starting point of this liturgical strategy was Harold's conviction that the Sunday morning main service was the most valuable asset that any mainline church had in terms of evangelism. Sunday morning was the time when anyone who had left church or was unchurched was most likely to engage with a new church to see what the experience was like. Part of the reason for this was that they could remain anonymous in the pew. It was important, therefore, that these visitors should feel comfortable and unthreatened.

We worked from the assumption that most of the people who visited our church came because the Holy Spirit had drawn them. In 1990s' Canada, there were many alternatives for Sunday morning activity and very little societal compulsion to attend church. These people had come for a reason, looking for something. It seemed reasonable, therefore, to try to ensure that if they did not find what they were seeking, it was not because we had got in the way. We surmised that people would only come back a second time if they had a good experience the first time, so we tried to make sure we did not do anything that might alienate them. We used contemporary language, avoided Anglican jargon, explained everything that was happening, and employed music that contemporary people found pleasant and singable.

We recognized that these "seekers" might not have extensive knowledge of Christianity or a background in church membership, so we tried to communicate in ways that contemporary people found familiar and effective. We tried to be sensitive to shorter attention spans and the fact that people were used to receiving information in "bites," usually with an appeal to the emotions as well as the intellect.

We also worked from the assumption that what people were seeking, and needed, was to know that God loved them and wanted to have a relationship with them. This was the first message we tried to get across, and we found that it was a good place to begin. We found that when people discovered, in the words of Adrian Plass, "God is nice and he likes me,"[52] they began to blossom. In terms of liturgy, we found that an open, celebratory style was most helpful in reaching these newcomers with a sense of God's goodness. After all, we were trying to share good news.

---

[52] Adrian Plass, *The Secret Diary of Adrian Plass, Aged 37¾* (1997; Grand Rapids: Zondervan, 2005), 10.

Section C: Congregational Ministry

Of course, these liturgical changes affected the congregation of Trinity directly. Some people did not like them and either chose to attend the traditional Communion service with hymns that Trinity offered every Sunday at 8:00 a.m. or found worship that they preferred in other churches nearby. However, through Harold's careful preaching, vision-casting, and explanation, most of the congregation gladly accepted the vision of Christian life being about spreading the good news, and they were excited by the new life that was emerging at Trinity.

We were learning as we went and trying new things. Some worked, while others did not. Over the course of ten years, Harold's model for worship was refined as Trinity grew from one small service to three every Sunday morning and then, for a period of time, also met in a school gymnasium. In this chapter, we explore some of the liturgical changes that we discovered were useful in evangelism.

SOME PRINCIPLES OF PURPOSE-DRIVEN WORSHIP

Many people make the mistake of assuming that contemporary celebratory worship is relaxed or casual. In our case, this was far from the truth. We thought it was necessary for newcomers to see that we valued worship and considered it important. Like it or not, contemporary people are very familiar with highly polished presentations on television, through other media, in advertising, and in business. They know that sloppiness indicates amateurishness or a lack of care. We therefore placed a high value on thoughtful planning and adequate practice to make sure there was not even a suggestion of carelessness. This attention to detail affected everyone involved in the liturgy—even lay people doing readings. They had to learn how to time their movement so that they would be in place before the music stopped, and they eventually were required to come to a mid-week rehearsal.

In the same way, we did not want people to feel that we were wasting their time, so we were careful to manage the energy of the service. Congregational singing at the beginning of the service creates an energy that, if managed properly, can carry through the whole service and assist people in worshipping. This does not mean that activity is non-stop or that there is no silence. It does mean that every aspect of the worship is intentional and is carried out carefully. Things that can break the flow of this energy are gaps between music and liturgy, times when it seems that people do not know what they are doing, ill-considered remarks, insensitivity to the moment, or anything else that can break the mood. Drops in energy are difficult to recover from, and they introduce a lackadaisical element that undermines the hard work of other participants. We assumed that if we ourselves were bored or distracted, so was the congregation. It is difficult to be specific about this, as managing energy is more of an art than a science, but it is something that wonderful liturgy always requires, whatever the style of worship. It might be argued that this kind of energy management is manipulative or that it leaves little room for the action of the Holy Spirit. Our experience convinced us that the opposite was true.

Worship at Trinity under Harold's leadership was purposeful, engaging, and conducted with the goal of forming Christian identity. We thought and prayed about what the outcomes of the worship experience would be. What would the people there know as a result of the worship? What would they feel? What would they do? So, in addition to removing obstacles to engagement, we also tried to present the gospel to the best of our ability.

PRESENTING THE GOSPEL

What were some of the things we changed? While the shape of the traditional Anglican service remained the same—gathering, the ministry of the Word, the ministry of the table, and being sent out—changes gradually appeared, especially in the first two parts of the service. The style and amount of music increased; the number of readings decreased. The readings were presented in different ways, sometimes as choral readings and sometimes with music underneath. The creed was omitted as something that might make unchurched people uncomfortable. The sermon was longer than in most Anglican churches.

We replaced prayer books and hymn books with an overhead projector for the songs and prayers. This was partly to enhance the corporate experience, because looking up when singing helps to bring people together. Another reason was that for the gathering and liturgy of the Word, we used very little of the prayer book service. From the offering on, however, the service was taken from the *Book of Alternative Services*, using the overhead projector.

Working from our assumption that new people were brought by the Holy Spirit, we also recognized that people tend to "try church" in order to find answers to some of the big questions and issues in their lives. In response to this realization, Harold started preaching on themes rather than following the lectionary. In order to deal thoroughly with different themes, we developed the practice of presenting sermon series that stretched over several weeks.

One sermon series, lasting seven weeks, was entitled "Misconceptions about God." The individual sermons dealt with common misunderstandings about God: God's love must be earned, God is angry and vindictive, everything that happens is a part of God's purpose, my concerns are too trivial to be important to God, God has given up on me, God thinks sex is dirty, and God doesn't want me to have money. Another sermon series was entitled "Developing a Christian Worldview," charting the story of the Bible: God's creation of earth and humankind, the fall and the introduction of evil and temptation, the promise of redemption, the birth of the redeemer, reconciliation, and fulfillment. Another series was "Life in the Shadows," and it dealt with issues such as illness, depression, poverty, loss, grief, and death.

These sermons did not stand on their own, however. The theme would be introduced by a Scripture reading, the sermon would unpack the relevant issues, and all the music was chosen with the same theme in mind. We also started occasionally using drama to illustrate a key point in the sermon. When the sermon was finished, an anthem would comment on the theme.

MUSIC AT TRINITY

In our culture, music is the medium by which messages with emotional content are conveyed. At Trinity, the role of music in worship was to help the congregation celebrate and praise God for who God is and what God could do in their lives, to communicate directly the message of new life in Jesus Christ, to create an environment for worship, and to provide transitions between the different parts of the service.

We began to introduce contemporary songs and anthems, accompanied by piano and guitar rather than the organ. We did this intentionally, because people without a church background, or with a different church background, are not familiar with Anglican hymns, no matter how much we "cradle Anglicans" love them. The music that people listen to daily is the music that they feel comfortable singing. Although the traditional style of worship using hymns, chants, and the organ can meet the needs of some parishes, we found that folk, country, and soft rock styles of music were preferred by most unchurched people at that time and place. This style of music also supported the more open, celebratory liturgical style that is required to grow congregations. In terms of blending styles, we found that a traditional piece inserted into a contemporary service works much better than a contemporary piece inserted into a traditional service. Also, contemporary pieces should never be accompanied by the organ—save that for the occasional hymn!

When we started changing the music, it seemed that singers and instrumentalists emerged from the woodwork. Everyone who could play guitar wanted to, and it was quite amusing when we had a "guitar corps" of up to six people crammed into the old choir stalls, which really were not big enough for them. It gave the effect of a bouquet of guitar players, joined at the hips but bursting out above. However, as a rule there were usually only about three guitars at a time. We purchased a high-end electronic keyboard that could sound like a piano, electric piano, or organ. Eventually, as other instrumentalists were attracted to the group, we added electric bass, drums, and other instruments. We also replaced the traditional robed choir with a "folk group," which rapidly grew to about twenty people, named itself Newsong, and insisted on learning four-part harmony. So, although the choice of music was different, the quality of music remained substantial. This vocal group did not robe or process. As the group grew, we outgrew the choir stalls and eventually removed them. The singers were then seated in chairs facing the congregation on one side of the aisle, with the guitarists on the other side, also in chairs.

The musical shape of the service at Trinity usually followed the same pattern each week. At the beginning of the service, the musicians assembled at the front of the church and led the congregation in three songs: one in celebratory style, one to reinforce the theme of the service, and another upbeat song to cover Sunday school departure. We would employ reflective piano music between readings or under readings. After the sermon, there was usually a piece reinforcing the service theme, either by the choir or from a soloist. At the offertory, we sang an upbeat congregational song to mark the transition to the Eucharist. Our Eucharistic responses were upbeat and simple. During Communion, we sang two or three reflective congregational songs and a praise song, expressing our thanks for God's love and the gift of his Son. Sometimes, instead of the praise song the musicians would perform a short four-part piece reflecting the same theme. The closing worship was another upbeat celebratory congregational song. As time went by, a prelude song was added at the beginning of the service and another song after the closing for people to leave by (or, when we were in the gymnasium, to stack chairs by!).

As with all music, quality is everything. Contemporary music done badly is as bad as, or perhaps worse than, traditional hymns done badly. We aimed for energetic instrumental leadership that required both competence and rehearsal. We also aimed for strong vocal leadership. Rehearsals were two hours long, and there was a general rule that if you did not rehearse, you did not sing.

We also tried to find music of quality. There is a lot of contemporary music out there, and not all of it is good. We had the enormous good fortune to have a musician who took on herself the job of finding new songs for us, under the guidance of the music director. Our guidelines were to look for good biblical content, solid theology, and stimulating music in good taste. Our experience was that music from the mid-twentieth century was already too dated. We avoided songs with repetitive verses, songs that dealt more with the singer than with God, and songs with overly simple music. The same guidelines were followed in selecting choral music.

While we welcomed singers into Newsong, we were choosy about soloists. Occasionally people would volunteer to sing solos or duets. We followed our guidelines and only allowed them if the content and quality of the performance were going to add to the worship service and contribute to the theme for the day.

As well as aiming for high musical quality, we also asked our musicians to be aware that they could be seen. They were seated at the front of the church, behind the preacher. It was not appropriate for someone to struggle his way out of a bright red sweater, waving his arms in the air, during the sermon (or to do anything else that might take the focus off the liturgy)! Musicians and singers had to be fully engaged throughout the whole service. It might seem self-evident, but we encouraged the worship leaders to look as if they enjoyed what they were doing and understood what they were singing. Fortunately, this was not difficult, because they entered into the worship wholeheartedly, as did the congregation.

THE ROLE OF DRAMA IN WORSHIP

Almost as soon as we started this experiment with liturgical evangelism, Harold asked us to provide dramas to assist with the message. This started quite simply, with one person (John) playing the detective Columbo, interrupting the sermon to ask Harold a few questions. Another time, Socrates the Sock demanded to come off John's foot and be heard. These were obviously not examples of high art—more like elaborate sermon illustrations. But they worked. People would come to church more regularly because they did not want to miss something good. There was a sense of surprise and expectation about the worship experience. Once again, Harold's instinct for how best to communicate to contemporary people was right. Dramatic illustration is almost indispensable in modern communications, as marketers have discovered. It enables people to relate to issues, to identify with characters, to participate in their experiences, to laugh at their absurdities, and to cry at their sorrows. Stories and illustrations make an idea come alive. Drama is able to sidestep intellectual barriers and touch the emotions.

Many of the sketches we produced for Sunday mornings were funny. This was not only because Harold, John, and I enjoyed a good laugh but because humour is a powerful language in our culture. Our sketches were designed to resemble the kind of fast, punchy "bites" that we saw on television and radio. In other words, we were trying to talk to people in a language they understood, as well as to give them a way to remember the message.

Not all of our drama was humorous, however. Some of our sketches were retellings of parables or Bible stories, but with a twist. For instance, we told the story of the prodigal son as a modern-day prodigal daughter who rebels against her mother. Our aim was to bring the Bible stories closer to our own experience. Drama helps people make connections between the gospel and their own lives. We wanted people to see the Scripture in a way that was pertinent to them today and not only to people two thousand years ago, in a country far away.

THE FAMILY SERVICE

One day, when Newsong was still new, John came to the music rehearsal and asked that the singers help him come up with a drama about the church as the body of Christ. We decided to base it on the old parlour game "Family Coach." Everyone in the congregation was involved, representing a part of the body. For instance, boys were feet and girls were hands. Each part of the body had an action: boys stamped, girls clapped. Someone narrated the story, and every time a body part was named, those with that part performed their action. Every time the body of Christ was mentioned, everyone stood up, did the wave, and said, "Hallelujah!" It was a great success, especially with the children. While not really drama, it was our first group effort at creating a drama-like sketch. It was also a "drama" that replaced the sermon at one of our early family services.

At Trinity, the children usually left the service during the third song and rejoined the adults when the offering was being brought forward. Once a month, we had a family service when the children would stay with the adults. The main difference between this and a regular service was that a drama about ten minutes in length would replace the sermon. These services were hugely popular with children and adults. These dramas could be Bible stories, parables, or explorations of some aspect of Christian life or teaching. Some of the more memorable dramas from these services were "David and Goliath," in which the giant was a nine-foot puppet; "Foundations," which was a modern take on the parable of the houses built on sand and rock (Matt 7:24–27; Luke 6:47–49); "Good Fruit," which explained how the Holy Spirit can change us; and "A Walking Tour of the Parthenon by Night," which was a modern adaptation of the parable of the sower (Mark 4:3–8).

THE PLANNING PROCESS

Sometimes there was no applicable parable or the topic was more abstract. There were times when it was hard for us to grasp quite what Harold wanted the drama to be about. By trial and error, we came up with a way to handle these situations. We called it the point statement. A point statement is a one-sentence statement of the principle or concept that the preacher wants to have illustrated or that he or she really wants people to remember. It is a focused idea—a complete thought. It is not a paragraph, a phrase, or a theme. While the sermon deals with a theme, the drama needs to be more focused. For instance, if you are asked to produce a drama about creation, where would you start? It is a huge topic and can be approached from many different angles. However, if you are asked to illustrate the point that God created people to be like him, you would have an idea of where to begin. These are some other examples of point statements that Harold came up with:

- People are afraid of God because they don't know him.
- Until a person says yes to God, the relationship can't begin.
- True happiness can be found in God's plan for you.
- Introducing people to Jesus is similar to introducing your friends to each other.

Each of these statements can be illustrated dramatically.

Obviously, planning a sermon series, developing point statements, writing and rehearsing drama—all this takes time. It cannot be done at the last minute. We found that the best way to set aside the necessary time was to go away on a planning retreat twice a year. Harold, John and I, and Diane Toycen, director of programming and parish life, would spend a weekend working on the plans for worship for the next six months. Harold would present his sermon series ideas and themes, and together we would decide which ones would require dramas, which ones would be family services, and so on. It was vital to have Diane there because she was able to tie in the children's programs with the plans—besides which, she had a wicked sense of humour! Sometimes we were able to come up with the point statements at these retreats, but other times, Harold's ideas would develop over time and we would need to get together a couple of weeks before the sermon in question to finalize and fine-tune things. That gave us two weeks to develop and rehearse a sketch.

MUSIC AND DRAMA AT CHRISTMAS, EASTER, AND OTHER SPECIAL OCCASIONS

Drama and music came to play a significant role on special occasions and at high festivals. Over time, our annual lessons and carols service evolved into a Christmas play that ran for three nights in mid-December. Every year, John wrote a new play that retold the nativity story, embedded in a story of modern life. Newsong was seated in the chancel behind the acting area, and each scene was followed by a choral number. We found that many people who came to the play would return on Christmas Eve for a service of worship. Harold regarded the Christmas Eve service as another excellent opportunity for evangelism, so he would select a particularly moving scene from the play that year for us to perform during the service.

John also wrote three passion plays that were performed during the services of Holy Week. The play would begin on Palm Sunday, continue on Maundy Thursday, and culminate on Good Friday. We found that people would attend the Holy Week services partly to see the drama. In fact, during Holy Week, drama became a large part of the liturgy. Eventually, we were having to do the Good Friday service twice to accommodate all the people who came to see it. As with the Christmas plays, scenes would be interspersed with music.

To help spread the gospel, Trinity also tried to address cultural events that were not included in the liturgical calendar. One of these was Valentine's Day. We would have a dinner-dance on the closest Saturday to February 14, at a location away from the church. Congregants were encouraged to invite friends, which was relatively easy to do, since this was a fairly non-threatening event. At some point in the evening between the dinner and the dance, the drama team would perform a sketch about love, and Newsong would sing. Harold would then say a few words—and it really was only a few—about human love and God's love and then encourage people to consider attending Trinity on a Sunday.

VISIONARY LEADERSHIP

We worked with Harold for ten years at Trinity, concentrating on drama and music in liturgy in order to fulfill the goal of creating worship that was open and impactful and that brought people back to church and to Christ. It has now been seventeen years since we left Trinity, and in those years we have been involved in other churches. We believe in "blooming where we are planted," so whenever we move into a community we attend the nearest Anglican church. Every one of the churches we have joined has been experiencing a crisis, and in each case the crisis could have been helped by a plan for growth. Yet none of these churches has moved in that direction. What is wrong? In our estimation, the issue is not one of location or money or neighbourhood or fighting among the congregation—or even one of worship style. The issue is one of leadership.

In 2010, Harold wrote an article entitled "What Makes a Vital Church?" for the Wycliffe College Institute of Evangelism.[53] In it, he explains five things a congregation needs in order to revitalize our congregations and carry on effective ministries. The first is visionary leadership. In our experience with Harold, it was his visionary leadership that created the church's growth. Because he had a vision of what the church should be, and the will to create the structures that would bring that vision into being, the church grew. In John's work life, he often tells his employees that there are managers and there are leaders. Managers do things right, and leaders do the right things. In our experience, many church pastors are focused on doing things right (as they were taught in theological college) and are not even aware what the "right things" are to which they should be giving attention.

In our experience at Trinity Streetsville, it was clear that our objective was to make new Christians by creating a worship space and a church community that was "fuzzy at the edges, but solid at the core," which is to say, accessible and welcoming but still standing for core Christian principles and values. Our aim was always to maximize our ability to fulfill the goal of attracting and keeping more people, so that we could incorporate them into the community and ultimately make new Christians—as Christ calls us to do.

Harold was focused on the vision of creating a vital church and was willing to do whatever it took to get it there. What we created in terms of worship and drama was one key outworking of that vision.

---

[53] Harold Percy, "What Makes a Vital Church?" *good idea!*, April 13, 2010, http://institute.wycliffecollege.ca/2010/04/what-makes-a-vital-church/.

BECOMING AN EFFECTIVE COMMUNICATOR OF THE GOSPEL
LANCE B. DIXON

THIS CHAPTER HIGHLIGHTS FOUR IMPORTANT LESSONS FROM HAROLD PERCY'S PREACHING ministry that, I believe, offer practical insights into the creation of effective sermons for today's generation. Looking back on Harold's preaching ministry provides an opportunity to admire a person who showed imagination in the proclamation of the gospel and who took tremendous risks in the face of fierce criticism to redefine preaching within the context of traditional worship.

At the outset, it is helpful to note that the context in which Harold flourished differs in many respects from the cultural landscape preachers are trying to navigate today. Harold's sermons certainly had an impact across generational lines, as former parishioners to whom I spoke while writing this chapter could attest. Nonetheless, cultural shifts between one generation and the next inevitably change our outlook on matters of faith. In this chapter, the term "Millennial generation" will refer broadly to the social era in which we now find ourselves, an era defined by political, technological, and social realities that did not significantly shape the outlook of those to whom Harold ministered. At the same time, there are two qualities of Harold's preaching that remain essential today and are highlighted in this chapter.

First, Harold realized that the most important quality for preaching is that it be *effective*; what we say should actually *change* lives. Harold was deeply concerned about the critical decline of many churches and their inability to respond effectively to the social changes taking place around them. Preachers today face the same problem. As a result, they cannot be content with merely going through the motions of preaching. We must expect *results*. Preachers must communicate the gospel in a way that moves the person in the pew to action in a way that will reinforce their commitment to Christ.

Second, preaching is fundamentally *theological* in nature. Harold often lamented the reduction of preaching to storytelling and self-help seminars. If the crucified and risen Christ is not proclaimed through the sermon, then we as preachers have lost sight of what is truly the life-changing message. Harold was well-known for adding unconventional moments into the worship service, but he never failed to preach Christ. He regarded this as essential to a pastor's call. It is important to note that Harold was by no means fundamentalist in his theology, despite being perceived as such by many in his denomination. Rather, he held to an orthodox faith and believed that the eternal God had called him to bear witness to the gospel for his generation. Many other preachers, by contrast, have shied away from proclaiming the crucified Christ because of the inevitable conflict this creates with contemporary culture. Harold was at odds with the theology of pastors who wanted to create a message acceptable to the wider society. He recognized the conflict inherent in following Jesus today and was prepared to help his congregation navigate this tension.

With these principles in mind, we now turn our attention to practical insights on preaching. Of course, it is difficult to speak of Harold's preaching ministry apart from questions of discipleship, liturgical renewal, and evangelism, for all of the various dimensions of ministry at Trinity Streetsville were intended to serve the primary goal of reaching the unchurched. Nonetheless, it will be helpful to focus on *how* Harold effectively communicated the gospel to a generation increasingly disconnected from the Christian worldview.

LESSON #1: AN EFFECTIVE PREACHER INSPIRES THROUGH GENUINE CONVICTION ABOUT THE GOSPEL

First of all, I stand here totally unrepentant as one who is . . . absolutely convinced that we're talking here about a literal resurrection . . . [as] the only thing that explains the fact we have the rest of the New Testament, and a church throughout the world, and the testimony of those apostles . . . who all went to their deaths and prison . . . I'm convinced the only thing that explains this is that Jesus came back to life.[54]

While some preachers have failed to maintain a commitment to theological orthodoxy, others have responded nobly to the call to proclaim the crucified and resurrected Christ to this generation. In this regard, Harold Percy takes his place among such well-known contemporary preachers as William Willimon, Haddon Robinson, John Stott, and Marva Dawn. In fact, much of Harold's ministry was spent trying to help other pastors, myself included, recognize that preaching is a dangerous business, that conflict between gospel and culture is inevitable, and that following Jesus entails a difficult choice. He was thoroughly evangelical in his sensibilities, believing that the Christian faith was founded on a personal and committed relationship to Jesus Christ as Lord. For Harold, this made the presentation of the gospel relatively simple. As he saw it, one is either prepared to follow Jesus on his or her own terms or one is not, and it is the preacher's responsibility to help the listener take whatever steps the Word of God has placed before him or her.

As a result, Harold would confront the listener with some kind of decision in every sermon, whether it was the choice to investigate Christian faith through a Christianity 101 course or the ultimate choice to follow Jesus as Lord and Saviour. After listening to Harold for even a short time, people understood the concrete implications of being a Christian. Harold made it clear that he expected people's lives to be different as a result of following Jesus. Listeners responded, and the congregation grew as a result.

At this point, some background regarding the setting of Harold's ministry might be helpful. Harold's first wife, Kathy, had deep family roots in Streetsville, then a quiet town just west of Toronto. Whether or not this was the main reason he agreed to serve as the pastor of its Anglican congregation, it was evident early on that this was where he belonged. In a short time

---

[54] Harold Percy, "Resurrection Means Hope" (Easter sermon at Trinity Streetsville, April 3, 1994).

after he arrived in the late 1980s, he managed to transform a declining, sleepy parish church into one of the most innovative and fastest-growing Anglican congregations in Toronto—and arguably in the country as a whole.

Granted, he was not without help. By then, Streetsville was being subsumed within the burgeoning and affluent suburban community of Mississauga, which was earning a reputation as a vibrant hub for high-tech and pharmaceutical companies. Harold's leadership attracted a number of gifted business and community leaders, who in turn helped gather a dynamic group of lay people who longed to see a vital community of faith at the heart of their growing city. For example, Dave Toycen, then president of World Vision Canada, hockey legend Paul Henderson, and the formidable mayor herself, Hazel McCallion, were three of the key supporters behind Harold's efforts.

One could argue that without prominent lay people supporting its pastor, Trinity would not have become what it was in its heyday. But that misses the point of how leadership works and of how Harold's role was essential for the transformation that took place. Without his vision for ministry and his exceptional ability at communicating it, key lay leaders would likely have looked elsewhere for something worthy of their time and energy. The fact is that leaders attract people willing to follow them, and there is no question that Harold was (and is) a gifted leader.

Harold quickly established a reputation as one who valued innovation in ministry and who was not afraid to take risks. Neither was he hesitant in dealing with the conflict that invariably accompanies breaking new ground. Harold had a strong conviction that God was calling the church to grow, and he surprised many people by his uncompromising position on what needed to be done. He initially faced harsh and widespread criticism for his apparent disregard of Anglican convention in his conduct of Sunday worship. Yet he was such an effective communicator that he was able to counter his critics with compelling arguments (evidenced by his numerous editorials in the national Anglican newspaper), which left people either persuaded by his views or resigned to the fact that Harold was going to press on regardless. His singular focus on building a faith community that was centred on the task of reaching the unchurched remained unchanged.

His preaching reflected this vision for the ministry of Trinity. Harold was unapologetic about placing the person of Jesus at the centre of the message. He was explicit that people did not show up for more "religion," and he never backed away from criticizing churches that neglected the work of evangelism. Indeed, Harold's conviction as to the truth of the gospel was the source of his strength and inspiration. Today, in a postmodern society increasingly ambivalent about the role of institutional Christianity, it is all the more important that preaching and pastoral leadership be rooted in such conviction. More than ever, we need preachers who are prepared to stand in the pulpit and, like Harold, be altogether unrepentant in proclaiming a crucified and risen Christ as the Saviour of all.

LESSON #2: AN EFFECTIVE PREACHER DEVELOPS INTO A LEADER

> The number one job of leadership is to explain why the organization exists and to communicate this clearly and effectively. We have congregations all across this country who don't know why they exist, with leaders who are unable to tell them.[55]

Even before arriving at Trinity, Harold had established himself as a hard-nosed and visionary pastor. He had a remarkable ability for identifying "people of influence" and for gaining their trust. This trust was largely built on the consistency with which he communicated his vision and the competency he demonstrated in accomplishing it. As a result, when Harold said something in a sermon, the congregation knew that he was convinced of it and was prepared to follow through with it. This gave him substantial authority as a preacher.

I started attending Trinity a year after I had left parish ministry to teach at a Christian secondary school. The year was 2002, at the height of Harold's ministry. The new facility had just been built, the congregation had increased to over twelve hundred people, and his national reputation had been established with the publication of a third book on church growth.[56] Sitting in the pews among hundreds of others, we could feel his confidence flow from the pulpit. In the eyes of the congregation, he was unmistakably their leader. As a young pastor, I could clearly see that Harold had earned their respect.

---

[55] Percy, "What Makes A Vital Church?"
[56] Percy, *Your Church Can Thrive*.

In analyzing the nature of Harold's leadership, it is again important to recognize the social and cultural landscape in which Trinity existed at the time. In this relatively affluent suburban city, we were still functioning on the edge of Christendom. Many families that were drawn to Trinity still possessed a "memory" of the Christian faith. Harold was brilliant in connecting to this large "unchurched" segment of his congregation.[57] Sixteen years later, it is important for any leader seeking to be effective to be aware of how dramatically the religious landscape has changed. For example, since 1971 there has been a steady increase of Canadians who are disaffiliating from organized religion, particularly so as one moves west across Canada.[58]

Regarding the changing perception of churches, research has shown that Millennials are less likely to view religious organizations positively compared to five years ago and compared to older generations.[59] A generation ago, the effectiveness of a pastor was still largely measured in terms of ability to create numerical growth. Today, however, many people have different ideas of what a spiritual leader looks like and does.

This generation does not measure leadership simply in terms of how large a leader is able to grow the size of a congregation or building.[60] In fact, pastors who emphasize this aspect of their leadership arouse suspicion, as Millennials are capable of organizing their social and

---

[57] The term "unchurched" identifies those with no prior religious background, as distinct from the "de-churched," which refers to those who have left church at some point. Since these were the terms used during Harold's ministry, I continue to employ them, although I recommend considering other, more inclusive, categories, such as "newcomers," "returners," and "regulars."

[58] "Canada's Changing Religious Landscape," PEW Research Center, June 27, 2013, http://www.pewforum.org/2013/06/27/canadas-changing-religious-landscape/. See also the perspective by Aaron Hutchins, "What Canadians Really Believe: A Surprising Poll," *Maclean's*, March 26, 2015, http://www.macleans.ca/society/life/what-canadians-really-believe/ based on an Angus Reid survey available at www.angusreid.org/religion-in-canada/.

[59] Hannah Fingerhut, "Millennials' Views of News Media, Religious Organizations Grow More Negative," Pew Research Center, January 4, 2016, http://www.pewresearch.org/fact-tank/2016/01/04/millennials-views-of-news-media-religious-organizations-grow-more-negative/.

[60] After conducting a survey of Millennials, Thom Rainer and Mark Dance identified four vital foci for spiritual leadership among this generation: mentoring, a gentle spirit, transparency and authenticity, and integrity. See Thom Rainer, "What Millennials Want in Leaders," *Lifeway*, May 12, 2014, http://www.lifeway.com/pastors/2014/05/12/what-millennials-want-in-leaders/.

political worlds through social media, without the need for hierarchical structures. They value the collaborative and democratic process of movements. Accordingly, it is important to recognize that younger audiences listen carefully to rhetoric. They are attentive to whom a leader claims to represent, what their personal motivations for leadership are, and how their personal experiences validate the leadership values being claimed. In other words, they are looking and listening for authenticity.

Growing up as the son of a pastor, I sat in many church office hallways as a child, waiting for my father to appear from an adjacent meeting room. Slouched in an oversized chair, I would observe clergy down the corridor chastising a deacon or server for failing to genuflect at the proper moment during a service earlier in the week or berating a secretary for not following through on a task or dismissing a couple for neglecting to fill out proper paperwork for a wedding or baptism. Today, people are not as inclined to tolerate such conduct on the part of a spiritual leader, regardless of how competent they may be in the pulpit or boardroom. Integrity of character has become a key factor by which Millennials decide whether or not to trust a pastor with their souls.

A 2016 *Globe and Mail* article highlighted a recent study by two sociologists of the decreasing involvement of Millennials in government elections. They compared this trend to a similar decline witnessed in churches across the country a decade earlier. Their insight speaks to the growing distrust in leadership:

> The decline of voting in the 21st century may become as striking a phenomenon as the decline of church attendance in the latter part of the 20th. Baby Boomers left the church; their children and grandchildren seem to be drifting away from the state.
>
> Why is this happening? One reason for declining turnout is a deep shift in social values away from deference to institutional authority. It used to be that if society's leaders told us to do something, we did as we were told. . . . Canadians are also less driven by a sense of duty than they once were.[61]

---

[61] Michael Adams and Maryantonett Flumian, "Many Canadians Aren't Voting. Have They Stopped Caring about Democracy?" *The Globe and Mail*, January 26, 2016, updated March 25, 2017, https://www.theglobeandmail.com/globe-debate/the-young-are-quitting-politics-and-thats-a-danger-to-our-democracy/article22633913/.

For those who preach to a generation that inherently mistrusts authority, the words of Marshall McLuhan could not be truer: the medium *is* the message.[62] Millennials are seeking integrity of leadership. A leader who claims to be acting in the interests of democracy must first prove it. A leader who is claiming to be speaking for the interests of a God of love and grace must first make their lives a testimony to what they preach. Ask a leader in any profession—trying to prove integrity of leadership is difficult amidst ongoing scrutiny through social media and catastrophic when we fail at it. But that consistent witness of integrity as a leader is precisely why it earns greater respect and authority among those seeking spiritual guidance. As the *Globe and Mail* article points out, while today's society is showing little trust in democratic institutions, they have not given up on democracy—just as they have not given up on "the quest for spiritual meaning." Leaders dedicated to being effective witnesses of the faith should proceed with tremendous hope.

As we move forward, the following questions may help a preacher develop his or her leadership role in our contemporary world: How do we convey authenticity from the pulpit? How does a preacher develop opportunities for mentoring? How do we go about empowering others in their own gifts of proclamation? To what extent does collaboration in preaching become more important than competency? How do we communicate a gracious and vulnerable spirit without diminishing our conviction of the truth of the gospel? How do we foster a social movement through a kerygmatic ministry? These are the kinds of questions, I believe, that we must be prepared to respond to as we seek to attract this generation to the message of Christ.

LESSON #3: AN EFFECTIVE PREACHER PREPARES WELL FOR THE MOMENT

> *Jesus knows your name; he knows who you are, he knows where you are, and he knows how you are. And he is inviting you to follow him: to make "follower of Jesus" your primary identity, and to arrange*

---

[62] It would be worth reflecting on the implications of McLuhan's principle for the shaping of the sermon itself and the pitfalls it helps the preacher avoid in preparation. For a helpful discussion, see Kenton Anderson, *Choosing to Preach: A Comprehensive Introduction to Sermon Options and Structures* (Grand Rapids: Zondervan, 2006), 38–39.

everything else in your life around this. This is the beginning of the great adventure of faith.[63]

So the [apostles] went around and said, "What does it mean if the powers of this world have been defeated?" Out of all their sermons, I want to just take three of the things that it meant for them and for us . . . The first thing they said is we don't have to be afraid of death anymore. . . . The second thing is that Jesus' resurrection means you can be forgiven. . . . The other thing that the resurrection means is that you and I are loved beyond our ability to comprehend.[64]

There is no doubt that Harold was heavily influenced by the tradition of expository preaching. When speaking about sermon preparation, he would often repeat the famous dictum "Tell them what you are going to say, say it, then tell them what they heard." Harold adopted Haddon Robinson's approach of building the sermon around one main "homiletical idea."[65] Harold would prepare bulletin inserts with his main ideas presented in logical order, as a result of which there were few surprises as to where he was going in his sermons. There was also little doubt that this approach worked; his points almost always seemed to hit the mark and motivate people to respond. What, then, are some of the practical things that made his preaching effective?

First, he understood that preachers don't *write* sermons, as if the act of preaching were essentially that of reading out a written text. Effective preachers, by contrast, prepare their sermons to be *heard in the moment.* Early in my teaching career, a school administrator commented on my zeal to build relationships but reminded me of the students' need for structure to help them learn. When students were able to hear the lesson objectives in advance, so that they could think through ahead of time

---

[63] Harold Percy, "The Heart of a Vital Church: Five Suggestions for Developing Passionate Spirituality in Your Congregation," *good idea!* (May 11, 2015), http://institute.wycliffecollege.ca/2015/05/the-heart-of-a-vital-church-five-suggestions-for-developing-passionate-spirituality-in-your-congregation, emphasis original.

[64] Percy, "Resurrection Means Hope."

[65] Here is Haddon Robinson's famous advice regarding sermon preparation: "A sermon should be a bullet, not buckshot" (*Biblical Preaching: The Development and Delivery of Expository Messages*, 3rd ed. [Grand Rapids: Baker Academic, 2014], 17).

both how they were going to learn and what they would do with that learning, they were able to absorb the material much more effectively. They could determine what information was essential and what was not. This discipline challenged me as an educator to be more efficient with my words, and I then became more conscious that students were actually listening for the information they needed. It shifted the focus, and rightly so, away from me as the messenger and toward the content of the message itself. It was not important for students to be impressed by my eloquence. What mattered was for them to learn and for us to accomplish our learning goals together.

This shift in emphasis eventually defined my success as an educator, and Harold used this same measure to define success as a preacher. After all, preaching is not about us as preachers; it is about enabling listeners to become followers of Jesus. But preachers face an added challenge. As a teacher, I have a full year in which to gradually convince my captive audience of the genius of Shakespeare's sonnets and to instruct them in the art of writing their own. The pulpit, however, offers no such luxury. Instead of months, we have only minutes in which to motivate and inspire a generation raised on Twitter and Snapchat to follow Jesus—using a text immersed in a worldview far removed from the secularized and technology-driven reality of today's Millennials. How, then, can preachers instruct Millennials to become followers of Jesus by means of a sermon?

First, Harold had a remarkable insight into the mind of the unchurched. He never took for granted those who showed up to attend a religious service, knowing that this is not something most people do on a Sunday morning. So he insisted that we begin each service the same way—by thanking them for coming. In fact, the simple strategy of making visitors feel appreciated has a profound effect. When they are acknowledged, people become more aware of why they have chosen to attend and consciously begin the process of making a connection with what is going on around them. Likewise, people are more inclined to invest in the people who take time to acknowledge them. This is especially important when we think of the level of suspicion most Millennials have toward those in authority. We do well to tell them that they are both seen and *appreciated*. Harold was also aware of how much people value their personal time, so he assured them he was not going to waste it. At the very beginning, he would tell listeners the point of the message he was going to share with them and how their lives would change as a result of hearing it.

Second, it is important to keep in mind that since Scripture was written by human beings for the purpose of communicating God's Word to other human beings, most of what is happening in a given text can be explained fairly succinctly. The key, of course, is the willingness of the preacher to spend the time carefully thinking through how best to explain the text to one's modern listeners. John Stott describes this critical work as "bridging two worlds."[66] We ourselves stand with one foot in each world and seek a way to convince modern listeners that their lives are not so distant from the lives of those whom Jesus encountered.

Third, it is important for preachers to accept the fact that they themselves ultimately have no control over whether or not their listeners will be willing or ready to receive the gospel message. Jesus emphasizes this point through his parable of the sower (Mark 4:1–23). For today's preacher, the moral of the story is that we are called to be faithful in casting the seed as widely as possible, without discrimination as to where it lands. As preachers, we are to treat all hearers equally, for we do not know in which soil the seed will eventually take root. Of course, preachers and farmers alike take great delight in seeing the fruit of their labours, so we work tirelessly to make the soil as fertile and receptive as possible. And Isaiah declares that God's Word does not return to him empty (Isa 55:11). So as preachers, we prepare our sermons in such a way that people who are willing and ready to listen are able to hear the invitation clearly, confident that they will respond. For Harold, every message was meant to focus on the same salient point, leading its hearers to the foot of Jesus' cross and inviting them to share in his risen life.

In a postmodern context, Harold's direct, expository style of preaching is often regarded as ineffective. There is an increasing call for the church to abandon any attempt to make the message relevant for the consumer culture and to aim for something more radical instead. According to this view, our preaching should lean toward the creation of a distinct society, since the Christian faith has its own distinctive language and finds true meaning only in the context of a community whose life is shaped by the Word.

---

[66] John Stott, *Between Two Worlds: The Challenge of Preaching Today* (Grand Rapids: Eerdmans, 1982), 137.

One influential preacher and theologian who has held firmly to this trajectory for the past thirty years is William Willimon, who teaches at Duke Divinity School. Willimon begins his book *Proclamation and Theology* by arguing that the problem with preaching today is essentially theological in nature. He is critical of preaching that rushes to present the Christian message in the most culturally effective manner possible. In fact, Willimon views most contemporary styles of preaching as "marketing strategies" that amount to an unfortunate "selling out" of Jesus.[67] He insists that we cannot compromise the theological language of the church: "Theology makes preaching as difficult and as demanding as it ought to be. [It] tests whether or not what we preach is Christ Jesus and him crucified rather than humanity and it slightly improved."[68]

In his earlier work *Peculiar Speech*, Willimon insisted that the church speaks not to the general human condition but to a particular Christian audience with a particular language of its own: "Conversation among the baptized is ecclesial in nature, political. A particular *polis* is being formed here, a family, a holy nation."[69] And, he insists, "No matter our style of preaching, there is no way for us preachers to weasel out of the baptismal truth that we preach within a distinctive universe of discourse. We talk funny."[70]

To this point, Willimon offers a uniquely biblical paradigm for the preacher. He presents Pentecost as the reversal of Babel and the inauguration of a prophetic community. The Spirit has given the world a prophetic community and created a particular *polis*, a people from strange and varied walks of life who learn to speak, think, and act differently from others. The real test of a preacher, then, is not so much the ability to preach as to call forth the prophetic community of which Willimon speaks.

One year, Willimon was the keynote speaker at a clergy conference that Harold and I attended together. On our drive home, I recall Harold commenting that he didn't think Willimon had suggested anything very different from what he himself was trying to offer his congregation. In

---

[67] William Willimon, *Proclamation and Theology*, Horizons in Theology 1 (Nashville: Abingdon, 2005), 4.

[68] Willimon, *Proclamation and Theology*, 5.

[69] William Willimon, *Peculiar Speech: Preaching to the Baptized* (Grand Rapids: Eerdmans, 1992), 4.

[70] Willimon, *Peculiar Speech*, 6.

some measure I had to agree. Harold always made the biblical narrative a priority. He spoke unequivocally about the distinction between Christian life and secular culture. He did not avoid controversial topics or capitulate to doctrinal accommodation. In terms of Christology, he was thoroughly in line with Willimon's language of the cross.

Yet he did not share Willimon's ecclesiology. Harold understood Jesus' call to be salt and light as the church's mandate to redeem and evangelize culture from within. Consequently, he resisted any notion of radical separation between church and culture. His heart was set on connecting to the unchurched, and he was not prepared to risk the social segregation of his congregation at the expense of his church's mission to share the gospel with those who were within their reach. For this reason, Harold's sermons consistently provided practical guidance to his congregation on how to be "ordinary people learning to follow Jesus in our time," which was the vision statement for Trinity throughout his tenure.

Might this emphasis on meeting the needs of the unchurched risk neglecting the deeper spiritual growth on the part of those already within the church? Toward the end of my time at Trinity, Harold was concerned with the challenge of fostering deeper discipleship. Yet despite the obvious importance of spiritual growth, he was not prepared to risk diverting attention from his primary focus on evangelizing the unchurched. Indeed, he continued to measure the effectiveness of his preaching in terms of the number of people who decided to follow Jesus. Whatever the focus of a particular sermon, Harold always brought a decisive word to each situation. This, in my estimation, remains his most enduring legacy as a preacher. Countless people can recall a time when they felt Harold's words make a spiritual incision into their heart or mind, like that of a surgeon who knows precisely where the inner wound or affliction lies hidden.

LESSON #4: AN EFFECTIVE PREACHER IS INCISIVE IN COMMUNICATING THE GOSPEL

> What the resurrection of Jesus means is that you can be forgiven. In our age we [have] lost so much of the language of guilt, but we haven't lost the experience: we just search for ways to express it.

> The good news of the resurrection is that God offers forgiveness to all those who embrace Jesus. . . .
>
> Many of us this morning would go through great psychological and spiritual healing if one of two things would happen to us—if someone could come embrace you and say, "I forgive you," or if you could go to that someone and embrace them and say, "I forgive you." The apostles went around and said, "This isn't some kind of new psychology—Jesus is making forgiveness real."[71]

Ultimately, an effective preacher is one who has listened, prayed, and studied the Word long enough to grasp an insight from God that will speak right to the hearts of his or her listeners. Listeners will become conscious that they are being confronted with a truth about themselves, suddenly aware that God knows them even better than they know themselves. This incisive word is how the Holy Spirit pierces through "joints and marrow" (Heb 4:12, NIV) to the very heart of a human being. Long before a preacher steps into a pulpit, he or she seeks out this incisive word, yearns for it, and prays and asks God for it, because the preacher understands that his or her calling is defined by a willingness to "wait upon the Lord" until it has been received.

Rob Bell, founder of the Mars Hill Bible Church in Grandville, Michigan, and one of the most influential pastors of the Millennial generation, recounts a remarkable moment during his ministry. One Sunday morning, as over five thousand people were filling the hall to begin the worship service, Rob locked himself into the bathroom down the hall from his office. The burden of preaching had become so great that he was desperate to hear from God. He explains, "I was exhausted. I was burned out. I was full of doubt. I was done. *I had nothing more to say.*"[72]

This moment says a tremendous amount about the burden of responsibility all preachers ought to feel, regardless of their church's size. And, as Rob Bell did, we should embrace such moments as timely reminders of our constant need for the Holy Spirit as we seek to be faithful in carrying into the pulpit that word that, when spoken, will cut into the hearts of God's people.

---

[71] Percy, "Resurrection Means Hope."
[72] Rob Bell, *Velvet Elvis: Repainting the Christian Faith* (Grand Rapids: Zondervan, 2005), 104, emphasis original.

Isaiah 6 recounts the prophet's vision in the Jerusalem temple of God in all his glory. When Isaiah confesses that he is not holy enough to serve as the Lord's messenger, God sends an angel to place a burning coal on his lips. Faced with our own inadequacy, every preacher should ask for similar "burning"—not only to be purified but also so that we may enter the pulpit with words set on fire by the Holy Spirit to pierce the very heart of his people before us.

The incisive preacher is never content simply to go through the motions of sermon preparation. Through prayer, study, and intense listening, the incisive preacher digs deep into the Word and does not relent until he or she has heard what God desires to speak to *his* people. The incisive preacher believes that he or she is an instrument of divine revelation. On the basis of that revelation, the effective preacher prepares a sermon that enables every willing listener to live a changed life as a result of hearing it.

When that word is clear, the effective preacher removes all other distractions from the sermon and centres his or her thoughts around this one message. Many pastors will talk about Saturday night as the time to sit down and "write my sermon." There are a couple of problems with this. First of all, Saturday night is not the time to start the process of listening to God. God doesn't schedule moments of revelation according to our weekly planner. There are far too many moments of grace and failure through the week to miss out on. We need God's Word continually in front of us as we encounter people in our travels through city streets, hospitals, and homes. Furthermore, as preachers we don't just listen to what God is speaking to us in isolation. Good preachers listen to how God is revealing the Word to others in the community as well. Harold had the pastoral staff discussing themes and issues related to his message, sometimes weeks in advance. Harold pressed us for insights and shared his ideas at length while listening for what idea resonated among us. For Harold, preaching was about seeking that one word from God that could change a life.

I close with an example of Harold's own incisive preaching of the gospel. At the end of the Easter sermon cited throughout this chapter, he softly spoke these words:

The other thing that the resurrection means is that you and I are loved beyond our ability to comprehend. For this God, you may ask, is there no price too great to save us? The answer is, none. Many people die in loneliness, and of loneliness. Jesus said, "I'm with you always; I'll never leave you." Sometimes that's not a great consolation, but the other side . . . is that he has left a community of people who live in the power of the resurrection, who have experienced forgiveness and freedom to love fully, and form ourselves, as we're learning to do here at Trinity, into a community of people that loves truly, a place for the lonely and broken to come and to be embraced and to experience God's love through us. That's the kind of community we're trying to create in this place.

May it be so for each of us who responds to the call to preach the gospel today.

GRACIOUS FORMS OF YES: INVITATIONAL DOORS IN PREACHING AND WORSHIP
JOHN H. MCNALLY

WHAT CAN HAPPEN WHEN FOLLOWERS OF CHRIST START PRAYING FOR GOD TO SEND spiritually searching people across our paths so that God can open doors for us to share the good news of Jesus?

It is hard to describe the joy of seeing the wonderful ways that God answers such prayers. When I have been leading "exploration sessions" for people considering baptism and church membership, I have been delighted to see and hear how God opens doors for people to meet Jesus. In one such session, a woman described how she had said yes to following Jesus at our Christmas Eve service. My joy overflowed when I baptized her several weeks later, having had the delight of baptizing her two adult daughters several months earlier.

Let me rewind that story. To begin with, one of the daughters had contacted our church with questions about Christianity. This contact was out of the blue as far as we were concerned, but she had clearly been prompted by the Spirit to connect with our church. If we were an answer to her prayers, she was certainly an answer to ours. She started attending and invited her sister. Then they both joined an Alpha group, accepted Christ, and were baptized. They started praying for their mom and invited her to accompany them to a special seasonal service. Devoted prayers, gracious words and deeds, and the power of God came together to open doors for all three women to accept Christ.

Harold Percy's teaching, modelling, and writing have contributed to such exciting stories by providing a faithful framework for fruitful ministry. Students and others who have been influenced by Harold have benefited from clear explanations and examples of the power of the gospel and of people saying yes to Jesus:

> In church services in my congregation, I frequently invite those who are ready to turn to Christ to pray this one-word prayer—to simply say "Yes" to Jesus. Sometimes it seems more appropriate to say a longer prayer that spells out in more detail the commitment that is being made.[73]

Harold highlights the value of inviting people both to "simply say 'Yes'" and to share "a longer prayer" for exploring the scope of the commitment being considered.

Harold describes crucial attitudes and actions that are necessary to respect the freedom of the respondent. Communicating the gospel of grace starts with asking permission to graciously share the gospel, rather than aggressively demanding an audience or a response: "Asking permission sets a more gracious climate."[74] Another effective evangelist notes how tone is an essential aspect of a gospel presentation and insists, "At all times be courteous."[75] As they share the message of God's grace and mercy, preachers and worship leaders invite a response with "gentleness and respect" (1 Pet 3:15, NIV), regardless of what that response may be.

Emphasizing the importance of courtesy is not a reason to avoid inviting people to make a commitment to Christ. Summarizing the argument of Romans 10, John Stott identifies a crucial question and then answers it from the text:

> What then, according to this section, is necessary for salvation? First the fact of the historic Christ, incarnate, crucified, risen, reigning as Lord, and accessible. Secondly, the apostolic gospel,

---

[73] Harold Percy, *Good News People: An Introduction to Evangelism for Tongue-Tied Christians* (Toronto: Anglican Book Centre, 1996), 128.
[74] Percy, *Good News People*, 123.
[75] Ramesh Richard, *Preparing Evangelistic Sermons: A Seven-Step Method for Preaching Salvation*, rev. ed. (Grand Rapids: Baker Books, 2005, 2015), 186.

the word of faith (8), which makes him known. Thirdly, simple trust on the part of the hearers, calling on the name of the Lord, combining faith in the heart and confession with the mouth. But still something is missing. There is, fourthly, the evangelist who proclaims Christ and urges people to put their trust in him.[76]

Given the importance of proclaiming Christ, this chapter describes some gracious ways of inviting people to say yes to Jesus, providing invitational "doors" that fit within the contexts of preaching and worship.[77] I underline the importance of clarity, creativity, and courtesy in offering such opportunities. All "top ten" ways of saying yes to Jesus are derived in one way or another from my twenty years of pastoral ministry. In exploring each option, readers can assess which of these invitational approaches might be most fruitful within their own contexts.[78]

1. DIRECTIONAL YES: WHEN READY, SHARE THE JOURNEY

The first gracious form of response can be categorized as a *directional yes*. This invitational door emphasizes how a pivotal commitment to Christ is part of an ongoing journey toward maturity. Harold's sample of "a longer prayer" serves as an example of this form:

> When a friend indicates a readiness to turn to Christ, the following prayer might provide a helpful model to follow: *Jesus, I realize that you already know me and that you love me. Now I want to get to know you too. Please forgive me for everything in my life that comes*

---

[76] John Stott, *The Message of Romans: Christ the Controversialist*, The Bible Speaks Today (Downers Grove: InterVarsity, 2001), available at http://us.langham.org/bible_studies/13-may-2016/, emphasis original.

[77] Various authors reflect on the evangelistic implications of the biblical picture of the door in such verses as Colossians 4:3. See, for example, Jenny Andison, *Doors into Faith: Inviting Friends to Join the Big Game*, Wycliffe Booklets on Evangelism 4 (Richmond: Digory, 2005); John Bowen, *Evangelism for "Normal" People: Good News for Those Looking for a Fresh Approach* (Minneapolis: Augsburg Fortress, 2002), 195–97; Michael Green, *Evangelism through the Local Church* (London: Hodder and Stoughton, 1990), 272.

[78] Along with other wise guidance, Ramesh Richard also offers "some don'ts of an evangelistic invitation" and includes an appendix entitled, "The Evangelistic Invitation: A Preparation Checklist" that contains numerous questions for assessing the faithfulness and effectiveness of potential invitations (*Preparing Evangelistic Sermons*, 189–91, 247–49).

between us, and help me to renounce it as I learn to live the life of God's kingdom. Help me to follow you faithfully, and to grow to love you more and more. Amen.[79]

In this prayer, the emphasis of the invitation is directional. Saying yes involves moving in the direction of God's love, forgiveness, reign, and much more on the journey of faithfully following Jesus. The wording of this prayer reinforces the fact that evangelism and discipleship are inseparable, as is so evident throughout Harold's own work. Such a directional yes can be shared individually between friends or within the context of preaching and worship. Preachers and worship leaders can invite others to share the journey with Jesus whenever they are ready.

Another advantage of this directional approach is the implication that the movement toward Christ probably includes several steps or stages. Os Guinness offers insightful and playful descriptions of persuasive communication that includes an invitation to respond to Christ in four stages:

> Questions have created a seeker and spurred a search for answers (stage 1). In its turn the discovery of what is thought to be a meaningful and adequate answer (stage 2) has pointed toward the question of whether there were solid reasons to believe that answer. If that issue is resolved and belief in the answer can be found to be a warranted belief (stage 3), then everything comes together to make the seeker step forward as a whole person to place their trust wholeheartedly in God (stage 4).
>
> Faith then becomes personal and experiential, not just a matter of knowing about God, but knowing God as reality . . . What God himself does through his Spirit is what counts and what makes it real.[80]

If one affirms that such stages are helpful ways of picturing the process of drawing closer to Christ, then the directional tone of the prayer can address next steps. The preacher or worship leader can encourage people

---

[79] Percy, *Good News People*, 128, emphasis original.
[80] Os Guinness, *Fool's Talk: Recovering the Art of Christian Persuasion* (Downers Grove: InterVarsity, 2015), 247–48.

to make a move into the next stage from questions toward answers, from answers toward assessment, and from assessment to commitment. As we ask people to consider next steps, we can trust the Spirit to spur on listeners in a way, as Guinness says, that "makes it real."

2. DIALOGICAL YES: IN DIALOGUE, OFFER A PRAYER PROMPTER

A second gracious form of response can be called a *dialogical yes.* This invitational door opens up dialogue and prompts prayer. For example, in *Becoming a Contagious Christian: Participant's Guide*, Bill Hybels, Mark Mittelberg, and Lee Strobel simplify saying yes to Jesus by first identifying where people see themselves spiritually and then prompting them to pray to Jesus in their own words for "crossing the line of faith":

> Have you come to the point of trusting Christ, or are you still in the process of thinking it through? . . . Is there any reason you wouldn't want to ask Jesus for his forgiveness and leadership right now? . . . Ask for the forgiveness of Christ. Ask for the leadership of Christ. Give thanks for God's forgiveness and leadership.[81]

This form of prayer can be introduced within the context of imagining a discussion about where a person sees him or herself in relation to Jesus. In my own experience of equipping a congregation for evangelism, people feel empowered by the idea of a dialogical approach that includes "commitment-advancing questions."[82]

These authors find that people are interested in discussing what it means to accept Christ as "Saviour" and "Lord." Their paraphrase of "forgiver" and "life leader" can serve as a catalyst for conversation between the individual and God. The worship leader could say something like "Through the Scriptures, the sermon, and the songs, Jesus is speaking about being our forgiver and life leader. How are you going to respond?" The leader can prompt people in a guided prayer about these themes in their own lives or share a sample prayer with the same themes. Either way,

---

[81] Bill Hybels, Mark Mittelberg, and Lee Strobel, *Becoming A Contagious Christian: Participant's Guide: Communicating Your Faith in a Style that Fits You* (Grand Rapids: Zondervan, rev. ed., 2007), 80–81.

[82] Daniel Meyer, *Witness Essentials: Evangelism that Makes Disciples* (Downers Grove: InterVarsity, 2012), 193–208. Meyer offers additional questions and suggestions for such dialogue.

a sermon can explain the meaning of such titles for Christ and help people explore implications for their lives. The response prayer can continue the "dialogue" that has already been underway throughout the service.

Framing the invitation in a dialogical form introduces an important image for the spiritual life. As seasoned spiritual directors William Barry and William Connolly explain, "Life could thus be readily seen as a dialogue of both word and action between God and ourselves."[83] From the outset, then, we can invite people to enter into a heartfelt dialogue with God.

3. RELATIONAL YES: PRAY WITH "SORRY," "THANK YOU," AND "PLEASE"

With a similar concern to make faith accessible, this third invitational door seeks to open a *relational yes.* This gracious approach has proven very fruitful during years of using the multi-week Alpha course for exploring Christianity. Nicky Gumbel describes the process as accepting the gift that God offers with the relational words of "sorry," "thank you," and "please." Then he shares this "suggested prayer of commitment to Jesus Christ":

> "Lord Jesus Christ, I am sorry for the things I have done wrong in my life. [Take a few moments to ask His forgiveness for anything particular that is on your conscience.] Please forgive me. I now turn from everything which I know is wrong. Thank You that You died on the cross for me so that I could be forgiven and set free. Thank You that You offer me forgiveness and the gift of Your Spirit. I now receive that gift. Please come into my life by Your Holy Spirit to be with me forever. Thank You, Lord Jesus. Amen."[84]

In my experience, people easily grasp the relational language within this prayer as an accessible way to connect to Christ. If carefully

---

[83] William Barry and William Connolly, *The Practice of Spiritual Direction*, rev. ed. (New York: HarperCollins, 2009), 26.

[84] Nicky Gumbel, *The Alpha Course Manual: A Practical Introduction to the Christian Faith* (Colorado Springs: David C. Cook, 1995), 75. In addition to appearing in the Alpha videos and participants' manual, this prayer was also published in shorter seasonal booklets for Christmas and Easter that were intended as helpful tools in a church welcome area or for use in conjunction with an Alpha course. For the latest version of such resources, consult the website of the Canadian branch (www.alphacanada.org) and click on the bookstore link.

explained in the context of preaching and worship, emphasis on the Spirit (prominent in the Alpha materials) encourages people to take a step of faith through God's empowering strength. The prayer is framed as a relational response to our Triune God, who helps the person say yes to Jesus.

A relational emphasis reminds us who is leading the conversation. God takes the initiative and gives us the opportunity to respond. In her classic book on relational evangelism, Rebecca Manley Pippert shares an incident that revealed both her own sense of inadequacy and God's overarching mercy. A student had started out trying to disrupt her exploratory Bible study. In a restaurant, a few weeks later, she was in the middle of an awkward conversation with this same student: "I think I was still speaking when Todd said, 'You're right. God is speaking, and I am saying yes.'"[85] Pippert's story reminds us that God is already speaking, already initiating the relationship for a Spirit-led yes.

Relational imagery also highlights the loving nature of the process. Rick Richardson uses marriage as a helpful analogy for this deepening relationship:

> Marriage usually happens only after someone pops the question, "Will you marry me?" and the other person says, "Yes!" In some cultures, the question might be popped parent to parent. But someone still needs to do it.
>
> Union with God most often has the same precursor—someone pops the question. "Do you want to follow Christ and commit your life to God?" What a joy to be part of the matchmaking and journey-guide process at this point of initiation![86]

As love between a couple blossoms into marriage, love for Christ naturally grows into a commitment to Christ in response to someone popping the relational question.

---

[85] Rebecca Manley Pippert, *Out of the Saltshaker and into the World: Evangelism as a Way of Life* (Downers Grove: InterVarsity, 1979, 1999), 149.

[86] Rick Richardson, *Reimagining Evangelism: Inviting Friends on a Spiritual Journey* (Downers Grove: InterVarsity, 2006), 137. In discussion with John Bowen, he extended this analogy, with the private "moment of decision" being like the engagement and baptism being like the public wedding.

4. MUSICAL YES: SELECT A SONG TO EXPRESS A RESPONSE

In the ongoing worship ministry of the church, one of the ways that some people sense God speaking is through music. This suggests the possibility of a fourth gracious form of response: the *musical yes*. This invitational door is opened by strategically selecting a congregational song, usually sung shortly after a gospel presentation, as a form of response. One famous example within evangelical circles is the Billy Graham Evangelistic Association's use of the hymn "Just as I Am" as a suitable response to the evangelistic message.

Over the years, and in consultation with musical family members and church leaders, I have compiled a list of songs that can be used to express initial or deeper commitment to Christ. Whether it is an older, cherished Easter hymn like "Christ the Lord Is Risen Today," a contemporary song like "In Christ Alone," or a new song that the Spirit can put in one's heart, people respond with a *musical yes*. There are online lists of seasonal suggestions related to Easter and Christmas. For example, the classic carol "O Little Town of Bethlehem" declares, "Where meek souls will receive him, still the dear Christ enters in." Ranging from a simple musical confession that "He is Lord" to Charles Wesley's rousing affirmation of faith "And can it be that I should gain / An interest in the Saviour's blood?," there are many ways to invite people to sing their response to the truth of Jesus. Contemporary songs (such as the Newsboys' moving creedal confession "We Believe") can continually be added to this repertoire of responses.

In order to open this "door," the preacher or worship leader can introduce the song by highlighting its depiction of Jesus and the response to him or her that the lyrics describe. After introducing these themes, the worship leader could say something like "If this song expresses how you feel and what you would like to say to Jesus, then sing it with all your heart. Turn this song into your personal prayer, singing your response to Jesus today." Whatever wording you use, it needs to be a clear invitation for people to respond by employing the lyrics as their prayer to God and proclaiming their faith in Christ.

5. HISTORICAL YES: TRY AN ANCIENT-FUTURE REMIX

Many different faithful responses to Christ throughout the long history of the church are available for adaptation and use today. Whether offering a fresh rendition of an ancient confession or reusing a classic prayer of commitment, this fifth form of response can be described as an *historical yes*. Depending on denominational traditions, creative usage of historical creeds is also an option. In this regard, Harold points out that "vitality in worship" is not usually about whether the actual wording of our worship is ancient or contemporary; rather, it is a matter of "whether or not the worshippers are truly experiencing God's presence among them."[87] Thus, depending on the setting or the sermon, it may be appropriate to facilitate an experience of God's presence by employing historical precedents as means of responding to God's mercy.

For example, the following prayers from Richard Foster's collection of current and classic prayers can provide invitational doors for responding to Jesus:

- Richard of Chichester (1197 to 1253): "O most merciful Redeemer, Friend and Brother, may I know Thee more clearly, love Thee more dearly, and follow Thee more nearly, day by day. Amen."
- Ignatius of Loyola (1491 to 1556): "Take, Lord, all my liberty, my memory, my understanding, and my whole will. You have given me all that I have, all that I am, and I surrender all to Your Divine will. Give me only Your love and Your grace. With this I am rich enough, and I have no more to ask. Amen."
- Teresa of Avila (1515 to 1582): "Govern everything by your wisdom, O Lord, so that my soul may always be serving you in the way you will and not as I choose. Let me die to myself so that I may serve you; let me live to you who are life itself. Amen."[88]

All of these historical forms of yes could be used as an ancient-future remix in preaching and worship as a fresh presentation of a classic prayer, a contemporary paraphrase, or as an inspiration for writing new prayers with similar themes.

---

[87] Percy, *Good News People*, 92. Harold expands the discussion of vitality in worship and other areas in his subsequent book, *Your Church Can Thrive*.

[88] Richard Foster, *Prayers from the Heart* (New York: HarperCollins, 1994), 25, 27, 46.

6. MISSIONAL YES: JOIN GOD ON MISSION

Even as we look for historical examples of prayers of commitment, the biblical narrative gives meaning to history as a whole by describing it as the unfolding of God's mission to a lost humanity. Along these lines, the sixth invitational door entails a *missional yes*, since accepting Christ inextricably involves us joining God in mission. Building on James Choung's award-winning work on evangelism,[89] a team linked to InterVarsity Christian Fellowship has developed excellent evangelism equipping materials, entitled *Reimagining Evangelism: Inviting Friends on a Spiritual Journey*. Within what they call the Big Story sharing guide, these authors coach Christians as follows:

> Whatever the response, help the person consider next steps. If your friend has not yet invited Jesus to forgive, heal, or lead him or her, you could ask whether he or she is ready to make that choice. If so, you can ask if your friend wants to pray now with you or later on, privately. If your friend wants to pray with you, you could use this prayer: Jesus, I know you are healing the world, and I want to be part of that healing mission. But I need you to heal and forgive and lead me first. I invite you to be my forgiver and healer and leader, and live in and through me to bring your healing to others.[90]

This approach recognizes different starting points and invites next steps, fitting for both worship and discipleship development. It frames the way the door of faith is also a door to becoming a follower of Christ on God's healing mission to the world.

As a pastor, I found this tool to be such a helpful gospel presentation and framework for invitation that it became an integral part of our "Believing and Belonging" sessions for those who were considering accepting Christ, being baptized, and joining the church on its mission

---

[89] See video clips with James Choung summarizing his book *True Story: A Christianity Worth Believing In* (Downers Grove: InterVarsity, 2008) at http://www.jameschoung.net/resources/big-story.

[90] Rick Richardson, Terry Erickson, and Judy Johnson, *Reimagining Evangelism Participant's Guide: Inviting Friends on a Spiritual Journey* (Downers Grove: InterVarsity, 2008), 49–50.

with God. More recently, I discovered that Tony Campolo often connects commitment to Christ to signing up for a mission trip, contributing to a charity, getting involved in a justice initiative, or some other means of joining God's larger mission.[91] We can learn from the way Campolo makes a direct connection between decision and action, especially in joining God's own mission.

7. INSTRUCTIONAL YES: EXPLORE GOD'S ACTION AND OUR RESPONSE

For those who are exploring faith commitment and church involvement, it is important to consider theological questions about the meaning of the cross in ways that are accessible and memorable. To meet this need (and as another resource in the worship and preaching toolkit), I developed a series of instructional sessions that we call "Believing and Belonging." Facilitating this gracious form of *instructional yes* has been a joy for me over the course of many years. This invitational door takes into account three primary aspects of the atonement.

Inspired by Jonathan Wilson's book *God So Loved the World*,[92] which describes and interprets the atonement, I wanted to formulate a prayer of commitment that could convey the meaning of Christ's work as victor, sacrifice, and example. I also wanted to be explicitly Trinitarian in describing the mystery of God's initiative and our response. On different occasions, I have used the following prayer as a bulletin insert to provide sermon notes on the meaning of the cross, as a sample prayer of commitment to be prayed on behalf of others following the sermon, as a tool to be taken home for later use as a personal prayer, and as a handout in the "Believing and Belonging" sessions:

- *Sacrifice:* Jesus, I accept you as the sacrifice, that you are the just judge who paid the penalty for my sin through your death on the cross. So I am sorry for the things I have done wrong and ask for your forgiveness.
- *Almighty:* Almighty Father, I accept that you sent your Son Jesus so that I could see your face and accept your grace. So I thank

---

[91] Tony Campolo and Mary Albert Darling, *Connecting Like Jesus: Practices for Healing, Teaching, and Preaching* (San Francisco: Jossey-Bass, 2010), 198–99.
[92] Jonathan Wilson, *God So Loved the World* (Grand Rapids: Baker, 2001), 97, 115, 132.

you for creating me in your image and coming to me in order to restore your fallen creation and reconcile our relationship.
- *Victor:* Jesus, I accept you as the victor, as you defeated Satan, sin, and all evil powers through your death on the cross. So I receive your liberating deliverance from the power of evil within, beyond, and around me that enslaves me in order to enter into the abundant life of your kingdom.
- *Example:* Jesus, I accept you as the example, as the supreme and perfect demonstration of God's love through your death on the cross. So I respond by committing to follow your example of the way of love on the disciple's lifelong journey to spiritual maturity in Christian community.
- *Spirit:* Holy Spirit, I accept that you have been working in me to enable me to take this step of faith. Holy Spirit, I receive your filling and ongoing empowering presence and guidance for following Jesus fully. I pray all this in the name of our one God: Father, Son, and Holy Spirit. Amen.

It has been exciting to see how God has used this prayer in different ways over a number of years of ministry. While the prayer as a whole has been a catalyst for conversation and conversion, it is more easily understood, and therefore more effective, when each part of the prayer is explained and discussed in detail. Such explanations can be offered by a preacher in the course of a sermon, by a worship leader in a transition between different parts of a sermon, by a small-group leader in a follow-up gathering, or simply by a friend in the course of discussion.

8. VISUAL YES: PICTURE THE PROCESS IN A SYMBOLIC ACTION
The next gracious form of *visual yes* shifts our attention from concepts and explanations to a more concrete embodiment of Christian confession. This invitational door works well for kinesthetic learners or those who respond well to symbolic imagery. For example, Bryan Chapell concludes his description of evangelistic messages with these words:

> Offer them some concrete way of expressing a commitment (e.g., offering a silent prayer in words the preacher supplies, pledging

to learn more, telling a loved one of their decision, meeting with a church leader after the service, coming to the front to receive prayer, raising a hand to affirm a decision, praying on knees at their bedside that night, etc.). The converted heart longs to affirm its faith.[93]

Chapell captures common ways to visually and physically express the heart's commitment with voices, feet, hands, or knees.

In similar fashion, Ramesh Richard employed "various methods of public acknowledgment":

With everyone's eyes closed, I said,
"Would you raise your head and make eye contact with me and nod your head?"
(Sometimes they even smile!)
"Give me a thumbs-up sign."
"Wave to me."
"Walk forward during the final song or after the meeting."
"Fill out a response card" ....
"Register on our website."
"Stay in your seat, and we'll come to you."
"Come to the front row, and I will meet you for additional questions and comments."[94]

The one element that unites this variety of responses is the importance of physically acknowledging one's acceptance of Christ. Any one of these methods is simply a visual means of saying yes to Jesus; each is one gracious form of symbolizing or embodying one's commitment.

With the potential for such visual and concrete forms in mind, I have experimented with ways to symbolize the exchange that is at the heart of the gospel of grace.[95] Each year, for example, we tried to share Communion on the Thursday night of Holy Week in different

---

[93] Bryan Chapell, *Christ-Centered Preaching: Redeeming the Expository Sermon*, 2nd ed. (Grand Rapids: Baker, 2005), 362.
[94] Richard, *Preparing Evangelistic Sermons*, 188.
[95] Depending on the example, before or after implementing the ideas I sometimes discovered others with similar suggestions for symbolic action. Searching the internet uncovers many more catalysts for creativity in responding to Christ.

ways, drawing on the richness of various Christian traditions and our own creativity. When people felt ready to say yes to Jesus as Lord and Saviour, either for the first time or in a deeper way, we invited people to come forward and symbolically give God their sin and receive the Lord's Supper in exchange, but without any pressure to participate.[96] How is that done in practice?

One year, we invited those in attendance to symbolically write their sins on a piece of scrap paper, feed the scrap into a paper shredder, and then receive the Communion elements in exchange. In another service, people dropped a nail—symbolic of their sin—into a large stainless-steel bowl with a reverberating clang; and in return they were given a wafer to dip into the Communion cup.

Another year, when the message explored the implications of Jesus washing the disciples' feet, people came forward and had water poured over their hands before Communion to symbolize cleansing from sin.

At other times, we have pounded our sins into the cross in the form of a symbolic nail or received God's grace by leaving our sins as trash in a garbage bag—both actions performed prior to receiving signs of grace in the form of the Communion elements. Depending on the congregation's level of comfort with creativity in the worship service, in small-group Bible studies, or in a retreat setting, more or less explanation may be needed beforehand. The possibilities for facilitating a visual yes to Jesus are almost limitless.

9. COMMUNAL YES: INVITE QUESTIONS AND OFFER PRAYER STATIONS

Another variation on the previous theme adds a somewhat different approach to the options under consideration. This ninth invitational door can be described as a *communal yes*. In my experience, people are sometimes initially hesitant to respond. There are various reasons for this. If the invitation is for a public response (perhaps in one of the ways described earlier), an individual may feel embarrassed about potentially being the only one to respond. Others may sense a desire to respond but are not yet sure how to do so. Still others may actually need support because of some internal struggle.

---

[96] Ramesh Richard emphasizes this point: "You will not manipulate a response.... Your presentation will be persuasive but not coercive, marked by urgency *for their sake* but not intimidating" (*Preparing Evangelistic Sermons*, 186).

Here it is helpful to recall the father struggling with whether or not Jesus can heal his son. He exclaims, "I do believe; help me overcome my unbelief!" (Mark 9:24, NIV). Just as Jesus highlights the importance of prayer in such situations (Mark 9:29), God continues to work through communal prayer stations or small-group prayer for various forms of healing, whether in regard to physical, emotional, or spiritual aspects of our lives. As an extension of the same principle, prayer can lead a person to the source of their healing and thereby help them to say yes to Jesus.

With whatever frequency fits the setting, prayer stations—pairs of people praying for others in a quiet corner of the church—in connection with communal worship can communicate the fact that both offering and receiving prayer are "normal" for wherever an individual may be on his or her spiritual journey. Normalizing the experience of receiving individual prayer can thus address the potential problem of someone feeling isolated or singled out in response to an invitation.

Katie Rawson, an expert in cross-cultural evangelism, writes, "Giving an invitation also allows any remaining blocks to surface."[97] For Rawson, the communal context of praying with two other people or in a small group provides a safe place to explore the grace expressed in the invitation, including related objections and questions that may be "blocks" in responding. As worship leaders and preachers respond to the Spirit's prompting and partner with trained prayer teams of two people offering support in the midst of struggle, they can graciously open the door to dynamic encounters with our living Lord.

10. CONTEXTUAL YES: HOW CAN YOU FRAME NEW DOORS?

In light of the importance of communal teamwork, every reader can add to this list of gracious forms of response with their own examples and ideas. This open-ended tenth invitational door is a *contextual yes*. In Harold's book on evangelism, the word "appropriate" keeps resurfacing. In his discussion about asking permission to make a presentation about the gospel or to ask for a response, Harold writes, "You will know best what is appropriate in your own particular situations."[98] His statement

---

[97] Katie Rawson, *Crossing Cultures with Jesus: Sharing Good News with Sensitivity and Grace* (Downers Grove: InterVarsity, 2015), 134. For another way of inviting and facilitating questions, see Richard, *Preparing Evangelistic Sermons*, 188.
[98] Percy, *Good News People*, 124.

implies that we can handcraft invitational doors to faith conversations in the Lord's house or in our own homes, in the context of congregational worship or personal discipleship, or wherever and whenever we sense the Spirit leading us.

If we are sufficiently aware of the personal, social, and cultural contexts of our ministry, we will be able to avoid the danger of being formulaic. Individual pastors and congregations will then feel free to use or adapt the forms proposed here or to develop their own forms of response. For example, Rawson raises an important question and offers her personal reflection on the use of the sinner's prayer:

> What should a "sinner's prayer" look like cross-culturally? I hesitate to provide printed prayers because people can so easily treat them as magical, but in general they should express sin in terms of breaking relationship with and dishonoring God, and repentance in terms of coming home to God and pledging allegiance or loyalty to Jesus . . . . If at all possible, people should pray this first prayer in their heart languages.[99]

Rawson advises us to employ key themes of the gospel for personal prayer in language that is authentic and true for each individual. She intentionally connects different aspects of Christ's identity with specific cultural contexts so as to avoid the implication that particular forms of prayer or commitment are somehow magical. Instead, Jesus' character provides the focus for each individual response. In this manner, the preacher, worship leader, or friend can encourage others to have a heart-to-heart conversation with God in ways that are authentic to their specific context and culture.

THE SIMPLICITY AND JOURNEY OF "YES"

Even as we seek to articulate the complexity and mystery of salvation, we do not want to undermine the simplicity and accessibility of the gospel. For Joel, Peter, and Paul, the message remains clear: "Everyone who calls on the name of the Lord shall be saved" (Joel 2:32; see Acts 2:21;

---

[99] Rawson, *Crossing Cultures with Jesus*, 134. While this example is quite specific, Rawson offers various other examples of connecting Christ with different cultural contexts.

Rom 10:13). We need to guard against making the process more complex than needed, especially with jargon from church subculture or "insider" language. All these gracious means of invitation open doors for the Spirit-empowered simple step of responding to the name of the Lord.

Depending on the individual in question, this response may be experienced as an event or as a process, with "conversions sudden and gradual" alike being the norm.[100] Rawson describes how invitations can help people relate to conversion either as an event or as a process, depending on their situation:

> Invitations provide opportunities for our friends to publicly respond to the Spirit's wooing with surrender and commitment. Even if the Spirit has already ushered them into the kingdom, openly confessing Jesus as their Lord seals in their hearts the reality of conversion.[101]

I, too, have seen the value of an intentional invitation both in facilitating such a response and in affirming a commitment that has already been unfolding for some time.

Preaching and worship provide opportunities to invite others to continue their spiritual journey by drawing closer to Christ with whatever next steps the Spirit is stirring them to take at the present time. As Paul insists, "No one can say 'Jesus is Lord' except by the Holy Spirit" (1 Cor 12:3). As Tony Campolo notes,

> It takes a certain amount of courage to ask for a decision, because listeners can say no. Always remember that as a speaker you have a responsibility to provide a well-planned and well-delivered call to decision, but you are not the one responsible for the outcome. That's between the Holy Spirit and the listener.[102]

Once we develop an appreciation of the roles of the person giving the invitation, of the listener, and of the work of the Spirit, we can

---

[100] Bowen, *Evangelism for "Normal" People*, 201–202.
[101] Rawson, *Crossing Cultures with Jesus*, 134.
[102] Campolo and Darling, *Connecting Like Jesus*, 199.

courageously issue the invitation without anxiously fretting about when or how the person actually walks through the door.

Whether the "door" is framed as contextual, communal, visual, instructional, missional, historical, musical, relational, dialogical, or directional, all the options in this chapter are simply gracious forms of saying yes to Jesus. At Wycliffe College in 2015, Harold Percy shared about the joy of people approaching him saying, "I said yes!"[103] May God give you many joyful experiences of seeing people walk through invitational doors in preaching and worship and in other areas of ministry to advance Christ's kingdom. With the foregoing suggestions and the following questions, may the Spirit spark your imagination about prayerfully framing gracious ways of saying yes to Jesus.

QUESTIONS FOR REFLECTION, DISCUSSION, AND ACTION

1. When have you seen God use an invitational door to help people say yes to Jesus?
2. If you have not seen such doors open, what might be some contributing factors that keep them closed (such as church culture, insider language, etc.)?
3. Which of the forms in the chapter seem most faithful to the gospel? Why?
4. How could you adapt a gracious form for fruitful ministry in your own situation?
5. How could you appropriately frame new invitational doors in your context?
6. How does Paul's prayer in Colossians 4:2–6 apply to your situation? In particular, how might you pray, with thanksgiving, for God to open doors to present the gospel with creativity, clarity, and graciousness?

---

[103] Related in a personal conversation with John Bowen.

SECTION D
REACHING OUT

THE EXIGENCIES OF OUR TIME: REFLECTIONS ON THE TWENTIETH ANNIVERSARY OF *GOOD NEWS PEOPLE*
ANDREW STIRLING

ONE OF THE MOST WINSOME FEATURES OF THE WRITINGS OF HAROLD PERCY IS HIS overwhelming sense of joy and enthusiasm. You cannot begin to read any of his publications without the impression that he enjoys the Christian faith. This characteristic is evident in his influential book *Good News People: An Introduction to Evangelism for Tongue-Tied Christians*. Harold consistently draws the reader into his own joy and, like the *perichoresis* of the Holy Trinity, makes his audience dance with him through the passion of the faith.

This joy manifests itself in the key ideas that permeate the work. For example, in the introduction he cites Alister McGrath: "The fundamental motivation for evangelism is generosity—the basic human concern to share the good things of life with those whom we love."[104] Harold is clear that a hurting world needs the Good News of God's love, culminating in the triumph of God over eternal death. For Harold, Christian faith is totally predicated on the life, death, and resurrection of Jesus Christ, and his desire is to draw as many people as possible into an experience of that joyful reality.

Evidence of this joyfulness is seen in two important sections of his work. First, his theology of joy is rooted in the biblical story that reveals

---

[104] Percy, *Good News People*, 12.

the appealing joy of God. For example, he concludes his first chapter on human need by retelling the story of the lost son from Luke 15. Harold recounts the story in a way that captures the simple essence of the parable. Jesus told the story to give us a "glimpse into the heart of God." For Harold, God's heart aches for the lost son. The thrust of the story, as of Jesus' ministry, is reconciliation between "a broken world and a loving God."[105]

Reconciliation and its resulting joy, however, are not Harold's only focus, for the book is also "about a God who invites those who have heard [the gospel] and responded to this news to share it with others until the whole world knows."[106] For most of the book, therefore, Harold addresses in concrete ways how "ordinary" people of faith can convey the Good News of Christ to the world.

His central conviction is that the local congregation of believers is to be "regarded as the primary evangelist."[107] Critical to the process of reaching out to the world is that all three components of congregational life must be committed to the process of evangelization. First, he believes that the *senior clergy or leadership team* must hold out the vision that God wants people to have faith in Jesus Christ. As a mentor, teacher, and encourager of disciples, the lead minister (or ministers) must be ready to share the good news.

The *congregation*, however, is not exempt from this healing and welcoming process. While Harold debunks the argument that "everything we [the church] do is evangelism,"[108] he nevertheless recognizes that the congregation needs to reflect the gospel both by what it teaches and in its social ministries. Where Harold is particularly perceptive is in his conviction that this form of ministry must be "intentional"—that it does not happen by chance or osmosis. Congregations have to think and act like evangelists. He realizes that, for many, this is a huge commitment that requires a paradigm shift: "For many mainline Christians, perhaps the first and greatest challenge will lie in making the necessary adjustments to begin thinking of their church as an evangelizing community."[109]

---

[105] Percy, *Good News People*, 26–27.
[106] Percy, *Good News People*, 27.
[107] Percy, *Good News People*, 73.
[108] Percy, *Good News People*, 29.
[109] Percy, *Good News People*, 75.

The third party involved in this process of evangelization is the *individual church member*. Belonging to a church necessitates sharing one's faith in every sphere of one's life. Feeling free to welcome those who belong to the network of contacts in family, work, and neighbourhood is essential to the mission of the church. Harold is aware, however, that not everyone has an extroverted personality that makes it easy to approach others with the good news and that introverted and shy people can also have a profound ministry. He believes that "availability" is more important than perceived "ability" and that God can use the former to sow the seeds of faith through an individual, regardless of his or her personality type.

When these three components work together with a single purpose, "good things will happen."[110] However, Harold doesn't see anything inevitable about the church's success in evangelizing the world. He is a pragmatist and realizes that significant factors inhibit and constrain the evangelizing process so that people are reluctant to embrace this vision.

Twenty years after the book's publication, it is still vital for church leaders to understand these constraints, for despite Harold's apparent optimism about the future, the church today is having to deal with even more aggressive and challenging issues that impede its ministry of evangelism. Therefore we must ask: What has changed? What are the external forces and internal influences that affect the witness of the church in the twenty-first century? Can Harold's work help us refocus our attention on the evangelistic imperative?

THE EXIGENCIES OF OUR TIME

1. Freedom
Central to understanding the current application of Harold's work is an appreciation of the importance of the connection between "evangelistic freedom" and "evangelical freedom." I am convinced that since Harold wrote his book, the social, political, and spiritual contexts in the world, and Canada in particular, are far less receptive to the Christian message. Indeed, it is at times hostile to Christian precepts and identity. This hostility has contributed to the lack of confidence that many Christians have in the good news. Some believers have decided to hide in the shadows

---

[110] Percy, *Good News People*, 74.

of our culture rather than openly share the light of God's presence in Jesus Christ. To use Harold's phrase, they are "tongue-tied."

As a corrective to this evangelistic restraint, I share John Webster's conviction that the church needs to understand the nature of God's own freedom. For Webster, God is not a remote being who left humanity (or the church) to its own devices. Rather, God moves towards us and is always present. Therefore any motivation for evangelism must come from God's own freedom as revealed in the Triune God. The gospel is rooted in this reality and is the "sovereign and majestic fullness with which God is himself."[111] Furthermore, Webster sees no hermeneutical distance between the witness of Scripture and those who interpret or preach it today. Therefore the Christian speaks God's Word in the context of God's radiant presence, and it is precisely in what he calls "evangelical freedom" that we find the "freedom announced in the gospel."[112] If Webster is correct, the church should not be worried or constrained by the response of culture but should announce the Good News of God's presence.

Another perspective, however, is expressed by Rex Ahdar and Ian Leigh, who argue that Christianity is inherently conflicted regarding its core message:

> "There is," as [Charles] Curran observes, "always a tension between passionate religious belief in salvation through one particular way and toleration of others as an acceptance of their religious liberty." If one conceded religious freedom, would this lead to the multifarious evils of relativism, indifferentism, scepticism and compromise in religion? Christian thinkers have struggled with these ongoing dilemmas.[113]

Rather than beginning with a doctrine of God, as Webster does, Ahdar and Leigh suggest that part of the inhibition Christians feel when sharing

---

[111] John Webster, *Confessing God: Essays in Christian Dogmatics II*, 2nd ed. (London: Bloomsbury T&T Clark, 2016), 2.
[112] Webster, *Confessing God*, 216.
[113] Rex Ahdar and Ian Leigh, *Religious Freedom in the Liberal State*, 2nd ed. (Oxford: Oxford University Press, 2013), citing Charles E. Curran, "Religious Freedom and Human Rights in the World and the Church: A Christian Perspective," in *Religious Liberty and Human Rights in Nations and Religions*, ed. Leonard J. Swidler (Philadelphia: Ecumenical; New York: Hippocrene, 1986), 143–65; here, 143.

their faith with others is born out of an uneasiness with the absolute claims of the faith in a pluralistic society. Ahdar and Leigh further argue that "the case for religious liberty is not one that can be explicitly derived from Scripture."[114] This negative view of Scripture's approach to religious freedom argues that Christianity has had to learn to promote Christian freedom, and, because of its propensity for intolerance, the church has had to find new ways of living in the world apart from the witness of Scripture. In other words, the church is constrained by its very own beliefs, and in a society that is often hostile to the gospel it feels reluctant to witness to its core beliefs. It is also unsure as to whether it can turn to the witness of Scripture for its inspiration and motivation.

So who is correct, and what are the implications for Harold's legacy? I suggest that Webster's interpretation of the gospel is a faithful analysis of the biblical Word and as such represents a call for us to re-examine our theology and practice in the light of the Word of God. Christians are called by Scripture to be free agents of God in the world because God is free within himself. His perspective also brings the church back to an appreciation of the importance of the Trinity by rediscovering the fact that its mission is always the *missio dei* that is rooted in divine self-disclosure. However, the church still needs to take into consideration the observation (and implied critique) offered by Ahdar and Leigh. Webster's assessment of the church is important because Christianity has clearly struggled with knowing precisely where it should stand on sharing its faith.

Christians today are unsure how much of their faith they should share with others in case they infringe on the freedom of other people's religious convictions. For many churches, the new orthodoxy is to "live and let live," as a result of which they cease to evangelize altogether. It is also an indictment of the church's lack of knowledge of the gospel itself. Many Christians conceive of the world as naturally divided between people who already have a faith of their own and those who have no faith at all. For them, the problems of past intolerance are like an anchor around their souls that prevents even the most faithful from sharing their convictions for fear of embarrassment or offence. Compounding this difficulty is an overwhelmingly negative portrayal of the church in popular media, to which Harold drew attention twenty years ago. He correctly

---

[114] Ahdar and Leigh, *Religious Freedom in the Liberal State*, ii.

affirms that "it is frightening to witness to the gospel. It is far easier to remain undercover."[115] Even in the latter part of the twentieth century, he recognized the timidity of the church in the face of the hostility of Western society.

In the twenty-first century, events throughout the world have contributed to this reluctance to evangelize. In particular, one cannot overestimate the cataclysmic impact of the terrorist attack on New York City on September 11, 2001. I think many Christians in North America were shocked to realize that some people throughout the world despise Western convictions and lifestyles. Both Canada and the United States had lived in the myth that their geographical distance from troubled spots in the world would protect and isolate them from danger. The myth was also constructed on the belief (though not expressly articulated) that North America is based on Christian principles. While society lived happily with its pluralism (something Harold appreciates as valuable), many Christians nevertheless thought that this openness was at least a by-product of Christian compassion. In other words, society and the church were comfortable with a benign and tolerant accommodation.

The events of 9/11 put a knife in many of these convictions. People from another faith and worldview had broken down the defences of isolationism. Subsequently, the West got involved in a protracted war in the Middle East and Afghanistan, and the resultant feeling of fear made everyone suspicious of the "other." Issues of freedom once again came to the forefront of social discourse. Today we are still challenged by a fundamental tension between liberty and security. Although they are both virtues, we treat them more like a difficult choice between the Scylla of freedom and the Charybdis of safety.

This latent fear and confusion has made many Christians reluctant to share the good news of Jesus. We seek to be inoffensive, and with the clash of Islamic and Western civilizations we are increasingly loath to speak about matters of faith and religion in the public sphere. We have seen this more recently with discussions about the number of migrants who are coming to Europe and North America after fleeing the violence of Syria and Iraq. There is a sense that our society wants to be welcoming and compassionate, thereby upholding the values of pluralism, but

---

[115] Percy, *Good News People*, 64.

underneath there is a suspicion of the exiles and a concern that their religious views will undermine our society from within. In a sense, we fear the coercion to which Ahdar and Leigh alluded. We are also now in a "post-secular" world, and, unlike twenty years ago, the challenge to Christians comes not only from secular or even scientific rationalism but also from competing religious worldviews that are spiritually derived and challenge the absoluteness of the Christian narrative.[116]

A second event, and applicable only in Canada, is the tragedy of First Nations residential schools. In the final report of the Truth and Reconciliation Commission (TRC), released in 2015, the authors concluded that the church had been instrumental in creating the abhorrent conditions that led to "cultural genocide." The TRC was critical of the way young First Nations children were taken from their parental homes on the reserves and forced to live in residential schools. In institutions that were often run jointly by the government and churches, children were forced to renounce their native spiritual practices and adopt Christian views. In a derogatory way, the TRC called this process "Christianizing." The pejorative language of the report implies that Christian acts of supposed kindness and charity actually became sources of oppression by removing people's basic freedoms. In the view of the authors, this is a classic case of religious freedom being jettisoned in favour of Christian enculturation.

These two examples characterize the challenge to evangelistic freedom today because Christians, even subconsciously, are conditioned by them. Harold rightly suggests that Christians should go into the "marketplace of ideas, proclaiming the Good News about Jesus and the resurrection."[117] Precisely how is this to be done today? The answer lies again with Webster's assertion that this is a theological issue. There is a need for the church in the twenty-first century to reclaim its mission by focusing not on the sins of the past but on the presence of the Triune God in the present. Christians must be willing to be different and not adhere to the constraints the world places upon them. Webster puts the challenge clearly before us in his description of evangelical freedom:

---

[116] An analysis of this change can be found in Charles Taylor, *A Secular Age* (Cambridge: Harvard University Press, 2007).
[117] Percy, *Good News People*, 62.

. . . evangelical freedom, for which we have been set free by the gloriously free God, our maker, redeemer and end. Whether such an account of freedom can commend itself to modern culture is not easy to know. Its persuasiveness depends on many factors: on a willingness to stand apart from dominant conventions; on the existence of forms of Christian common life which exemplify the practice of a freedom which is beyond autonomy or heteronomy; but above all on the coming of the Holy Spirit who is the agent of all persuasion in the matter of the gospel. To understand and practice freedom we need to become different people.[118]

Harold expressed a similar point when he claimed that Christians must stand apart simply because we are different.[119] Once we have reclaimed both the distinctive nature of the gospel we espouse and our confidence that it is actually true, can we engage a society that looks upon everything we do with suspicion? In terms of the TRC, it is vital that we take the church's apology seriously and ensure that the abused know that we repent (not just apologize) for past sins. We must also be open for Aboriginal Christians to evangelize non-Aboriginals by explaining how they have acquired and preserved their faith in Jesus. This will be a painful but powerful process, and it will demonstrate the gentleness and genuine humility that Harold advocates.[120] This process will also show that the church trusts completely in the power of the Holy Spirit to heal and restore brokenness.

How, and through whom, does the church present the gospel to the marketplace? This question is particularly poignant in the light of declining church attendance. What is the point of a vital church life, of programming and preaching, if no one is willing to participate? Should churches close their doors and take the gospel to the street?

I had a very interesting experience while on sabbatical in Oxford in 2016. On a Sunday morning, I attended three Christian events within the span of four hours. I began my worshipping sojourn in an historic Church of England parish for a sung Eucharist. It was serene and included a

---

[118] Webster, *Confessing God*, 226.
[119] Percy, *Good News People*, 26.
[120] Percy, *Good News People*, 65.

biblical sermon encouraging people to be disciples. There was a mixture of ages, but the congregation was predominantly older.

From there I went to the Hillsong church that meets in the Odeon movie theatre. The music was loud, the message was live-streamed from London, and the room was filled with young people from every ethnic group. It was vibrant, dynamic, and contemporary.

As I walked outside onto Cornmarket Street, there was a throng of shoppers. In their midst stood a young man on a box. He was proclaiming the gospel, inviting people to renounce their sins and turn to Jesus. Their eternal destiny was at stake. Afterwards, I spoke with him about his mission and the rejection he faces (most of the time) but also about people who were moved by his words (and the Holy Spirit!) to embrace the gospel.

The fascinating part of all three expressions of faith is how diverse their forms of evangelism were. They were all intentionally evangelistic in that they found their freedom in Jesus. Yet the manner in which they addressed the gospel, the outward form through which it was delivered, and the audiences they reached differed greatly. Harold would, I think, like them all, although the third approach did not represent evangelism via the congregation.

Despite the cultural changes of the past twenty years, I am completely in agreement with Harold that the congregation and its members are still the primary instruments of evangelism. Clearly, the church cannot rely on professional clergy to do their evangelizing for them. It requires the whole body working together in its many parts (as Paul insists in 1 Corinthians 12) to achieve this goal.

2. The Zeitgeist

Harold deals very sensibly with the contentious issue of precisely how Christians should share the gospel, espousing timeless principles that are particularly appropriate in the postmodern context and beyond. For example, he believes that the ability to listen is an integral part of the process of evangelization: "Generally, our efforts to influence others towards choosing Jesus and the life of God's kingdom will only be as effective as our willingness to listen to their story."[121] Clearly his

---

[121] Percy, *Good News People*, 121.

conception of evangelism is dialogical, whereas the propensity for many evangelicals is to deliver a monologue and in so doing treat the "other" as a passive object rather than an engaged subject. Listening is central, for instance, to the approach advocated by Jeff Clark:

> Active listening means what it implies. Rather than giving space for someone else to speak only so we can have time to formulate our response, active listening actually listens to the other. We don't position ourselves in order to unleash a counter-attack. No, we listen to others, reflecting on their words, asking questions when clarity is required, while seeking for the good, rather than the bad, in what they have to say.[122]

The challenge, however, is that while the Christian might listen, the response they hear may be hostile or derogatory in nature. For that reason, the evangelist needs to be both an apologist and a courageous disciple.

For example, in a seminar I attended recently in the UK, a sincere young Christian was talking about the peace that comes from knowing Jesus. No sooner had he begun than the conversation was abruptly interrupted and turned into a discussion of how religion is the source of most of the world's conflicts and therefore should be refused access to the public square. Some participants argued that because the followers of Jesus have created a religion, they are *ipso facto* a source of violence and must be looked upon with suspicion. I pointed out that if that is the rationale to remove religion from the public sphere, why do we bother singing national anthems? Surely historical evidence suggests that as many (if not more) wars are fought over national boundaries and secular views of the state than wars over anything else (the French Revolution, for example), so we should immediately refrain from singing "God Save the Queen" or "*Les Marseillaise*"! In spite of my intervention to assist the Christian student, the invective against religion continued. Evidently, the deconstruction of the Christian narrative in our society has led to something less than rational discourse. It is tinged with venom. Christianity, in particular, is being turned into a scapegoat on which to blame the violence, avarice,

---

[122] Jeff Clark, "Letting Go of the Defend and Conquer Mentality," *Christian Week*, January 24, 2016, https://www.christianweek.org/letting-go-defend-conquer-mentality/.

and sins of the world. The only way back for the young evangelist in this seminar was to talk once again about the person of Jesus.

The key, therefore, for helping Christians today to engage the "other" with the gospel is not only to revitalize our apologetics, as helpful as that is, but also to develop our catechetics so that Christians are prepared for the challenges of our time. Herein lies the great challenge for the church. Despite Harold's pleading that Christians need to know their faith,[123] we are easily intimidated by the rejection of the world. That is why in the light of Harold's views, I have always stressed the need for congregations to be places of learning. Borrowing from his model, the churches where I have served have developed introductory courses to Christianity, employing Bethel Bible materials, Alpha programs, Stephen Ministry groups, and regular Bible studies for specific age groups. Even with these, however, I realize they only touch the surface of the challenge. As time progresses and Christendom is broken apart, the church needs to stress the essentials and core of the faith to engage a world full of doubt. This is not easy.

Paradoxically, the difficulty is further compounded today by a contemporary appetite for the mystical and spiritual. Twenty years ago, Harold was correct in assessing the existential challenges of disintegration, loneliness, fear of death, and the fact that people want wholeness, forgiveness, and hope (as he argued in chapter one of *Good News People*). Today, however, rather than looking to formal religious expressions to address these needs, many young people turn to a vague and undefined "spirituality." Influenced by postmodern thinkers, our culture seeks a spirituality that does not require the existence of God and moves away from formal religious traditions. Like a Kafka parable, the only destination on this spiritual journey is, in Frederick Bauerschmidt's terminology, to be "away-from-here."[124] In other words, as long as one's spirituality is not encumbered by the history of a religion or its doctrines, one is free to find solutions to the psychological and existential dilemmas that one faces.

The danger in this exercise is that without a clear conceptual framework, almost any spirituality can be practised or promoted. The

---

[123] Percy, *Good News People*, 84.
[124] Frederick Christina Bauerschmidt, "Michel de Certeau (1925–1986): Introduction," in *The Postmodern God: A Theological Reader*, ed. Graham Ward, Blackwell Readings in Modern Theology (Oxford: Blackwell, 1998), 135.

great challenge for Christians, therefore, is to connect the issues of our day with the person of Jesus. Harold describes eloquently how the gospel intersects with spiritual needs, but his analysis is overly optimistic when it comes to communicating this reality amidst the priorities and spiritualities of the current zeitgeist.

One final obstacle that has clearly developed in the past twenty years is the "hybridization" of religious culture. We find this hybridization in the transient nature of the global community. For example, I am now finding that most of the weddings we perform for our urban congregation involve the union of two people from very different cultural, linguistic, and even religious traditions. In seeking to be relevant, the worship service is sometimes adapted to include some of the religious traditions represented by the different families and their respective cultural backgrounds. This is clearly a response to the pluralism of society.

It is, however, in the less formal experiences of people where hybridization comes to the fore. Many young Christians are torn between "belonging" and "believing." Some want a sense of belonging to a faith community because they feel a connection with God, family, or tradition. Even though they keep these connections, it is unclear as to precisely what they believe. They may adopt views on reincarnation or the after-life from Buddhism while maintaining a general appreciation of the social teaching of Jesus, but they see no evident contradiction between these two perspectives. They adopt ideas from the smorgasbord of religious views but still feel that they belong within their own tradition. Conversely, some people believe but do not belong. For practical reasons or because of feeling a sense of alienation from the church of their upbringing, they believe in Jesus and even identify with him publicly but feel no need to belong to a fellowship formed by his words.

In both of these polarities the process of hybridization takes place, and it is a great challenge to connect with this group and encourage them both to believe and to belong. For Harold's model of evangelism to work, hybridization needs to be transformed into a collective commitment. The interplay between believing and belonging is essential to create a community that can bear witness in word and deed to the lordship of Jesus. Some scholars are suggesting that this should lead to the adoption of a "liquid" church model, which Peter Ward describes as follows:

Liquid Church is characterized by an embracing of mediation. Through representation and discourse new ecclesial identities and relations are brought into being. These relationships can be described as networks of communication. What distinguishes these networks is that they are fluid.[125]

Ward sees a "liquid church" approach developing in Fresh Expressions in the UK and the emerging church movement in the US.[126] The challenge to these "liquid" forms is that they maintain their incarnational base in a God-centred community.

RECLAIMING CONFIDENCE AND JOY

How, then, should we reclaim the confidence and joy that Harold demonstrates in his work? I have visited a number of congregations who followed his guidance and have witnessed the positive influence his views had in their evangelism programs. It is a testimony to the efficacy of his goals of transformational leadership, the making of disciples, the importance of community, the pastoral care of the laity, and the need for celebratory worship that we are honouring his work in this book. Clearly, we must draw on his legacy and continue developing his ideas, while also recognizing that the world has changed in many ways. The challenge was clearly stated to me in a meeting I had recently with a Dominican friar from Burkina Faso. He told me that the motto of the friars is *Laudare, Benedicere, Praedicare* ("To Praise, To Bless, To Preach"), and it is precisely these things that the church in North America needs to reclaim. What he told me can be summarized thus:

- The church in the Global North needs to re-evangelize itself in order that it can engage the culture with the gospel in a spirit of freshness and peace.
- In Africa, we have had to hold on to our freedom even when persecuted by tyranny.

---

[125] Peter Ward, *Engaging Culture*, Regent's Park College Occasional Papers 1, ed. A. Clarke (Oxford: Regent's Park College, 2013), 47.

[126] The British website is www.freshexpressions.org.uk, and the Canadian one www.freshexpressions.ca.

- We have had to maintain our faith in Christ when surrounded by other powerful faiths such as Islam.
- We have had to show that new life in Christ actually makes a difference in our lives and that from this change, the world is changed. We know we have to be different from the mores of our world.
- We have had to bring Christ himself to people so that believers and non-believers can be embraced by him. This is our form of blessing.
- We have had to let go of our colonial past and rely only on the Holy Spirit for our protection.

He added that these same challenges face the whole of the Christian community.

In many ways, his comments summarize the challenge of evangelism today, and, as Good News people, Harold Percy would want us follow this path in the midst of the exigencies of our time.

HOW EVANGELISM CHANGES WITH CULTURE
JOHN P. BOWEN

THE ENGLISH EVANGELIST LOOKED OUT FROM THE TOP OF THE CLIFF, AND TEARS CAME TO his eyes. He had not been back to that spot since he had preached the gospel there some years before. He told me the story. His Kenyan hosts, knowing his reputation, had brought him there and told him to preach. He had looked down to the dense forest beneath and said, "But there's no one there!" "Do it anyway," they urged him. And, as he preached, one by one people emerged from the forest and stood at the bottom of the cliff, listening intently. At the end, he gave an altar call, and many responded and were baptized. Since that day, a church building had been erected at the top of the cliff, and now the members welcomed their spiritual father with open arms and joyful praise.

Would that approach to evangelism be effective in Western culture? Probably not. But then, there is a distinction to be made between evangelism, which will always be part of the life of a healthy church, and the way in which it is practised, which changes according to culture.

I want to argue that there have been five main forms of evangelism at work in the West in the past fifty years.[127] Each has some biblical basis. Each has helped people come to faith in Christ. But each is in part a reflection

---

[127] The original idea for this chapter came from an article by Tim Stafford ("Go and Plant Churches of All Peoples: Crusades and Personal Witnessing Are No Longer the Cutting Edge of Evangelism," *Christianity Today*, September 27, 2007, http://www.christianitytoday.com/ct/2007/september/36.68.html).

of the culture in which it was shaped and used. And its usefulness may therefore increase or decrease over time as culture changes. Wise church leaders will discern what is best in any given context.

1. CRUSADE EVANGELISM

Fifty years ago, the most popular form of evangelism among churches that cared about evangelism was the "crusade."[128] A number of evangelical churches from across a city would come together and invite a well-known evangelist to come and proclaim the gospel, usually in a large public setting, such as a sports stadium.

There were many such evangelists. Some spoke only for events in their denomination, while others strove for broad ecumenical support. Others had particular emphases in their ministry, such as healing. Some had a local reputation, others national, still others international. The events might run for a weekend or a week or (in at least one case) sixteen weeks.[129] Thousands would attend the events.

The format of a crusade evening was always roughly the same, that of a nonliturgical church service. A choir would sing, someone might give a testimony to the power of the gospel in their lives, there might be a Bible reading, and there would be prayer, often by a local church official. Then came the preaching, with a focus on personal sin and repentance and the redeeming work of Christ. And at the end of the sermon would come the altar call, when those who wished to respond to the call of Christ were invited to come to the front of the auditorium, to meet with a trained "counsellor," who would hear their story, offer advice, and pray with them to help them find their way to Christian faith. The counsellor would also endeavour to get contact information for the responder so that there could be follow-up shortly afterwards.

This kind of evangelism has several things to recommend it.

It uses people's strengths in evangelism. I worked with the Billy Graham Crusade in Toronto in 1978, and I remember one of the team saying, "Dr. Graham doesn't believe in mass evangelism. The only

---

[128] The word is seldom used now because of its culturally offensive overtones. It is often replaced with terms such as "festival" or "celebration."
[129] Billy Graham held an event at Madison Square Garden, New York, from May 15 to September 1, 1957; see further Billy Graham, *Just as I Am: The Autobiography of Billy Graham* (Toronto: HarperCollins, 1996), 367–79.

reason he can do what he does is because every Christian involved in this event has done what they can do, things which Dr. Graham can't do." Christians who brought their friends had lived a Christian life before them for months and maybe years. They had prayed and cared and spoken as they were able. And through such acts of witness they prepared the ground for Billy Graham's preaching of the gospel to bear fruit. The thing Billy Graham was particularly gifted to do was to invite people to make a commitment to Jesus, clearly, firmly, and without manipulation—something most Christians are not gifted to do. So the event as a whole was a powerful expression of the body of Christ at work to do the work of evangelism.

The preaching of the Word also happened in a rich context. The naked Word was dressed in clothing of Christian fellowship and Christian worship. By the time the sermon began, visitors had already had a rich taste of what it is like to be part of the kingdom. The spoken Word in part explained the experience people had had in the meeting to that point and made the message more credible.

However, there was also a downside to crusade evangelism.

The most commonly levelled criticism is that for many who go forward, this is merely a flash in the pan. Many have no clear sense of why they are going forward and seldom understand that they are entering into a lifetime of discipleship. In my first stint as a counsellor in 1978, I "counselled" six people, helped them say a prayer of commitment, and conscientiously took their contact information. In the following few days, I phoned every one of them, often more than once, and was very taken aback that not a single one wanted to talk to me, let alone meet and discuss what they had done.

This is not the whole story, of course. I have also met mature Christian leaders who came to a real and lasting faith through this kind of event. But it is a signal that we should be cautious.

A related criticism is that those who go forward in crusades do not always find their way into a local Christian community where they can grow and thrive. In spite of significant efforts to address this gap, the fact that the event by definition occurs at a special time and place means that forging a link with a local church requires extra effort at a later time. And if you have ever visited a place of worship for the first time—especially as a non-believer or a brand-new believer—you will know how overwhelmingly intimidating it can be. No wonder it did not always happen.

This problem also highlights the fact that the model of evangelism embedded in a crusade is that of the sudden decision. Perhaps in the background is the model of the apostle Paul's conversion—sudden, dramatic, and total (Acts 9:1–9). Yet the majority of new Christians say it took them between six months and five years to come to a clear commitment to Christ, and they did so while already involved with Christians, one way or another. Often they "belonged before they believed."[130] There may have been a crisis event, such as going forward at a crusade, but that was not the be-all and end-all. And, of course, it does not take much research to realize that Paul's conversion also took longer than that single event on the Damascus road. It had been growing for several years.

2. PERSONAL AND FRIENDSHIP EVANGELISM

It is tempting to suggest that the "invention" of personal and friendship evangelism was a reaction against the impersonality of mass evangelism—but that would be wrong. In fact, the two, mass and personal, had coexisted and to some extent reinforced one another for decades. That being said, the emphasis of personal and friendship evangelism, as the term implies, is small-scale—normally one-on-one—rather than large-scale.

The beauty of this approach is again what the name implies: it is personal, tailored to the needs and the questions of the individual—no "one-size-fits-all" here—and it is ideally in the context of ongoing friendship. What better way for good news of a personal relationship with God, a divine friendship with Jesus, to be communicated than by means of a personal relationship between friends? One could even say there is something sacramental about this approach; the friendship has already communicated a taste of the love of God.

How this small-scale evangelism has been practised varies wildly, from approaches that are tightly structured to those that have no structure at all.

At one end of the spectrum is the technique (I use the term deliberately) of one C. S. Lovett. His 1959 book *Soul-Winning Made Easy* recommends the following approach:

---

[130] John Finney, *Finding Faith Today: How Does It Happen?* (London: The Bible Society, 1992), 24–25, 43.

Your prospect has just said, "I don't know what a Christian is—you tell me." That's the moment you've been waiting for. Hold up your right hand so that FOUR FINGERS are showing as you say to him, "If it's all right with you, I'd like to read you four verses of Scripture and explain them to you—then you'll know what a Christian is. That would be okay, wouldn't it?" (Nod your head affirmatively.) The request sounds simple and harmless enough. Surely four verses wouldn't take too long. Your affirmative nod will prompt most people to say, "Go ahead," or, "Sure."

Your hand reaches to your shirt pocket. The movement is so natural your prospect doesn't notice it. You don't take your eyes from his face as you bring forth a copy of BEGINNING TO LIVE [a booklet containing relevant Bible verses]. As you are doing this, say to him . . . "God says that we are ALL sinners, as we see here in His Word . . ."

As he fixes his eyes on the verse, your words will carry more intimacy as they are spoken closer to his ear. Let your finger point to the verse so as to direct his eyes to the right place.[131]

C. S. Lewis observes that "God is, if I may say it, very unscrupulous."[132] Thus it is quite possible that people began a lifetime of joyful discipleship to Jesus by being evangelized in this way. But to most readers, this approach seems manipulative and depersonalizing in the extreme. It may be personal in one sense, but it has nothing to do with friendship!

There are other structured approaches to personal evangelism that are more benign. One of the best known is the four spiritual laws[133] of the organization Power to Change (formerly Campus Crusade for Christ). The four laws, often used in booklet form, summarize key aspects of the Christian message in a few words and can be used as an aid in explaining the message.

As with other structured approaches, of course, there is still the possibility of insensitivity. I have met people who have been deeply hurt

---

[131] C. S. Lovett, *Soul-Winning Made Easy* (Baldwin Park: Personal Christianity, 1959), 53–55.

[132] C. S. Lewis, *Surprised by Joy: The Shape of My Early Life* (London: Geoffrey Bles, 1955; Collins Fontana, 1960), 154.

[133] One explanation of the four laws is at http://www.4laws.com/laws/englishkgp/default.htm.

by an inappropriate use of the booklet. But I have also met people in senior church leadership positions who were brought to faith by *The Four Spiritual Laws*. Often this is because experienced evangelists know how to incorporate the booklet into a more relaxed, more relational approach to evangelism, when to use it and when to refrain from using it. In such cases, it can be very effective.

And then there are those friendships between a Christian and an unbelieving friend where "spiritual conversation" is not at all programmed or structured but is dependent on spontaneous opportunities.[134]

I think of James, a graduate student from Oxford who came to the University of Toronto one fall to do a master's degree. He was curious about Christian faith and through a series of connections ended up talking to me. We met weekly, and I tried to help him with his questions until, three months later, he decided to become a follower of Jesus. I was delighted. The tenor of our conversations then changed. Rather than "If this were true, what would I do?" the theme was "Now I'm following this way, what should I do?" We began reading and discussing the Bible together. To my surprise, the first time we met for Bible study, James brought a Bible. I had no idea he owned one. I pulled it across the table towards me and opened the front cover. There I read, "To James, from Dave." It was dated a few years earlier. "Who's Dave?" I asked.

"Oh, Dave was my best friend in high school," he replied. "He was a Christian, and we had lots of discussions about faith over the years. But he never managed to persuade me. Then, when we graduated, he gave me this."

Our Bible studies continued through the school year. They were lively, intriguing, edgy, and often humorous. As the spring drew on, he said one day, "By the way, I have a friend coming to see me at the end of term. I'd like you to meet her."

"Who's that?" I asked.

"Meredith and I dated through university," he replied. "She was a Christian. Towards the end of our undergraduate years, I asked her if she would marry me. She told me she couldn't marry someone who wasn't a Christian. At the time, I thought, what is this fascist religion

---

[134] The classic statement on friendship evangelism is Pippert's *Out of the Saltshaker and into the World*.

where you can't marry whoever you want?" James smiled ruefully. "Now I understand perfectly."

So one fine May morning, I was introduced to Meredith. And, as I shook her hand, I smiled and said, "Nice to be on the same team as you."

You might think I was the evangelist in this story, and in a sense, I was. But those long-term friendships with Dave and then Meredith had laid deep foundations in James' soul. They hadn't always talked about faith—I'm sure, like most friends, they talked about anything and everything—but Dave and Meredith had not hidden their faith and had borne witness to it as opportunity offered, and in the end, their witness bore fruit in James' life. That's how unstructured friendship evangelism works.

3. CONGREGATIONAL EVANGELISM

What is the best place for evangelism to happen? On a street corner, in a coffee shop, in a home? There is no right answer. And yet there is something appropriate about evangelism happening when the body of Christ gathers for worship. The Spirit of God is present in a special way as the Word of God is preached to a receptive audience. The worship space becomes "a thin place" where God and humankind intersect. An outsider stumbling into that place is likely to encounter the Word of God and the Spirit of God there and come to faith. The apostle Paul anticipates that an outsider entering such a worship service will exclaim, "God is really among you!" (1 Cor 14:25).

This kind of theology underlies congregational evangelism. Churches that have taken this understanding seriously have naturally tried to clear obstacles out of the way in order that this evangelistic encounter can happen. In the United States, Willow Creek Community Church in Chicago (started in 1975 by Bill Hybels) and Saddleback Community Church in California (started in 1980 by Rick Warren) came to prominence as large churches where this kind of evangelism was taking place. Terms such as "user-friendly," "seeker-friendly," and "seeker-sensitive" came into everyday discussions of church and evangelism. In Canada, Trinity Streetsville under Harold Percy's leadership was a model of how this kind of evangelism may be done and how God honours such evangelistic efforts.

The strengths of this form of evangelism are many and substantial. For one thing, congregational evangelism is an impossibility without a relatively healthy congregation. Crusade evangelism and personal evangelism could operate without healthy churches—though it would be a significant weakness in the background for both. With congregational evangelism, however, it has to be acknowledged from the get-go that only a church with a healthy spiritual life could be effective in this ministry. Throughout this book, you have been reading about different ways in which Trinity grew to be healthy: robust preaching, lively worship, significant participation by many members, prayerfulness, a warm welcoming program, and so on. The simplest definition I ever heard of evangelism was that it is "overflow." That is how congregational evangelism works: it is the overflow of a congregation's spiritual life to those who are thirsty for it.

If crusade evangelism depends for its effectiveness on the dynamic preaching of a single individual, congregational evangelism depends far less on any one single factor and almost entirely on a number of smaller factors—including preaching, naturally. If crusade evangelism depends on the power of a single special occasion, congregational evangelism relies on the power of every Sunday morning. Evangelism is no longer one week in the year but continuous, week by week. It is no longer an optional extra added on to the schedule of an already-busy congregation; it reflects the DNA of normal church life. And it is no longer dependent on the visiting "expert." These are healthy things.

Congregational evangelism has not been without its critics, however. The most basic objection is that traditionally evangelism has not been the purpose of Sunday worship. Worship is worship, and evangelism is evangelism, and, if the latter takes over the former, the former will suffer. Critics point out how, in order to be "sensitive" to guests, "difficult" parts of the liturgy are simply dropped—the creed and the confession of sin, for example. In traditions where the minister typically wears liturgical robes, these are often set aside in favour of a suit and tie or something less formal. Regular readings from the lectionary are rejected in favour of sermon series that speak to people's "real-life problems." Some seeker churches do not offer Communion during Sunday services.[135] While this may make the worship more accessible to new folk, it is the regular churchgoers who will not be nurtured and fed. Willow Creek, acknowledging this problem early

---

[135] Trinity Streetsville always did.

on, moved its main service for feeding existing believers to a Wednesday evening.

Having said that, I have known many mature Christians from Trinity Streetsville over the years, some of whom who have contributed to this book. They do not appear to have suffered from the evangelistic emphasis of Trinity. Indeed, it seems to have whetted their appetite for spiritual growth and service—more than some Christians from churches where the traditions have been honoured to the letter. Being involved in evangelism is itself a catalyst to one's own spiritual growth.

At Trinity, however, the weight of evangelism did not fall entirely on Sunday mornings. Harold also introduced the following.

4. TEACHING EVANGELISM

I first heard the phrase "teaching evangelism" in the 1970s and was immediately struck by its cultural aptness. The term refers to evangelism that is more than a single sermon followed by an appeal for an immediate decision, which was often the crusade model. It is evangelism that seeks to convey information before there is any talk of a decision. I cannot be asked to commit my life to Jesus before I have a clear sense of who Jesus is—and many people in our culture do not. This approach is therefore all the more important in a world where people know little about Jesus or the Bible and certainly could not tell you what the "good news" of Christianity is meant to be. This is the equivalent of catechism in the early centuries of the church when there was no general cultural memory of the content of Christian faith, and so enquirers were instructed for up to a year before they were allowed to be baptized. We assume that after a year of instruction they knew what they were getting into!

Catechism, however, where it exists at all, has for many years become little more than a form of instruction for teenagers who have grown up in the church and are considered ready to take on their faith as adults. They therefore need a more mature understanding than they had as children, and catechism is intended to supply this lack. It is not designed for unchurched people with no Christian background to speak of.

Many evangelical churches have over the years created their own courses to introduce genuine newcomers to the faith, even if those courses were simply described as membership classes. But the idea of an evangelistic teaching course came to the world's attention in 1990 through the birth of the Alpha course. It is worth noting, however, that the course had been pioneered at Holy Trinity, Brompton, for some years before it went viral. The idea did not appear out of the blue. It was just a natural function of an evangelical church trying to provide instruction to converts and potential converts.

As Alpha has spread all over the world, so, too, have imitators arisen. *Christianity Explored*, out of All Souls, Langham Place, in London, features more Bible exposition and is not as explicitly charismatic as Alpha. The *Emmaus* course expresses a more Anglo-Catholic theology. And *Living the Questions*, featuring Bishop John Spong, incorporated a more liberal theology.[136]

At Trinity, Harold created his own course, entitled Christianity 101,[137] which ran for four weeks two or three times a year as there was interest. There was a simple but crucial connection between Sunday worship and Christianity 101. At some point in the service, Harold would say, "If you are new to church and trying to figure out what you believe, there is a four-part course beginning this coming Wednesday that is just for you." He would often add, "And if you have been in church all your life and feel you could use a refresher course in the basics of Christianity, then you would be welcome too." The beauty of this rider was that it enabled long-term members who were secretly uncertain of their faith to attend with dignity. It was not that, after all those years, they were still beginners; rather, it was just an opportunity for a refresher course. Harold told me,

> I would often also ask, "How many of you here have already participated in the Christianity 101 course?" Hands would go up all over the place, and I think that might have made it easier for

---

[136] *Emmaus* is available at www.chpublishing.co.uk/uploads/documents/0715149946.pdf and *Living the Questions* at www.livingthequestions.com. Other courses include *Start*, from the Church Pastoral-Aid Society in the UK (www.cpas.org.uk); *Via Media*, which, as the name implies, is designed to appeal to more middle-of-the-road Anglicans in the US (http://www.everyvoice.net); and *Introducing God*, from Australia (www.introducinggod.org).

[137] Harold and I wrote a booklet on how to create and teach such a course: Harold Percy and John Bowen, *Just the Basics: Teaching the Faith to Beginners*, Wycliffe Booklets on Evangelism 2 (Richmond: Digory, 2004). It is available for free download at http://institute.wycliffecollege.ca/2004/10/just-the-basics-teaching-the-faith-to-beginners.

some to make the decision to attend who might otherwise have been a bit reluctant to do so.[138]

For those who decided to become disciples of Jesus through Christianity 101, there were then opportunities to be baptized or (if they had been baptized as babies) either to be confirmed in the main service or simply to renew their baptismal vows.

The advantages of this approach to evangelism are many. Ideally, it does not assume any prior knowledge of Christian faith or of the Bible; it can start from the beginning. Teaching the faith over a number of weeks is also good for the church and for the inquirer. It is good for the church because it is a chance to show the breadth and depth of the gospel and how it forms a coherent whole. It also demonstrates Christian respect for the mind; we want a new Christian to know from the beginning that loving God with their mind is part of the package. Teaching evangelism is good for the inquirer because it respects the fact that evangelism is a process, and it gives them an opportunity to weigh what is being said and to ask their questions without any pressure to make a hasty decision.

Many such courses include a meal and encourage people to sit at the same table, eat, and discuss the talks with the same people each week. This facilitates the growth of community. I do not know who first coined the phrase "belonging before believing,"[139] but it captures an important reality. Most people do not figure out what they believe in private and then search out a community that believes similarly. Rather, we work out what we believe in relationship with others. Evangelistic courses that offer teaching in the context of community (and food!) are creating a healthy loam in which the seed of the gospel can take root and grow.

This kind of teaching the gospel has few flaws in principle. One that occurs occasionally in practice is that people who come to faith through such a course are then expected to graduate into "real" church—but struggle to do so. In the case of Trinity, the culture of Christianity 101 and that of Sunday worship were integral parts of a seamless whole, and many who went to Christianity 101 were already attending on Sunday mornings anyway, so there was no problem. But there are sometimes

---

[138] Personal email, August 5, 2017.
[139] The earliest source, to my knowledge, is John Finney.

instances where the church is (to put it bluntly) lifeless and discouraging compared with the vitality and joy of the evangelistic group, and new Christians fail to make a connection. I did hear of one English bishop who, faced with this problem in a group who had done Alpha, decided to assign a priest to the Alpha group and so acknowledge that this was now a new church.

5. CHURCH PLANTING AND FRESH EXPRESSIONS OF CHURCH

I remember hearing some years ago that the Church of England was planting one new church every two weeks. I was incredulous. Then a report emerged that revealed that the report was greatly exaggerated: the true number was closer to one new church every three weeks![140] This was early in what is now known as the "Fresh Expressions" movement. Of course, not all of those "churches" were full-fledged, recognizable churches with traditional denominational characteristics. Many were embryonic or experimental. Not all survived. But it was an indication that something new was happening. At one point, over seven hundred of these fresh expressions of church were detailed on the Fresh Expressions website.

There is a clear connection between church planting and evangelism. George Hunter of Asbury Seminary summarizes it thus: "Churches after fifteen years typically plateau. After thirty-five years, they typically can't even replace those [members] they lose. New congregations reach a lot more pre-Christian people."[141] Tim Stafford documents this tendency by pointing out that Southern Baptists, who for years majored on crusades as the most effective form of evangelism, are now putting more effort into church planting, with the result that "established Southern Baptist Churches report 3.4 baptisms per 100 resident members, whereas new churches average 11.7," adding, "It's not hard to conclude that more new churches would lead more people to Christ."[142]

Why is there this connection? Apart from anything else, as Hunter points out, older churches tend to become more introverted. The popular

---

[140] "We already know of 177 church plants which have come about since statistics began to be collected in 1985" (Church of England, *Breaking New Ground: Church Planting in the Church of England* [London: Church House, 1994], 1).
[141] Stafford, "Go and Plant Churches."
[142] Stafford, "Go and Plant Churches."

definition of sin as "humankind turned in on itself" (variously attributed to Augustine or Luther) applies to churches as much as to individuals. They develop their own way of doing things—their own culture—and it is difficult for new people to fit in. By the same token, those churches may not represent the culture of the communities around them. For historical reasons, they may be (for example) a commuter congregation of older white people whereas their building is in an area of mixed race young families—a common enough scenario.

Lesslie Newbigin foresaw this problem decades ago and suggested a solution:

> There may be elements in the local reality which are so alien to the present membership of the local church—by reason of language, race, culture, occupation or other factors—that the existing church is incapable of functioning as sign, instrument and first-fruit of God's purpose to embrace *that* element in the local reality in his new creation. It is not enough in this situation for the Church to say "Come—all are welcome." A few may accept the invitation, but only to become assimilated to the language, culture, style of the already existing congregation. This is not to take seriously the full reality of the "place." . . . The existing congregation must be willing also to *go* outside the walls of the Church in order to become part of that other reality—in language, culture, style of life. Only so does there appear in the midst of *that* reality the sign and first-fruit of God's all-embracing purpose.
>
> At this point we begin to tread on very controversial ground. What do we expect as the result of this going, of this mission? We ought to expect that there is brought to birth within that "place," outside the walls of the Church as it now is, a community which is the first-fruit of the Gospel in that place. It should have its own proper character as distinct from that of the community from which the mission came.[143]

---

[143] Lesslie Newbigin, "'What is "a Local Church Truly United"?,' 1976," in *The Ecumenical Movement: An Anthology of Key Texts and Voices*, eds. Michael Kinnamon and Brian E. Cope (Grand Rapids: Eerdmans, 1996), 118.

What is that new community? A new church. It is interesting that he considered the idea "controversial" back in 1961; now it seems like a no-brainer. If the local church cannot connect with its neighbourhood, then let's start a daughter church that can.

This, of course, is how the early church grew. More than twenty churches are mentioned as having been founded in the book of Acts alone. One friend says, "Churches are like people: every day some die and others are born." To many Christians, this is an alien thought, but both things are true. Philip Jenkins' book *The Lost History of Christianity*[144] describes how whole historic denominations died out in the Middle East after centuries of thriving. On the other side of the coin, I remember a Kenyan bishop telling me that he had temporarily ordered his evangelists to stop planting churches because they were doing so too fast for the new communities to become stable and grow to maturity.

Church planting enables the church to go into places and cultures where there is no gospel witness. New churches have been planted among narrow interest groups that traditionally have no connection to church—Goths, skateboarders, taxi drivers, and sports networks, for a start. It is the principle of the Incarnation that the gospel takes on the flesh and blood of a neighbourhood, a community, a culture. This is what cross-cultural missionaries have always done, planting churches that are expressions of local culture. Only now it is happening in the West and not just in far-off mission fields.

Is there a downside to church planting? Again, the concerns are more pragmatic than principial. For example, not all church plants survive. And when they die, there is always hurt and disillusionment. One friend whose church plant failed said that was when he began to be an agnostic. This is a real concern.

There is also this important question: if the church is really inclusive of all peoples, when do the Goths get to worship and fellowship with the skateboarders and the taxi drivers? What happens to the biblical vision of a richly diverse cross-cultural church? It is not dodging the issue to say that this is an issue for more traditional churches too: after all, when do the staid English Anglicans get to worship and fellowship with the

---

[144] Philip Jenkins, *The Lost History of Christianity: The Thousand-Year Golden Age of the Church in the Middle East, Africa, and Asia—and How It Died* (San Francisco: HarperOne, 2008).

Pentecostals down the road? Such examples could be readily multiplied. These are questions that need to be in the back of our minds always, even though the answers will not come quickly or easily. But they are not sufficient to warrant a moratorium on church planting.

WHAT'S NEXT?

This kind of review inevitably invites the question "So what's coming next?" Yet the job of the historian is always easier than that of the prophet.

My guess is that crusade evangelism is never going to make a comeback in contemporary Canada. Apart from anything else, it goes against what I see as the very healthy trend in church life in recent years that small is beautiful and local is beautiful.[145] Large, impersonal events in a public venue are not culturally attractive to this generation. They are too redolent of a Christendom we prefer to leave behind.

What of friendship and personal evangelism? It seems to me that as long as Christians have friends who are not churchgoers—and that cannot be taken for granted, sadly—there will be, as in all friendships, a sharing of the most important things in life. And as a result, friends will ask questions of each other, and some non-Christians will come to share the faith of their Christian friends.

My question about the future of congregational evangelism is whether there are Christian leaders willing to pay the price to do what Harold did at Trinity. In the years since Harold began to draw national attention through what was happening at Trinity, I cannot think of many churches, certainly in the Anglican world, that have followed his example, in spite of books, seminars, and coaching to that end. In any case, as I suggested previously, I believe that congregational evangelism is most effective among the dechurched—those who have some church exposure in their background—and their number is decreasing by the year.

Teaching evangelism will, I believe, always have a place among the church's most effective evangelistic resources. Yet it will likely happen more often away from an actual church building, which is not a comfortable venue for most non-church folk. I think of a Baptist church in Toronto that offers Alpha in the "upper room" of a local pub called the Yellow

---

[145] See, for example, Paul Sparks, Tim Soerens, and Dwight Friesen, *The New Parish: How Neighborhood Churches Are Transforming Mission, Discipleship and Community* (Downers Grove: InterVarsity, 2014).

Griffin. People pay a hundred dollars for the course—not for Alpha materials, which are always free, but for a weekly burger and beer. Do people come to faith that way? Yes, they do, and then they make their way to the sponsoring church—and to baptism and incorporation into the body of Christ.

As for church planting, I believe we are only just beginning to see how effective this will be in evangelism. How far it will be accompanied by evangelism depends, I believe, in large part on whether the church plant adopts a top-down approach or a grassroots-up methodology. In the former, a group buys or rents a building, starts Sunday services, and invites the neighbours to attend. That is the heart of the top-down church plant. This worked in the 1950s, when newcomers to Canada were looking for friends and community.[146] It can still work among immigrant communities. It may also be effective among the diminishing numbers of the unchurched.

The grassroots approach, on the other hand, does not start with Sunday worship. It begins with Christians moving into the neighbourhood, building relationships, meeting needs, talking about Jesus when appropriate, and waiting to see what grows. It may take a year before the time seems right for Sunday worship. But when it does, it will represent the new community that has come into existence, and evangelism will already have been happening organically. Cam Roxburgh summarizes the distinction between the two methodologies: "It depends whether you are planting a church or a Sunday morning worship service."[147] The former is more likely to be fruitful in evangelism than the latter, though it will take longer.

So will there be anything new in evangelism in the coming years? I believe that the current missional shift, inspired by Lesslie Newbigin and others—the rediscovery of the truth that a central purpose of the church is to engage in God's mission to renew all things through Christ—will continue to change everything. Paradigm shifts are like that: their implications take time to penetrate and transform different parts of the old way of thinking and being. The dominoes fall slowly.

---

[146] For the story of one such church plant, see Reginald Stackhouse, "Church Planting in the 1950s: A Historical Perspective," in John Bowen, ed., *Green Shoots out of Dry Ground: Growing a New Future for the Church in Canada* (Eugene: Wipf and Stock, 2013), 35–41.
[147] Personal conversation, September 2016.

This suggests to me that evangelism will be less and less a thing in its own right and more and more one natural overflow of the church's involvement in mission. Sociologist Rodney Stark describes this kind of integration of mission and evangelism in the early centuries of the church's life.[148]

For one thing, he observes the early Christians' commitment to caring. In times of plague, for example, many people would flee the cities, abandoning even friends and relatives in order to save their own lives. The Christians, however, buoyed by their belief in the resurrection and the certainty of an after-life, did not experience the same panic and were willing to stay and care for the sick—not only their own but also others who had been abandoned by their families and friends. Even if they possessed few medical resources, the very fact that they cared in practical ways such as offering food and drink meant that more sufferers survived. You can see how this kind of activity would enhance the reputation of the church and cause people to be attracted to this faith, where there was a different and life-giving way of doing things. Imagine the conversation: "Why are you doing this?"

"Because Jesus commanded us to do so."

"Aren't you afraid?"

"Jesus has defeated death, so everything is different."

"Tell me more!"

A more contemporary story of how mission leads naturally to evangelism comes from Cam Roxburgh, director of Forge Canada and himself a church planter:

> Randy . . . thought he would never darken the doors of a church building. A number of his friends were involved in a mission group from our church who were helping a lower income apartment complex to do life a little differently. They painted, gardened, and worked hard at sprucing up the place. They brought food into the complex and held a banquet for the people, many of whom could never afford to go out for a nice meal. They found many ways to make a difference. Randy noticed—and he participated. He had a

---

[148] Rodney Stark, *The Rise of Christianity: How the Obscure, Marginal Jesus Movement Became the Dominant Religious Force in the Western World in a Few Centuries* (San Francisco: HarperCollins, 1996), 73–94.

huge heart and wanted to make a difference, so he began to join in with his friends who were doing these good deeds.

Before long, Randy was not only helping serve this apartment complex, but was socially involved with the entire group. He began to participate in other events when the group would get together to do life well. He began to notice that some of his behaviours and patterns began to change and be shaped by the life of the group as well. It took a while longer, but eventually this belonging to the group, and then behaving like the group led to him being introduced to Jesus, and making a decision to follow him.[149]

I earlier used the phrase "belonging before believing." Randy took a step further and began "behaving before believing." C. S. Lewis warned that this could happen: "You must not do, you must not even try to do, the will of the Father unless you are prepared to 'know of the doctrine.'"[150] Randy was, without realizing it, learning to do "the will of the Father" and, as a result, stumbled into knowing "the doctrine." When people of no Christian faith get involved with Christians who are actively serving God and serving people, evangelism will not be far behind.

If the church is recovering its sense of mission, as seems to be the case, then I do not fear for the future of evangelism. Evangelism always thrives best as the offspring of mission. The church that lives out its faith in public will always be in the position of needing to "be ready to speak up and tell anyone who asks why you're living the way you are, and always with the utmost courtesy" (1 Pet 3:15–18, MSG). And people will be drawn to the Christ who inspires and directs this mission.

---

[149] Cam Roxburgh, "The Invitation to Follow Christ: A New Approach," *good idea!* (March 9, 2015), http://institute.wycliffecollege.ca/2015/03/the-invitation-to-follow-christ-a-fresh-approach/.

[150] Lewis, *Surprised by Joy*, 180–81. Lewis is referring to his own experience, that trying to "behave" like his Christian friends catalyzed his growing into belief. There is nothing new under the sun.

ENGAGING OUR COMMUNITIES IN THE POWER OF GOD'S SPIRIT
DEBBIE JOHNSON

"God's mission has a church," not "God's church has a mission."
—Harold Percy

IN 2005 TO 2006, THE CONGREGATION OF NORTH BRAMALEA UNITED CHURCH (NBUC) FOUND itself engaged and inspired by a new vision: "Imagine God building . . . better lives, better families, a better Brampton . . . WE DO!" We imagined what God can do in an individual's life and how that changes a family and can transform a city. Right from the beginning, we heard this vision as a call to expand the ministry we had been given (which included obtaining a larger building and additional staff) so that we could serve our neighbourhood and the city of Brampton more faithfully and effectively. In 2016, again after much prayer and discernment, we added the words "and beyond" to the vision statement, so that it then read, "Imagine God building . . . better lives, better families, a better Brampton and beyond . . . WE DO!" This addition reflected our more deliberate engagement in mission to the wider world.

ENGAGING OUR COMMUNITIES: WHO?

Sometimes people ask how we get our congregants to be so involved and engaged in the life of the local community. Although involvement certainly requires strategies and programs, they are not at the heart of our engagement. Rather, engagement involves vision. We believe that we exist as a church "to enable everyday people to grow in The Way of Jesus and to follow the living God out into the community." As a mark of what it means to be a follower of Jesus, we encourage serving both within and beyond our faith community, inspired by Jesus' statement that he "came not to be served but to serve" (Mark 10:45). In fact, it is safe to say that serving is part of our congregational DNA.

How did we get started? In 1983, what was then the Dufferin-Peel Presbytery of the Toronto Conference of the United Church of Canada called Rev. Norm Greene to assist with the closing of Harrison United Church so as to enable the birth of North Bramalea United. That decision by the presbytery and congregation reflected the core of the gospel, which reveals that through the life, death, and resurrection of Jesus death does not have the last word—God's last word is new, resurrection life. The rural community that had once been Harrison's neighbourhood was now giving way to urban development. The fields around North Bramalea were being transformed into suburban neighbourhoods, and, as the first NBUC vision stated, we were being called there to "enable spiritually hungry people to share the life of Christ."

Stories of our first years of worship in Chinguacousy Secondary School continue to shape our community today. At the beginning, Rev. Greene knocked on doors in order to introduce himself and the church to new neighbours. He often dropped by after Sunday service to thank newcomers for being part of the worshipping community and to ask how the church could be of service. His persistence in making personal contact attracted people of all ages to become part of what God was doing in their neighbourhood, and as neighbours invited other neighbours and friends, the church grew.

In *The Message*, John 1:14 states, "The Word became flesh and blood, and moved into the neighbourhood." This verse is foundational to our understanding of what it means to engage with our community and the wider world. We believe that Jesus is still moving into the neighbourhood as hearts and minds are transformed by the experience of the power and presence of his Spirit, filling us with his love and compassion. As people both within and beyond the walls of our church building commit (or commit anew) to following Jesus, we discover the power of Christ's Spirit alive and at work in us today, reflecting the truth of Ephesians 3:20 that "the power at work within us is able to accomplish abundantly far more than all we can ask or imagine."

ENGAGING OUR COMMUNITIES: HOW AND WHY?

Why do faith communities need to be committed to helping followers of Jesus live out their faith in the world? Is it too simple to say it is because that is how Jesus showed us we should live? Jesus was shaped by his own faith tradition and was ready to engage in challenging dialogue with the religious leaders of his day, but he did not spend all his time within the walls of the temple or synagogue. He went to where people lived, gathered, worked, and played, extending loving-kindness to others as an expression of God's love. He shared his vision of how God intended the world to be. In the Gospel of Mark, Jesus sent out his twelve disciples with the words "Don't think you need a lot of extra equipment for this. *You* are the equipment" (Mark 6:8–9, MSG). He still invites us, if we are willing, to be part of God's healing and restoration of the world, brought about through the power of Christ's Spirit alive in those who choose to follow him.

Too often, faith communities turn inward, limiting Christ's mission solely to the care of their own members or to the maintenance of their church buildings. Yet Jesus has invited us to much more. A number of years ago, in Atlanta, I had an opportunity to visit the church where Rev. Dr. Martin Luther King Jr. had been the pastor. Across the street from the original building is the new Ebenezer Baptist Church. Clear windows run the length of both sides of the sanctuary. We were told that when the new church was being constructed, there was a great desire to have beautiful stained glass windows on either side of the sanctuary, and there was great disappointment when funds for the project could not be raised. But sorrow turned to joy once the building was completed and the people of that church realized that stained glass windows, as beautiful as they would have been, would have been out of place. Since Ebenezer Baptist Church is located in one of the poorest districts of Atlanta, stained glass windows would have visibly separated the congregation from the surrounding neighbourhood. Perhaps the windows would have even kept the church community insulated from the neighbourhood around them.

But with clear glass, they could not help but look out and see the world that Christ still calls them to serve.

Going into the world, sharing Christ, and living out our faith in both word and deed have been foundational to Harold Percy's understanding of the mission in which the gospel of Jesus Christ invites us to participate today. On more than one occasion, I have heard Harold say, "'God's mission has a church,' not 'God's church has a mission.'"

It helps to ask, "What would happen to our neighbourhood if our church community wasn't there?" If the answer is that it would make no difference—or worse, that the community would be better off—then it is safe to say that we have lost sight of what it means to be the church. Of course, we can sometimes feel overwhelmed by the enormous need and the endless opportunities to serve. At such times, it helps to remember a saying often attributed to Mother Teresa: "We can do no great things, only small things with great love."[151]

ENGAGING OUR COMMUNITIES: WHERE TO BEGIN?

The best place to start is always with prayer and Scripture study. Gather some folks together in your church community for a conversation about the vision and mission to which you believe Christ has called you and about how you are living out that mission. Here I would offer two passages in particular for prayer and reflection. The first is Jesus' statement at the beginning of his ministry, as he stands before the hometown crowd in Nazareth reading from the scroll of the prophet Isaiah:

> "The Spirit of the Lord is upon me,
>   because he has anointed me
>   to bring good news to the poor.
> He has sent me to proclaim release to the captives
>   and recovery of sight to the blind,
>   to let the oppressed go free,
> to proclaim the year of the Lord's favor." (Luke 4:18–19)

---

[151] See, for instance, Mother Teresa, *Everything Starts from Prayer: Mother Teresa's Meditations on Spiritual Life for People of All Faiths*, ed. Anthony Stern, 2nd ed. (Ashland: White Cloud, 2009), 33.

Of course, this does not mean that we ourselves can equal all that Jesus himself accomplished. Yet the Spirit of the Lord is on us as we follow him, enabling us to minister in his name with compassion and power.

The second passage for prayer and reflection comes from the end of Jesus' life on earth, as he describes what the kingdom of God looks like:

> "Then the king will say to those at his right hand, 'Come, you that are blessed by my Father, inherit the kingdom prepared for you from the foundation of the world; for I was hungry and you gave me food, I was thirsty and you gave me something to drink, I was a stranger and you welcomed me, I was naked and you gave me clothing, I was sick and you took care of me, I was in prison and you visited me.' Then the righteous will answer him, 'Lord, when was it that we saw you hungry and gave you food, or thirsty and gave you something to drink? And when was it that we saw you a stranger and welcomed you, or naked and gave you clothing? And when was it that we saw you sick or in prison and visited you?' And the king will answer them, 'Truly I tell you, just as you did it to one of the least of these who are members of my family, you did it to me.' Then he will say to those at his left hand, 'You that are accursed, depart from me into the eternal fire prepared for the devil and his angels; for I was hungry and you gave me no food, I was thirsty and you gave me nothing to drink, I was a stranger and you did not welcome me, naked and you did not give me clothing, sick and in prison and you did not visit me.' Then they also will answer, 'Lord, when was it that we saw you hungry or thirsty or a stranger or naked or sick or in prison, and did not take care of you?' Then he will answer them, 'Truly I tell you, just as you did not do it to one of the least of these, you did not do it to me.'" (Matt 25:34-45)

As Mother Teresa would tell us, those around us who are hungry and thirsty, strangers, naked, sick, or in prison provide ample opportunity for us to act with compassion in the name of Christ and for the sake of his kingdom. If it is true that "God's church has a mission," then this passage provides a practical, straightforward answer to what that mission can look like.

There are lots of good people, agencies, and organizations without any stated faith commitment who are working to make the world a better place for all people, and I give thanks to God for them all. Yet for those who choose to follow Jesus, these two passages offer us something more, a glimpse of Jesus' own ministry and the invitation to be part of what God is doing in the world even now. We do not have to be perfect (in fact, we cannot be). We do not have to accomplish everything (nor can we). But what we can do is to say yes to Jesus and discover that as our hearts and minds are transformed by that relationship, he calls us to share the Good News of God's great love with the people around us. Our faith—our words and works—enact that love in the power of God's Spirit.

For leaders of Christian communities, a second step, once we are grounded in prayer and compelled by Scripture, may be to go out in pairs for a "walkabout" in the community where the church is located. Simply walk (at most) fifteen minutes in all directions from your church. Notice who your neighbours are. What are some of the needs you see? Are you willing to knock on doors and talk with folks about the church and ways that we can work and serve the neighbourhood together? Once we have prayed, studied, and begun to recognize the needs of our neighbours, our passion for serving in Christ's name will come alive in praying the simple prayer of Bob Pierce, founder of World Vision: "Let my heart be broken by the things that break the heart of God."

What is breaking God's heart, and what breaks yours?

ENGAGING OUR COMMUNITIES: WHERE AND IN WHAT WAY?

In 2015, the image of the lifeless body of three-year-old Alan Kurdi, washed up on the beach after his family's failed and desperate attempt to escape Syria by boat, broke the hearts of many people, including the people at North Bramalea United Church. We had been talking for a few months about whether we could engage in refugee sponsorship. The loss of that young life compelled us to act.

We did our homework and studied and prayed, then came to the conclusion we could sponsor a family of up to six people. One January afternoon, the call came in from the United Church of Canada. Could we sponsor a Syrian family of seven who were on the United Nations refugee list, currently living in Jordan and wanting to move to Brampton? A flurry of emails, phone calls, and further prayer led us to say yes.

All our plans and preparations, hopes and dreams, and fears and trepidations culminated with the arrival of the Al-Mahameed family on February 15, 2016, which was Family Day in Ontario! To say that we have been blessed as a congregation by our sponsorship of this family is an understatement. On the very first Sunday after their arrival, the whole family came to church. The husband and father, Amer, spoke to us of his family's deep gratitude for our sponsorship. He spoke of the power and goodness of faith in his own Islamic practices and in our Christian ones. He spoke of the God—known by many names—whose love had drawn us together. There wasn't a dry eye in the house as the congregation stood in ovation and solidarity with our new brothers and sisters.

What breaks God's heart, and what breaks yours?

A few years ago, at the invitation of Ted Brown, who became the executive director of Regeneration Outreach Community in Brampton, my colleague Jamie Holtom was taken for a ride through the Ardglen and Orenda neighbourhoods in Brampton. Members of our congregation taught at the local school, and Jamie's ministry as the chaplain for the Brampton Fire Department had already made him aware of some of the challenges this neighbourhood faced. So from the beginning, we understood that this was not a "do-gooder" one-off initiative. If God was calling us to "move into the neighbourhood," then we would need to commit to ministry over the long haul.

At first, we launched a few simple outreach projects in the neighbourhood, such as a Christmas drop-off, and events at the local school. Then in January of 2013, nine-year-old Kesean Williams was shot and killed by an unknown drive-by assailant while sitting in his living room. His family had just moved into the neighbourhood a few days before. The outrage and pain that we felt in response to his death strengthened the belief that God was calling us to move into the neighbourhood—literally.

We found a vacant bakery in a local plaza. Every week, people from our church gathered at the plaza and walked through the local neighbourhood, praying and seeking to discern whether this was where Christ wanted us to serve. Through the power of the Holy Spirit, together with the fierce determination, persistence, and sweat of many church and community members, that run-down bakery was transformed into The Journey Neighbourhood Centre,[152] which opened in November of 2013.

Then, in the early morning of June 8, 2014, fire broke out in one of the townhouse units down the road from The Journey. An entire row of homes was destroyed, claiming the life of ten-year-old Nicholas Gabriel and leaving eighteen families homeless. The Journey became the hub for a community once again wracked by pain and grief. The outpouring of support was overwhelming. In partnership with Regeneration Outreach Community,[153] members of our congregation offered love and support in Jesus' name in ways too numerous to count. Words alone cannot express the depths of pain and loss that those families experienced, yet words and loving actions offered in and through the power of Jesus helped to bring hope and healing to the Gabriel family, their immediate neighbours, and the community as a whole.

What is breaking God's heart and yours—right now?

The Holy Spirit moves both on a big scale and in the smaller relationships that we form. I was invited to be part of the Superstars Reading Program at Sir Winston Churchill Public School, also located in the Ardglen/Orenda area of Brampton. As part of our involvement in the community, we partnered with the school so that reading mentors could offer an hour each week to students who needed some extra reading support. We saw this as one way to live out the mandate of John 1:14. Having prayed about it, I decided that this was something I could do.

I will never forget the two years that I spent reading with Jack. The first day I went into his classroom, he eyed me with great suspicion but came over to the table where we were to read and picked out a very simple book. He struggled with the three-letter words, even as I tried to encourage him in all the ways that I had been taught. I thought our time had gone well until the next week when I arrived and he began chanting, "No, no, no!" It was only at his teacher's insistence that he came over to

---

[152] For further information, see www.thejourneyneighbourhoodcentre.ca.
[153] For further information, see www.regenbrampton.com.

the table to read. You can appreciate that this session was harder than the first. The next week, I was greeted in the same way and decided to end his/our pain—after only fifteen minutes together.

All through the following week I prayed that I would find a way to reach this child so that he could improve his reading abilities and perhaps even discover some of the joy that I myself find in reading. Truthfully, though, I also prayed for a way to reach this child that would stop the pain of walking into that classroom one more time, only to be greeted by the words "no, no, no." In prayer, I told God that one of the reasons I was doing this was John 1:14; surely if God had called me to put faith and work together in this way, God could give me and my student Jack what we needed to make it succeed.

As only God can do, the answer was provided. I went to the bookstore and picked out a new book with vibrant colours and pop-ups. I came to the classroom door and was greeted by the usual chant. I walked in, filled with Spirit-given strength, and told my young friend that he did not have to read with me, even though I had bought a new book for him. I would be happy to read with someone else today, and he could continue doing what he was doing. The chanting stopped. I sat down with a young girl who loved to read. Out of the corner of my eye, I saw Jack watching my every move. I settled in with the girl and pulled the new book out of the bag. Jack got up from his desk. When I showed the girl my book, she made sounds of delight at being able to read it. Jack came a little closer. I started to read with her; Jack stood by my side.

I told him that he could look at the book when I was finished reading with his schoolmate. Then I smiled and prayed some more. He stayed near me and, as soon as she was finished, hopped into the chair beside me, pulling the book out of my hands and into his.

"Did you really buy this book for me?"

"Yes," I said.

"Why?" he asked.

Why do we do this? Why would I spend time mentoring a young boy to read when he clearly didn't want that help? Why would I pray for a way to reach him? That's the question people of faith have to answer at one time or another. Reading a book with a young boy in school is not going to change the world—at least I don't think so . . . But what I do know is that every act of kindness and compassion, every willingness to step out in faith and to love the people of this world with the power of Christ's love and compassion at work within us, makes a difference. Never again did I hear "no, no, no." Instead, I was greeted by a big smile and Jack jumping out of his chair to join me reading. Over the next two years, Jack and I continued a friendship that I would never have enjoyed if I had not obeyed the nudge to serve others with consistency, love, and compassion. Mine was a very small act of service in a neighbourhood with very great needs. Yet it was motivated by the desire to serve and follow Jesus wherever he might lead. In the end, it did help Jack with his reading, but, as so often is the case where faith and works are joined together, it also made me aware of the great privilege of serving in the power and name of Jesus.

The encouragement to practice our faith by following Jesus wherever he leads continues to challenge and grow our community. Although this is not a complete list, North Bramalea United Church is currently involved in the following ministry initiatives:

- The Lucas Holtom Carnival
- Biannual free clothing exchanges
- The Journey Neighbourhood Centre
- Love Brampton
- The Christmas Caring and Sharing program (serving over 100 families)
- Back-to-school backpacks and supplies (for over 100 children)
- Wellspring Chinguacousy Cancer Support Centre
- Superstars Reading Program at Sir Winston Churchill Public School
- L'Église du Christ au Congo, a mission partner of the United Church of Canada
- Sponsorship of a Syrian refugee family of seven and partnership with Heart Lake United Church to bring a second, related, family to Brampton

As a community of faith, we know that there is so much more that can and needs to be done. Some of the initiatives we've tried have failed. Every week people come to our churches looking for financial as well as spiritual support. Every week we encounter people who are facing mental health challenges in an under-supported and overstretched health care system. Every week we have people asking if we can sponsor one more family or help raise funds for worthy causes. Every week we do what we can even though we must sometimes turn people away or refer them to others for the assistance that we are unable to provide. Every week our hearts are broken by the things that break the heart of God.

But the disappointments, the failures, and even the overwhelming needs of the communities around us do not prevent God from acting. Every week we pray, "Thy kingdom come, thy will be done, on earth as it is in heaven," and find that we are renewed in our hope and strength to reach out in Jesus' name. As we listen for Christ's call and respond to his invitation to follow him, we must never doubt the power of doing small things with great love. Each action we take in Jesus' name changes the world, one heart at a time. We are encouraged to lean into him more for strength and courage to take the next step, to reach out again with love and compassion, to work for justice and reconciliation, to be the bearers of his good news, and to act with loving-kindness in a world that is desperate to experience the power of God's love. Eugene Peterson has Jesus saying it this way:

> "Let me tell you why you are here. You're here to be salt-seasoning that brings out the God-flavors of this earth. If you lose your saltiness, how will people taste godliness? You've lost your usefulness and will end up in the garbage.
>
> "Here's another way to put it: You're here to be light, bringing out the God-colors in the world. God is not a secret to be kept. We're going public with this, as public as a city on a hill. If I make you light-bearers, you don't think I'm going to hide you under a bucket, do you? I'm putting you on a light stand. Now that I've put you there on a hilltop, on a light stand—shine! Keep open house; be generous with your lives. By opening up to others, you'll prompt people to open up with God, this generous Father in heaven." (Matt 5:13–16, MSG)

Every day, through our words and actions, we reveal the ways that our relationship with Jesus transforms our own lives and the lives of others.

Christ's invitation is for us to go out into the world that God so loves to be salt and light as we share the good news that he embodies. We may not know where to start. We may not believe at first that we have anything to offer that will make a difference. We may even think that we are too busy to serve. So let me encourage you to pray a prayer that Harold Percy has invited me and countless others to pray, perhaps the shortest and most powerful prayer you will ever utter. It is a prayer with the power to change each of our lives, our families, our communities, and the world, in ways we cannot even begin to imagine. It will not guarantee success, and it will certainly not insulate us from the world's suffering and pain. Quite the opposite: our hearts will be broken by what breaks the heart of God. It consists of a single word: "yes." Say yes to Jesus and follow him wherever he leads.

ALL DOORS OPEN: GOD'S CHILDREN, PEOPLE, AND REIGN— A VIEW FROM A PROGRESSIVE URBAN PARISH
PETER G. ELLIOTT

HOW DID A THEOLOGICALLY PROGRESSIVE ANGLICAN CATHEDRAL GROW IN NUMBERS DURING a period of ecclesiastical conflict? In this context, how does an inclusive church or congregation understand evangelism?

Change began with a strategic-planning exercise. In 2003, the wardens and parish council of Christ Church Cathedral, Vancouver, accepted an invitation from the diocese to engage in a planning process that would include both hard data (e.g., attendance figures) and soft data (gained through focus groups and personal interviews with members of the parish). In preparation for this task, the parish council chose to dedicate a portion of their meetings throughout 2004 to discussing the book *Your Church Can Thrive: Making the Connections that Build Healthy Congregations*, by Harold Percy.

Out of a series of meetings came several documents: a detailed plan for parish ministry, an articulation of goals and objectives, a poetic vision statement, and a bumper-sticker-length slogan, "Open Doors, Open Hearts, Open Minds." It was a most useful exercise, and several of these components remain in place at the time of this writing. Above all, it was the slogan that caught the imagination of the congregation, as well as— if imitation is the sincerest form of flattery—of several other Anglican parishes in the diocese of New Westminster and beyond. "Open Doors,

Open Hearts, Open Minds" was proposed because the very first sermon preached at Christ Church, Vancouver, by the Reverend Hugh Pooley Hobson on December 23, 1888, had taken Revelation 3:8 as its text: "I have set before you an open door, which no one is able to shut."[154]

An open door serves as a compelling vision for this church, which began its life in a residential neighbourhood and is now at the heart of the downtown of the largest city on Canada's west coast. With Christ Church serving as a parish church, a diocesan cathedral (since 1929), a place for civic events, and a venue for the performing and visual arts, the congregation has grown significantly since that strategic-planning process. While growth in numbers is not the only measure of a congregation's faithful response to the gospel, it is nonetheless a valid indicator of positive change. One reason for the significant impact of the cathedral's ministry on people from many places is an insight regarding what Harold calls the dimensions of discipleship. These dimensions apply to "people who are in the beginning, intermediate, and even advanced stages of discipleship."[155] There are three dimensions:

- Understanding yourself as a child of God.
- Understanding yourself as a member of the people of God.
- Understanding yourself as participating in the reign of God.

What makes Percy's model so intriguing is the notion that growth in discipleship is not restricted sequentially: it is not, as too many models of evangelism seem to propose, that you need first to understand yourself as a child of God and then become incorporated into the people of God in order, finally, to participate in God's reign. Rather, Percy proposes an "all doors open" approach, in which any one of these models can serve as a point of access and new growth.

Sometimes—and this has been our experience at Christ Church Cathedral—people join because they are attracted to the worship life of the community and discover, while at worship with the people of God, their deepest identity as a beloved child of God. Others are drawn by

---

[154] Neale Adams, *Living Stones: A History of Christ Church Cathedral, Vancouver, BC* (Vancouver: Christ Church Cathedral, 2006), 13.
[155] Percy, *Your Church Can Thrive*, 38.

the cathedral's outreach ministries (refugee sponsorship, meals for the downtown poor, and affordable housing initiatives, to name but three) and discover the spiritual depth that brings people into work that expresses God's reign of equity and fairness.

"All doors open" is implicit in the cathedral's slogan "Open Doors, Open Hearts, Open Minds."

CHILD OF GOD

> You are God's work of art: created in Jesus the Christ.
> —David Haas, "You Are God's Work of Art"[156]

Roman Catholic priest Henri Nouwen (1932 to 1996) was among the most influential theologians of the late twentieth century. Combining insights from psychology with spiritual theology and social justice, Nouwen published more than forty books that were (and still are) read by countless numbers of clergy and lay leaders in the church. Key to his theology was his understanding that the core identity of human beings is as beloved daughters and sons of God. Near the end of his life, Nouwen was drawn to Rembrandt's painting of the parable of the prodigal son. He preached and lectured on this compelling work of art extensively throughout North America and wrote about it in his bestselling book *The Return of the Prodigal Son: A Story of Homecoming*. In it, he writes, "The Father is always looking for me with outstretched arms to receive me back and whisper again in my ear: 'You are my Beloved, on you my favor rests.'"[157]

The powerful affirmation that each and every human being is God's beloved child resonates deeply in the lives of many in Vancouver. In the final decades of the twentieth century and opening decades of the twenty-first, Vancouver's highly secular community has been deeply scarred by the illnesses and deaths of many gay men. As are many other major metropolitan centres throughout North America, Vancouver is home

---

[156] David Haas, "You Are God's Work of Art," *Common Praise* (Toronto: Anglican Book Centre, 1998), hymn 39.

[157] Henri Nouwen, *The Return of the Prodigal Son: A Story of Homecoming* (New York: Doubleday, 1992), 44.

to a large community of sexual and gender minorities,[158] with the AIDS epidemic having an acute impact on the lives of many men, along with their partners, friends, and families. Some churches and some families, sadly, closed their doors to those whose lives were affected by HIV-AIDS. Under the leadership of then dean Jim Cruickshank, Christ Church Cathedral took a different stance. Supported by the cathedral's lay leadership, Jim and associate clergy welcomed members of the gay community into the cathedral. With characteristic warmth and intelligence—Catholic at the altar, Evangelical in the pulpit—Jim communicated a message of God's unconditional love for all of God's beloved daughters and sons. Jim regularly referred to the way in which Henri Nouwen's books and teaching had inspired him.[159]

Cruickshank's legacy was strengthened by his successor, dean—and subsequently bishop—Michael Ingham. A prominent physician described it this way:

> "I was baptized as an Anglican and God's presence continued to be in my life: but I could not come to churches where my identity as a gay man could not be affirmed. I felt my spirit lift when I read an address by Michael Ingham affirming the dignity and worth of all of God's children. I returned and Christ Church Cathedral became my home."[160]

---

[158] Rather than employing an acronym such as LGBTQI+, I have chosen to follow the example of Dr. Mark Henrickson in employing the description "sexual and gender minorities." See M. Henrickson, "Sexuality and Social Work," *International Encyclopedia of the Social and Behavioral Sciences*, 2nd ed., ed. James Wright (Oxford: Elsevier, 2015), 21:802–807.

[159] Ironically, the proclamation of God's unconditional love that Nouwen preached so powerfully, declaring that we are God's beloved, could not resonate within Nouwen's own tortured soul. His friend Nathan Ball explains as follows: "Now there were people in the gay community who felt that the most important contribution he (Nouwen) could make would be to become more public as a gay priest, given his prominence, credibility and influence. He was tempted to do this, because he felt that the more public he was about his own sexual orientation and his personal struggles to remain faithful to his priestly vow, the greater the personal healing . . . . He lived with this enormous tension and did achieve something of a resolution after his breakdown" (Michael Higgins and Kevin Burns, *Genius Born of Anguish: The Life and Legacy of Henri Nouwen* [Toronto: Novalis, 2012], 101–102).

[160] From a personal conversation with Dr. Jack Forbes.

In the early 1990s, it was the health care workers who first came to the cathedral: nurses, social workers, psychologists, and physicians, all grateful for our acknowledgement that the human lives for and about whom they had cared with such compassion had been a blessing to them. A psychotherapist, now a deacon, had been active within the traditions of Wicca. She described her experience this way: "In my prayer life, one message kept repeating—*go to Christ Church Cathedral*. There I heard the message of God's unconditional love for all human beings—straight and gay. As a lesbian feminist, I had not heard this proclamation from a church before. It changed my world: I was baptized and began to study for ordained ministry."[161] For us, an "open door" means being genuinely "open." In the late 1990s, well-known environmentalist David Suzuki was invited to address the congregation during the sermon time on a Sunday morning. After his address, a newcomer commented, "If an agnostic like Suzuki can preach here, then this is the church for me!" Later, this same "newcomer" reaffirmed his faith in Christ in the diocesan confirmation liturgy and served as co-chair of the parish council that engaged the aforementioned strategic plan.

Feminists, sexual and gender minorities with their families and friends, health care workers, and atheists all heard in their hearts' core the Good News of God in Christ: that, as Henri Nouwen would say, "We are beloved daughters and sons of God." Harold Percy explains, "The personal dimension has to do with my understanding of myself as a child of God and my personal relationship with God, my growing understanding of the gospel and its implications, and the process of transformation through which I am becoming more like Jesus."[162]

PEOPLE OF GOD

Who are we who stand and sing? We are God's people.
—Herbert O'Driscoll, "Who Are We Who Stand and Sing?"[163]

---

[161] From a personal conversation with the Reverend Dixie Black.

[162] Percy, *Your Church Can Thrive*, 38.

[163] Herbert O'Driscoll, "Who Are We Who Stand and Sing?," *Hymns Ancient and Modern: New Standard*, Hymns Ancient and Modern Editorial Board, ed. (Norwich: Canterbury, 1983), hymn 529.

Church attendance is far from popular in British Columbia. Only 34 percent of the population affirm that they "embrace religion," while another 22 percent are inclined to reject religion.[164] Western Canada does not have the longer, established traditions of eastern or central Canada. Consequently, the church's rapid rise and fall in the 1950s and 1960s affected British Columbia churches to a profound extent.

In the last few decades, many have been discouraged by their encounters with congregations that focus more on meeting the budget than on embracing the gospel's twin call to evangelism and peacemaking. In addition, a long simmering conflict sparked a decade of contentious debate (from 1999 until 2009) over extending all sacramental rights to all disciples of Christ—including sexual and gender minorities. More conservative-minded evangelical and charismatic Christians objected, but they faced ever-increasing majorities voting for change at successive diocesan synods.

The dispute culminated in costly litigation. Some Anglican clergy and laity sued their bishop and synod, claiming that individual congregations had the right to dissent on the basis of conscience. The petitioners lost their case, for civil law judged that the bishop's rights trumped congregational control. In the aftermath of this decision, those who had initiated the lawsuits seceded from the diocese, leaving behind church buildings they had worshipped in and cared about for many years. It was a difficult time marked by strained friendships and broken relationships.

It was in the midst of this difficult period that the cathedral embraced its ministry plan with the motto "Open Doors, Open Hearts, Open Minds." Already buoyed by the presence of members of the helping professions, the cathedral now attracted others inspired by the worship and witness of a community dedicated to living out the baptismal promise to "respect the dignity of every human being."[165]

At around the same time, a long-planned interior renovation of the cathedral required the congregation to vacate the building for at least six months (in fact, it turned out to be twelve). This period of dislocation and absence from an historic and much-loved building turned out to

---

[164] "Dr. Reid's Keynote Address at BC Leadership Prayer Breakfast," Angus Reid Institute, April 22, 2016, http://angusreid.org/angus-reid-keynote-address-bc-leadership-prayer-breakfast/.
[165] *The Book of Alternative Services*, 159.

be a blessing. The parish council organized a series of neighbourhood "house churches" where parishioners could gather for Bible study and pastoral care. Over two hundred people participated in these home-based communities, building relationships that have lasted over the years and strengthened their experience of being part of the people of God.

The numbers of those who identified themselves as members of the parish grew unexpectedly during this period of dislocation. Just so, Harold Percy writes, "The gospel is certainly about the salvation of people as individuals, but it is about much more than that. It is about the new community that God is forming and calling to live to the praise of his glory."[166] For us, the vision of what Percy calls a "new community" became powerful and compelling in this time of controversy and dislocation.

Key to the numerical growth of the cathedral community have been ministry groups led by lay people. Connecting with people in the busyness of urban life is a challenge for all city churches. The cathedral's long-standing practice of healing prayer through the laying on of hands is a core element of the ministry of the congregation. Women and men, supported by clergy, regularly offer the ministry of healing at Eucharistic liturgies each Thursday at noon and on Sunday during the principal liturgy. People from all walks of life come forward week by week, bringing with them the complicated circumstances of their lives—stories of illness and conflicts in spousal or family relationships predominate—and the simple act of standing with and praying for those in distress brings the real lives of real people into the worship of the church.

Out of this commitment to and practice of ministries of healing, more intentional pastoral care ministries and a ministry of healing touch have developed. Based on principles from the therapeutic touch movement, the ministry of healing touch brought together a vibrant group of about twenty women who supplemented clergy and lay pastoral care visits to the acutely and terminally ill, with silent, loving attention grounded in prayer. Many were given temporary relief from stress and pain and have spoken eloquently about how helpful this ministry was. More recently, a mental health ministry has been established, seeking to change attitudes towards individuals and families who live with mental illnesses. With mental illness becoming epidemic in the digital age, those who suffer

---

[166] Percy, *Your Church Can Thrive*, 39.

with such challenges have too often been ostracized by both church and community organizations. The end of stigmatization is an important goal of this emerging ministry.

Defining who we are as people of God took on a more tangible form when, in the late 1990s, a prominent leader of the congregation was diagnosed with kidney disease. Only a kidney transplant would prevent a life of having to rely on dialysis. A member of the congregation volunteered to be considered as a donor: there was a match. On the Sunday prior to the surgery, these two women asked for public prayer as they approached the procedure. After surgery, they both confirmed that through this experience they gained an especially vivid realization that we are one body in Christ (Rom 12:5).

These and many other ministries brought people together, increasing their commitment to the life of the church. Gatherings of the community have been undergirded by a rich and vibrant liturgical life, supported by an excellent music program and inspired by faithful preaching. Throughout this period, a favourite congregational hymn— "All Are Welcome," by Lutheran Marty Haugen—has served to express our lived experience of community in Christ:

> Let us build a house where hands will reach beyond the wood and stone
> to heal and strengthen, serve and teach, and live the Word they've known.
> Here the outcast and the stranger bear the image of God's face;
> let us bring an end to fear and danger.
> All are welcome, all are welcome, all are welcome in this place.
> —Marty Haugen, "All Are Welcome"[167]

THE REIGN OF GOD

> As servant church you follow Christ's own way.
> —Sylvia G. Dunstan, "Go to the World"[168]

---

[167] Marty Haugen, "All Are Welcome" (Chicago: GIA Publications, 1994).
[168] Sylvia Dunstan, "Go to the World," *Common Praise*, hymn 598.

A servant church ecclesiology undergirds the pastoral ministry of Christ Church Cathedral. Mindful of Christ's words "From everyone to whom much has been given, much will be required" (Luke 12:48), generations of lay and clergy leaders have acted on the baptismal promise "to strive for justice and peace among all people and respect the dignity of every human being."[169] For us, keeping this promise has taken the form of advocacy for the civil rights of women and sexual and gender minorities in a city where cultural diversity flourishes.

Vancouver is a seaport with a long history of employing manual labourers. Technological advances in all the resource-based industries (forestry, mining, and fishing) have resulted in the reduction—or in some cases, elimination—of manual labour. This attrition, combined with increased levels in the number of people addicted to illegal drugs, has contributed to the large number of unemployed people living in downtown Vancouver—some in small rooms, others in shelters, many on the streets.

The problems of the homeless and destitute—many afflicted with the triple dose of poverty, addiction, and mental illness—are compounded by the fact that property values have continued to skyrocket since the late 1990s. Weightwatchers, a commercial program that helps people overcome weight problems due to overeating, holds weekly sessions in the cathedral buildings, where, ironically, the hungry poor come seeking food and other forms of assistance.

The Sandwich Project was born from the compassion of a widowed mother and her adult daughter who heard of cathedral staff and volunteers turning away people who sought food and assistance because they themselves had so little to offer. The pair made sandwiches at home and brought them to the office for office volunteers to distribute.

Requests for help grew so much that the congregation was invited to join this ministry of sandwich making. For five years, parishioners contributed bags of sandwiches for this project. An outbreak of food poisoning among street residents led the Vancouver Health Department to enforce city bylaws stipulating that all distributed food be prepared in certified kitchens that employ food safety protocols. Consequently, the cathedral became a hive of food preparation, gathering groups of women

---

[169] *The Book of Alternative Services*, 159.

and men who prepare sandwiches in the cathedral's recently enlarged kitchen and serve them weekly.

"Why not add a bowl of soup?" someone asked innocently, as a result of which a served meal of soup and sandwiches has now become standard. We now call it the Maundy Project. Currently, some sixty volunteers participate in this ministry of compassionate service, serving about a hundred people each day. Again, this is one of many ways by which people are drawn into the life of the church.

In the mid-1970s, the Church of the Savior in Washington, DC,[170] held a seminar that inspired the cathedral leadership of the time with stories of welcoming radical diversity, calling all those in attendance to a generous sacrifice of their time, energy, and resources. At the end of the seminar, participants were invited to write down and commit to one practical action that would further the reign of God in the world.

One participant identified affordable housing for the inner-city poor as her objective. Others joined her. They opened a bank account and within a year had formed the not-for-profit 127 Society for Housing. The name referred to a line from the Psalms that had inspired them: "Unless the LORD builds the house, those who build it labor in vain" (Psalm 127:1). From this modest beginning, three buildings in Vancouver's downtown south, still managed by a board comprised mainly of members of Christ Church Cathedral, now house more than two hundred individuals. As one board member told me, "It's a way I can bring what I learn from Jesus' teaching and from the sacraments of the church into a living reality for the poor."

These are but three examples of the many ways in which members of the cathedral congregation have engaged the social dimension of the gospel. Harold Percy writes, "As surely as the gospel has both a personal and corporate dimension, so it has a public dimension as well. God's purposes in the gospel do not end with the individual and his or her salvation. . . . The ultimate concern of the gospel is the world and everything in it."[171]

---

[170] For an overview of the history of the Church of the Savior, visit http://io-sermons.org/church-history/.
[171] Percy, *Your Church Can Thrive*, 39.

WHAT DOES AN EVANGELIZED PERSON LOOK LIKE?

The most important lesson from these three dimensions of discipleship is how they resist unfolding in a predetermined sequence. We are not first children of God and then people of God who eventually learn to participate in the reign of God. Pastoral experience at Christ Church Cathedral has shown time and again that God uses all open doors to beckon his beloved into a deeper relationship. This insight, emerging during a tumultuous and turbulent period, provided a theological and pastoral lens through which to view what God was doing in the life of the congregation of Christ Church Cathedral.

As one of his more penetrating questions, Harold Percy asks, "What does an evangelized person look like?" Framing the question in terms of these three dimensions of discipleship makes the response fairly clear. The evangelized are those who understand themselves to be beloved children of God, full and equal members of God's people—Christ's body—and as such committed to being part of God's mission of establishing God's reign of peace, justice, equity, and goodness in the world.

RECOMMENDED RESOURCES

Anderson, Leith. *A Church for the 21st Century*. Minneapolis: Bethany House, 1992.
Andison, Jenny. *Doors into Faith: Inviting Friends to Join the Big Game*. Wycliffe Booklets on Evangelism 4. Richmond: Digory, 2005.
Bowen, John. *Evangelism for "Normal" People: Good News for Those Looking for a Fresh Approach*. Minneapolis: Augsburg Fortress, 2002.
———. *Making Disciples Today: What, Why and How . . . on Earth?* Richmond: Digory, 2013.
———, ed., *Green Shoots out of Dry Ground: Growing a New Future for the Church in Canada*. Eugene: Wipf and Stock, 2013.
Campolo, Tony, and Mary Albert Darling. *Connecting Like Jesus: Practices for Healing, Teaching, and Preaching*. San Francisco: Jossey-Bass, 2010.
Dawn, Marva. *Reaching Out Without Dumbing Down: A Theology of Worship for This Urgent Time*. Grand Rapids: Eerdmans, 1995.
Guinness, Os. *Fool's Talk: Recovering the Art of Christian Persuasion*. Downers Grove: InterVarsity, 2015.
Holtom, Jamie, and Debbie Johnson. *Bullseye: Aiming to Follow Jesus*. Toronto: United Church Publishing House, 2015.
Hybels, Bill. *Courageous Leadership: Field-Tested Strategy for the 360° Leader*. Grand Rapids: Zondervan, 2002.
Johnson, Darrell. *The Beatitudes: Living in Sync with the Reign of God*. Vancouver: Regent College, 2015.

Lamott, Anne. *Help Thanks Wow: The Three Essential Prayers.* New York: Random House, 2012.

Mallon, James. *Divine Renovation: Bringing your Parish from Maintenance to Mission.* New London: Twenty-Third Publications, 2014.

Maxwell, John. *The 15 Invaluable Laws of Growth: Live Them and Reach Your Potential.* New York: Center Street, 2012.

———. *The 21 Irrefutable Laws of Leadership: Follow Them and People Will Follow You.* Nashville: Thomas Nelson, 2007.

———. *Winning with People: Discover the People Principles that Work for You Every Time.* Nashville: Thomas Nelson, 2007.

Newbigin, Lesslie. *The Gospel in a Pluralist Society.* Grand Rapids: Eerdmans, 1989.

Nouwen, Henri. *The Return of the Prodigal Son: A Story of Homecoming.* New York: Doubleday, 1992.

Percy, Harold. "Evangelism and the Anglican Church of Canada." In *Anglican Essentials: Reclaiming Faith within the Anglican Church of Canada*, edited by George Egerton, 214–23. Toronto: Anglican Book Centre, 1995.

———. *Following Jesus: First Steps on the Way.* Toronto: Anglican Book Centre, 1993.

———. *Good News People: An Introduction to Evangelism for Tongue-Tied Christians.* Toronto: Anglican Book Centre, 1996.

———. "The Heart of a Vital Church: Five Suggestions for Developing Passionate Spirituality in Your Congregation." *good idea!*, May 11, 2015. http://institute.wycliffecollege.ca/2015/05/the-heart-of-a-vital-church-five-suggestions-for-developing-passionate-spirituality-in-your-congregation.

———. "What Makes a Vital Church?" *good idea!*, April 13, 2010. http://institute.wycliffecollege.ca/2010/04/what-makes-a-vital-church/.

———. "What's the Job and What Are the Skills Required?" In *The Future Shape of Anglican Ministry*, edited by Donald M. Lewis, 143–55. Vancouver: Regent College, 2004.

———. *Your Church Can Thrive: Making the Connections that Build Healthy Congregations.* Toronto: Anglican Book Centre; Nashville: Abingdon, 2003.

Percy, Harold, and John Bowen. *Just the Basics: Teaching the Faith to Beginners*. Wycliffe Booklets on Evangelism 2. Richmond: Digory, 2004.

Rawson, Katie. *Crossing Cultures with Jesus: Sharing Good News with Sensitivity and Grace*. Downers Grove: InterVarsity, 2015.

Richardson, Rick. *Reimagining Evangelism: Inviting Friends on a Spiritual Journey*. Downers Grove: InterVarsity, 2006.

Roxburgh, Alan, and Fred Romanuk. *The Missional Leader: Equipping Your Church to Reach a Changing World*. San Francisco: Jossey-Bass, 2006.

Schnase, Robert. *Five Practices for Fruitful Congregations*. Nashville: Abingdon, 2007.

Smith, Christopher, and John Pattison. *Slow Church: Cultivating Community in the Patient Way of Jesus*. Downers Grove: InterVarsity, 2014.

Sparks, Paul, Tim Soerens, and Dwight J. Friesen. *The New Parish: How Neighborhood Churches Are Transforming Mission, Discipleship and Community*. Downers Grove: InterVarsity, 2014.

Standish, N. Graham. *Becoming a Blessed Church: Forming a Church of Spiritual Purpose, Presence, and Power*, 2nd ed. Lanham: Rowman & Littlefield, 2016. First published 2005.

Vennard, Jane. *A Praying Congregation: The Art of Teaching Spiritual Practice*. Herndon: Alban Institute, 2005.

Willard, Dallas. *The Divine Conspiracy: Rediscovering Our Hidden Life in God*. New York: HarperCollins, 1997.

Willimon, William. *Peculiar Speech: Preaching to the Baptized*. Grand Rapids: Eerdmans, 1992.

OTHER BOOKS BY
CASTLE QUAY BOOKS

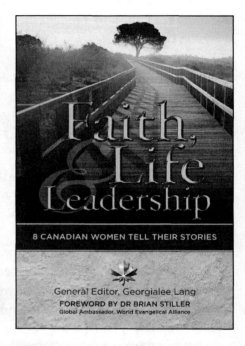

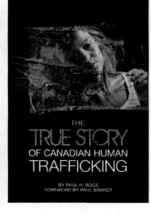
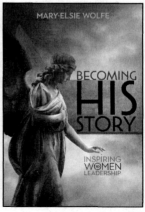